Rule of Thumb

Rule of Thumb

Ebert at the Movies

Todd Rendleman

continuum

Continuum International Publishing Group
80 Maiden Lane, New York, NY 10038
The Tower Building, 11 York Road, London SE1 7NX

www.continuumbooks.com

Library of Congress Cataloging-in-Publication Data
A catalog record for this book is available from the Library of Congress.

ISBN: PB: 978-1-4411-9221-9

Typeset by Fakenham Prepress Solutions, Fakenham, Norfolk NR21 8NN
Printed and bound in the United States of America

For my mother and father

Contents

Acknowledgments

There are so many people to thank, including Rani Ban, Walt and Liz Bennett, Ransom Cadorette, David Cho, Kerry Colburn, Richard and Sherie Dodson, Theodore Dubinsky, Christopher Edwards, Roger Feldman, Jim Ford, Liz Gruchala-Gilbert, Floyd and Marleen Gustafson, Rémi Fournier Lanzoni, Arianna Molloy, Linda and George Peters, Lois and Merwin Peters, Debbie Pope, Aaron Potratz, Rodney Powell, Kimberly Segall, Debra Sequeira, Cory Shepherd, Steve and Nadja Shoemaker, Jane Swanson, Andrea Taylor-Brochet, Art Tran, Ron and Susana Weigel, David Wicks, Rob and Carol Wingfield, and Jen Worick.

I thank my students, especially those in the Writing Film Criticism seminar, who allowed me to share my ideas with them and inspired me with their own, including Gabe Bentley, Chris Kyle, Meghan Landies, Sarah Long, Alex Nunn, Reed Probus, Michelle Reading, Grant Rehnberg, Jessie Roberts, and Matt Storm. I'm blessed by their discerning questions and unbridled passion for movies.

Trevor White, a fine writer himself, provided astute comments on an earlier draft of this book. Richard T. Jameson and Kathleen Murphy have nourished me with conversations about movies and writing, as have my French friends and film experts, Jean-Louis Capitaine and Alexandre Boyer. My gratitude, also, to my prized colleague Michelle Beauclair, who invited me to Paris to begin writing this book. Talking about movies with each is like a day in the country.

Jennifer Maier's support and confidence were instrumental in completing the project, and both she and Dave Kosloski offered wisdom at every turn. For camaraderie, I thank Eric Pierson and Robert Baird, my partners in crime at Ebertfest and beyond. David Bordwell and Kristin Thompson also provided spirited, helpful advice at critical junctures. Marilyn Hancock graciously assisted in preparing the index, and Dominic Williamson made the process of selecting the film frames a delight.

Nobody—not even the late Gene Siskel, in his day—spars with Roger Ebert more fervently than my dear friend Maggie Courtright. It's always a treat sitting next to her, watching the credits roll, and haggling over the latest movie—or Ebert's thoughts on it.

Year in, year out, I'm thankful for the love and support of Dale and Kelly Anderson, Gail and Jeff DeBell, and Fan and Jack Gates. These extraordinary people do not need cinematographers. They're lit from within.

And kudos as well to Katie Gallof and David Barker at Continuum, whose generous feedback, attention, and confidence have made this book a reality.

Two writers who hearten me are J. R. Moehringer and Craig Seligman. Moehringer's achievements in reporting, biography, and autobiography are spellbinding. His writings—so personable, so elegant—in every genre are like sublimated poetry. And Seligman, by seamlessly weaving together criticism and biography, is a master of each. Both are always leaning over my shoulder, moving me to write.

I gratefully thank my teachers. Carolyn Taylor, my graduate school advisor and first true-blue editor, has an infectious love of words and life. Ramona Curry taught me how to teach film and continues to model the life of a movie lover, scholar, and, above all, friend. Ruth Anne Clark is one of the reasons I became a professor; her integrity and support are mainstays in my life. Further back, I thank my high school Spanish instructor, Jill Pearce Bell, who always encouraged me to think deeply about the movies. And Bonnie Heidinger, my American lit teacher, surrendered countless lunch hours talking with me about books and film. It was more than lunch, though. We also chatted from 3:15 to 3:35—that fleeting window between school's end and the time needed to slip into my singlet for 3:45 wrestling practice. She urged me to write about movies, and our conversations—stolen moments, here and there—are cherished memories.

Deep gratitude goes to Luke Reinsma as well, who read and commented on every sentence of this book. He's the ultimate collaborator, and whether we're climbing *The Tree of Life* or checking out *The Girl With the Dragon Tattoo*, he's also been an ideal movie companion and a steadfast friend.

Finally, I thank my brother, Troy, who always has my back. And especially my parents, Bill and Brenda Rendleman, whose love and support are unwavering. While so many young people in my hometown of Anna, Illinois, spent their Friday nights driving up and down Main Street, circling a Dairy Queen, my parents bought me tickets to Africa with Robert Redford, to the Louisiana Bayou with Barbara Hershey, to a pub with Faye Dunaway, to heaven with Warren Beatty, to hell with Mickey Rourke, and to the stars with Jeff Bridges. They also bought me books by Roger Ebert and Pauline Kael, ensuring my own Algonquin Round Table in the hills and dales of Southern Illinois. They sacrificed much for me, and it's to them that I dedicate this book.

Foreword

It is a decidedly strange sensation to be writing the introduction to a critical analysis of my work. It is complicated still more because when Todd Rendleman first contacted me to discuss this book, I expressed some reluctance, saying I was in the process of writing my own memoirs. I confess that may have been so long ago that I hadn't yet started writing.

Online, Todd seemed like a nice man. To prove he was sincere, he sent me an early draft of this book. I was fascinated, as anyone would be when faced with the prospect of his own life seen through other eyes. I specified in advance that I felt he had every right to write whatever he wanted, and I didn't want to be placed in the position of approving or even correcting it. In that sense, this is an "unauthorized biography."

However, I did read several pages. I found no errors. I also found it encouraging that someone thought my movie reviews were worth writing a book about. I am not an academic critic or even, some days, a straight-faced one. I am a newspaperman. I went to work as a sports writer on one of my home-town dailies before I was sixteen, and I've worked for newspapers without interruption ever since; for the *Chicago Sun-Times*, since 1966. As is the nature of newspapers, most of my reviews have been written on deadline. By that I don't mean I was desperately hammering at the keys while the second hand ticked toward 12, but that I had a finite time available and then the review was in other hands.

The *Sun-Times* for many years, before the current economic downturn, was a robust and healthy paper, movies were a popular subject, and my editors without exception supported me. If a new movie was released that deserved lengthy discussion, that would mean a "Sunday piece," where I could turn in 2,000 words and actually see them in print. That's not much compared to many magazine critics, but it allowed me to dig a little deeper. That kind of space is no longer available, but luckily the internet and blogging have lifted all space limitations. In my case, that may have been a mixed blessing. I can write long, but sometimes I can write too long.

In the meantime, I actually did write my memoir, *Life Itself*, and it was published in September 2011. I was clear in my own mind it would not be a "movie book" but a personal book, so there must be hardly any overlap between this book and the memoir.

If you were to ask me what my influence has been, I would not make grandiose claims. My movie reviews have mostly fallen between 500 and sometimes 1,100 words, were written four to eight in a week, and there were a lot of them. We seem to have around 10,000 on my website, and many more have not been and may never be digitized. So instead of writing an earth-shaking essay like some others, I made hundreds and hundreds of smaller impressions, containing in aggregate how I look at movies, how I value them, and how many different ways they can be approached. Some of my reviews were dismissive and outright silly. Some very earnest. Some written in ecstasy, some in outrage.

This enterprise was complicated by the success of "Sneak Previews" and its reincarnations under several titles, sometimes condensed into "Siskel & Ebert & Roeper." Gene Siskel and I were a sight unseen on commercial TV: Two guys who didn't look like "celebrities" and debated in a rough but sincere style. Today I hear from a lot of our early viewers that we changed the way they thought about movies.

What we did on TV was television. It was not at the same depth as print, although it had many virtues. In the early days, some dismissed us as showbiz performers, and if anything that inspired me to work harder and write more in print. To have both opportunities was a godsend.

Altogether, I hope readers absorbed the idea that movies are important, they are to be loved, and they cannot all be held to the same measure. If Todd Rendleman has arrived at a similar conclusion, I will be most pleased. In any event, I am grateful to him for having gone to a great deal of effort for this book, and I will read it with great interest.

Roger Ebert
Chicago, November 2011

Introduction

"Keep driving, Bill. This doesn't look like a good idea," Mom said.

"Brenda, we're here," Dad sighed, pulling into the parking lot of the New Art Theater in Champaign, Illinois.

But let's back up for a moment. My family was on yet another mission prompted by myself and Roger Ebert. I was seventeen, and I'd traveled with my parents for three-and-a-half hours from Southern Illinois for a weekend visit with my brother, then a junior at the University of Illinois in Urbana-Champaign. Because of my affection for Faye Dunaway and Mickey Rourke, and Ebert's enthusiasm for their new film *Barfly*, I begged my family to catch the 9 p.m. screening.

As we found the theater, a long line had already formed in the icy February air. It was a young crowd, some with purple hair, wearing black leather, smoking cigarettes. Smug, I suspect, because they were waiting to see a movie about Charles Bukowski. We joined their ranks, the only well-scrubbed family of four in a long stretch of outsiders. We finally moved into the theater—and whatever one thought of that dingy movie house or the film itself, the lobby was warm. And, on a freezing night, the thick aroma of buttered popcorn was comforting. "This is nice," I thought, realizing my capital was sinking, feeling desperate to score a point. Dad bought our four tickets. In 1988, $22 was a lot of money to spend on a movie called *Barfly*.

The theater was packed. It would become a refuge to me during my years at the University of Illinois, but it would never again be as congested as it was that night. The lights lowered, the previews began, and a British invasion loomed. The first, for *Sammy and Rosie Get Laid*, was rowdy, earsplitting, and not a title that inspired confidence. A sigh of relief accompanied the next trailer for a Merchant-Ivory film—tranquil long shots of the British countryside and horse-drawn carriages. We were on safer ground. "1910, Cambridge, England ... They are friends ... with ... a special relationship." Cut to a chaste kiss between James Wilby and Hugh Grant, followed by plentiful handholding and stares, pregnant with longing. "A love story of unforgettable passion ... without ending." Appropriate, too, for a trailer without ending. The movie was *Maurice*—definitely not *A Room With a View*, which Mom had enjoyed. Among Sammy, Rosie, and Maurice—crudely or clandestinely, spiritedly or solemnly—sexual urges were taking flight. These were not the romances I was hoping for.

Two strikes. The lights dimmed, and the credits were splashed over a collage of LA bars and pubs. "Francis Ford Coppola Presents" was there to establish authority, I guess. He did, after all, direct *The Godfather*—what was I worried about? "Mickey Rourke" and "Faye Dunaway" followed suit. They wouldn't let us down, I knew it. *Barfly* began with an ugly, bloody back-alley fight. This was no slickly choreographed Bruce Willis tussle; these were scabbed fists penetrating flesh and teeth. Rourke, already spitting up blood, was unshorn. I wasn't expecting his natty stockbroker from *9½ Weeks*, but, here, he was even more soiled than in *Angel Heart*, where Pauline Kael felt he was so filthy he'd "sprout mushrooms." Mom, in turn, was already sighing—deeply and repeatedly. Feeling queasy, I leaned toward my brother Troy and whispered, "Maybe we should just go." But by now my head was on the guillotine and he replied with the satisfaction of an older brother: "No. You got us into this, and we're gonna sit through the whole thing."

I felt nauseated and trapped. The twenty-five minutes before Faye Dunaway arrived was like a year—a year of my brother's victory lap, Mom's river of sighs, and Dad's willingness to play the believing game. But then, at the far end of the bar, Dunaway appeared. Rourke approached, and a civilizing force entered his life and the film. At that moment I could relax, my mind leaving my family and entering Bukowski's strange world, as closed as the lips of a tightly-sealed jar. Finally, I understood why Ebert wanted us to see it so badly.

So my first visit to the Art Theater would move into family folklore, into that mysterious, permanent realm of teasing—another instance of my leading everyone down a precarious, possibly amoral, road with no clear destination. It's also a treasured moviegoing memory, which I owe in part to Ebert—and Dad, who never turned the car around—as well as another chapter in that theater's rich history of inviting viewers to great films. In 1958, at the age of sixteen, Ebert discovered *Citizen Kane* at the Art Theater and learned "that a movie could suggest the truth about a human life and that movies were the expression of the vision of those who made them." In both respects, *Barfly* soared.

We were not Chicago people. The six-hour drive that separates Chicago from Anna, Illinois, is infinite. Growing up along the Missouri and Kentucky borders, St. Louis was my family's city of choice. As it was for Judy Garland and Margaret O'Brien in *Meet Me in St. Louis*, it was the center of our universe; we merely shared a state with the Windy City. My father's paper was the *St. Louis Post-Dispatch*, so my first impression of Ebert wasn't in a newspaper column. Like many, it was on television, where Ebert and Gene Siskel duked it out each week. I always enjoyed Harper Barnes' and Joe Pollack's reviews in the *Post-Dispatch*—they were thoughtful, intelligent writers. But it was a godsend when Ebert began publishing his annual collection in 1985. Since this was the same year my parents bought our first VCR, the timing was impeccable. When a video store opened in town—a little hole in the wall called "Video World" that smelled like a bar—I could take Ebert with me and catch up on all kinds of films. His annual compilation of reviews was as pleasurable and necessary as going to the movies each weekend. In fact, it was a gift. Every Christmas my parents would buy me his latest collection, and those books remain the only presents I've never outgrown. With years, I would be stimulated by Pauline Kael, David Ansen, John Simon, Kathleen Murphy, and Richard T. Jameson, but it's Ebert who laid a foundation for me to appreciate critics and the movies that captured their imaginations. Nobody influenced my thinking about movies more thoroughly, or from an earlier age, than he. Consequently, my affection for him is, first and foremost, personal.

So, well before the night I saw *Barfly*, I had a history with Ebert, and he had a history with *Barfly*. He had visited the LA set during its production and covered its debut at Cannes the following year. From the get-go, he sensed something special in bringing together Dunaway, Rourke, Bukowski, and director Barbet Schroeder for this tough little movie. Moreover, Bukowski captured the experience of seeing his life recorded on film in his novel, *Hollywood*. Since his characters are barely veiled stand-ins for real-life counterparts, the book is a vigorous, dishy pleasure. In it, Bukowski is thoughtfully critical of every major film

Figure 1 Barbet Schroeder directing Mickey Rourke and Faye Dunaway in *Barfly*. Ebert visited the LA set and sensed excitement in the air. *Cannon/ Photofest*

industry player, with the exception of Rick Talbot, a popular Chicago film critic who visits the set. Talbot, of course, is Ebert, and what's fascinating is Bukowski's affection for the guy. In Talbot, Bukowski ("Chinaski" in the book) detects candor and sincerity — and a real joy in being a writer. After Talbot expresses his affection for the carnivalesque atmosphere on the movie set ("This is a great night"), Chinaski replies, "I loved Rick's lack of sophistication. That took guts, when you were on top, to say that you enjoyed what you did, that you were having fun while you did it." And this is Ebert: a critic of considerable standing who isn't afraid to express exhilaration on a movie set. That it's Bukowski — the most grizzled and jaded of poets — who's writing this is all the more resonant.

This book, by analyzing Ebert's critical sensibilities, is an effort to understand how he's earned the trust and appreciation of moviegoers and filmmakers, as well as hearts as hard-bitten as Bukowski's. "Pardon me," Talbot says to Chinaski in *Hollywood*, "but I have been studying you all evening, and you don't seem to be a vicious man." Chinaski's response: "And neither do you, Rick." Ebert has challenged our expectations of what it means to be a critic. Discerning and gifted with words? Absolutely—but not vicious or unapproachable. The following chapters seek to unpack Ebert's aesthetic sensibilities. Although there is much gained by comparing his writing with his colleagues, I'll resist the urge to declare a victor. If I've done my job, it should be clear that I adore Pauline Kael and John Simon every bit as much as Ebert. In fact, any discussion of movies is impoverished without the fullness of their points of view. Poet Jennifer Maier observes that we're pressed to choose "Either/Or when we yearn to settle/freely in Both/And." So while my focus will be on Ebert, my intention is to satisfy this yearning, to appreciate a range of critics in all of their complexity.

The first chapter, "Godchild," places Ebert in historical context, and "Rule of Thumb," "Close to Ebert," and "The Total Effect" elucidate his critical values. "Lit Crit" explores his affection for books and movies, and "And I Still Can See *Blue Velvet*, Through My Tears" considers Ebert's moral sensibilities in response to his most famous review. "Cross References" examines his feelings toward spirituality and religion at the movies, and "Turned On" explores his attitudes toward sex on film. "Misfires" considers moments when his critical faculties falter, and "I Ain't a Pretty Boy No More" elaborates on his championing of underdogs. Finally, the epilogue "Heroes" contemplates Ebert in the winter of his career. There's no question that Ebert's online presence and blog, as well as his autobiography, have allowed him to address all sorts of topics and events, from childhood memories to presidential debates to the effects of Rupert Murdoch on the media. The movies no longer dictate what he'll discuss each week. But the focus of this book is his film criticism, and it's my belief that his style, values, politics, and moral compass have always been there—at the movies.

Chapter 1
Godchild

Naked and restless in bed, Faye Dunaway finally stumbles to her second-story window to eye Warren Beatty, the contours of her back glistening with sweat. Another sweltering shot: a bird's-eye view of Paul Newman as the wily Cool Hand Luke, having consumed an unreasonable number of hard-boiled eggs, lying stretched atop a prison mess hall table like Christ on the cross. And then there's Jane Fonda, carrying Michael Sarrazin on her back—as well as the weight of the Great Depression and the metaphorical load of Vietnam—enduring a grueling 1930s dance marathon in *They Shoot Horses, Don't They?* Meanwhile, in *Point Blank*, Lee Marvin strides down a cavernous hallway with obdurate authority, each step hammering the floor like a nail through sheet metal, intent on revenge. These nonconformists summon the pulsating spirit of American film in the late 1960s. To movie lovers, they are instantly placeable.

Less recognizable but equally significant, American film critics shaped and embroidered the 60s cinematic landscape. Composing in longhand and hovering over her writer's easel, Pauline Kael describes Jane Fonda in *Barbarella*: "Her American-good-girl innocence makes her a marvellously apt heroine for pornographic comedy... According to [director Roger] Vadim, in 'Barbarella' she is supposed to be a kind of sexual Alice in Wonderland of the future, but she's more like a saucy Dorothy in an Oz gone bad." In a few paragraphs, Kael legitimates Fonda's work in a manner that even Fonda struggled to defend, suggesting the range of her blossoming talents. From these sensibilities, John Simon recoiled. It was never enough for him to ferret out moments of art or inspiration in the mundane. He demanded more from movies *and* critics. "Nothing succeeds better than highbrow endorsement of lowbrow tastes," he once wrote about Susan Sontag. "Who would not, at no extra cost, prefer to be a *justified* sinner?" (italics his). Now imagine a shot of the critic Rex Reed devouring a banana, along with peanut butter, jelly, and whipped cream, from the fingertips of the ingenue Farrah Fawcett (then a minor beauty, not yet one of the Majors). Of course it's a fantasy sequence. In *Myra Breckinridge* Reed *is* Myron Breckinridge. A sex change remakes him as Myra (Raquel Welch), and, together, the alter egos pursue movie stardom. Oddly, the analogy works, as Reed used his critic-cum-celebrity persona to cross over, however briefly, into movies, however awful. Meanwhile Roger Ebert was chasing his own romanticized vision of sweetness and sin: that of the consummate newspaper critic. Routinely, he would screen a film in the afternoon, effortlessly meet the evening deadline, then interview filmmakers at a favorite pub—a punishing bar crawl that would yield only to daylight. He was equally enticed by Hollywood, having penned the script for Russ Meyer's *Beyond the Valley of the Dolls*. The circle was complete: Like images on the big screen, the critics, too, were stars.

Figure 2 Time for a smoke: *The New Yorker*'s Pauline Kael, a few months after writing her review of *Bonnie and Clyde*. *Martha Holmes/ Time Life Pictures/Getty Images*

Figure 3 A sharp tongue and collar: Film critic John Simon in 1975, at the offices of *New York Magazine* in New York. *Michael Tighe/Hulton Archive/ Getty Images*

The vitality in American movies of the 60s was amplified by the influence and imagination of this new generation of critics. Fresh attitudes toward films were espoused with impassioned idealism, and the nation's bully pulpit was New York City. They made a colorful cast. Andrew Sarris began writing about film in 1955, mostly in obscure publications, and his first review for *The Village Voice* was of Alfred Hitchcock's *Psycho* in 1960. Everything about that film—its content, style, and production—signaled startling changes in American movies. And Sarris loved it, parting ways with the critical vanguard. By 1968, he published *The American Cinema: Directors and Directions, 1929–1968*, daring to organize and rank the accomplishments of filmmakers. Having interned at the Cinémathèque Française and translated an English version of *Cahiers du Cinéma*, Sarris was drawn to French auteurism, privileging the role of the director in shaping a film's expressive qualities. If Sarris was the courtier, Pauline Kael was the immigrant, whose piecemeal critical approach resisted frameworks. After managing and writing production notes for a theater in San Francisco and working in nonprofit radio, Kael developed her critical voice while freelancing for publications like *Sight & Sound*. In 1965, she reached larger audiences with *I Lost It at the Movies*, the first time that film criticism hit the best-seller list. That volume also reissued a critical appraisal of Sarris' auteurist point of view. Her spirited panning, coupled with a strike at *The New York Times* that increased readership of the *Voice*, brought Sarris to the critical fore. Kael soon uprooted to New York, briefly writing for *McCall's*, then for the *New Republic*, before settling into *The New Yorker*, where she remained for three decades. Ironically, while Sarris' baroque, gentlemanlike prose appeared in the edgy *Voice*, Kael's earthy, loopy style shook up the staid *New Yorker*. And all the while writing for *The New Leader*, the scrupulous John Simon maintained a vigilant eye, patrolling and protecting cultural and moral high ground from the antics of Sarris and Kael.

It was a changing of the guard. For decades, Bosley Crowther had reviewed films for *The New York Times*, yet by the 1960s his point of view had grown stodgy and stale. Although Kael and Sarris achieved notoriety through their aesthetic sparring, they were unified in their desire to establish a sturdy base of influence for critics. In 1966 and partly in opposition to Crowther and the conservative aesthetics of the New York Film Critics Circle, Kael and Sarris were two of twelve founding members of the National Society of Film Critics. Membership in the Circle was limited to newspaper writers. Redressing power imbalances, the National Society welcomed magazine writers as well.

Nowhere was the new epoch more evident than in stormy debates over Arthur Penn's *Bonnie and Clyde*. In every sense, this 1967 film packed a wallop. For some, it was a hair-raising, invigorating two hours; for others, a moral and aesthetic slap in the face. It's hard to tell which part of the film carried the most impact: its treatment of crime and sexuality, its violent *dénouement*, its visual distinction recalling the French New Wave, or its announcement of dynamic new talent. Even its influence on international fashion was unmistakable. As a cultural landmark, it had a gift for provoking debates among audiences and critics. Crowther despised it. He soon retired, passing the baton to Renata Adler, whose inimitable voice and unerring judgment revitalized criticism at the *Times*. Commencing a lasting partnership with *The New Yorker*, Kael was ecstatic, her analysis alive to new sensibilities in American movies, her opening line throwing down the gauntlet to her critics: "How do you make a good movie in this country without being jumped on?" And inevitably, Simon was appalled—not only at the movie, but also at Kael's avidity. Still, a polemic response to *Bonnie and Clyde* was unnecessary for membership in the new establishment. In *Life*, Richard Schickel was conflicted, inviting "all men of goodwill to join me here on the nice, soft grass of the middle ground."

But most declined the invitation. There simply wasn't much middle ground to be had. In the meantime, a young critic in the Midwest was electrified by *Bonnie and Clyde*, his ardor and geographic location signaling new directions for American movies. While Sarris and Kael made names for themselves in the early 60s, Roger Ebert was serving as editor-in-chief of *The Daily Illini*, the University of Illinois' student newspaper. He briefly attended graduate school at the University of Capetown and the University of Chicago, but academia would be the road not taken. Ebert eventually joined *The Chicago Sun-Times* as its film critic in April 1967, and, to this day, he says he was offered the position because he had long hair and had written a piece on underground films. One of the first movies he reviewed was *Bonnie and Clyde*, which he recognized as a cultural milestone. At twenty-five and one of the youngest film critics writing for a daily, Ebert was the embodiment of a new film generation—a generation raised on Saturday matinees and older movies on the *Late Show*. They carried their love of movies to college, forming film societies on university campuses, where cinema studies was a burgeoning academic field. And they relished the shifts in American movies that followed the demise of the studio system and the Production Code, permitting a broader array of content on the screen. Many were literate in foreign cinema and receptive to the gradual European influence on American film. Weathering the cultural shifts that defined the late 50s and 1960s, they romanticized movies and were unembarrassed to use grandiose language. Richard Schickel: "*The Wild Bunch* is the first masterpiece in the new tradition of what should probably be called the 'dirty western.'" Andrew Sarris: "Claude Chabrol's *La Femme Infidèle* is the most brilliantly expressive exercise in visual style I have seen on the screen all year." Pauline Kael: "Remember when the movie ads used to say, 'It will knock you out of your seat'? Well, *Z* damn near does." Brace yourself: imposing pronouncements were their lingua franca.

Ebert, the newest critic in Chicago, attended screenings at the Town Underground, a burlesque theater that briefly doubled as an art house under the direction of friend and cinephile John West. At the Clark Theater run by Bruce Tinz, he also devoured the classics of Welles, Hitchcock, von Sternberg, Minnelli, and Hawks. Ebert's take on American movies left an immediate impression: readers were captivated by his direct approach, his thoughtful point of view, and—depending on the film—his sense of humor, ranging from the subtle to gregarious. So much so that in 1975 he was the first film critic to receive a Pulitzer Prize for criticism. Given his talent and beat, it seemed natural that Ebert should walk away with the laurel that the muckraker Jack Anderson coined "the Academy Awards of Journalism." By any measure it was an auspicious year. Teaming with fellow film critic Gene Siskel of *The Chicago Tribune*, Ebert hosted a PBS television special, *Opening Soon at a Theater Near You*. They would soon share the balcony of PBS's *Sneak Previews* for a national audience. Though the nomenclatures changed—moving into syndication with Tribune Broadcasting they were *At the Movies*, then it was *Siskel and Ebert and the Movies* with Disney's Buena Vista Television, and finally *Siskel and Ebert*—their tart chemistry proved irresistible. For a time, their program was one of the most widely watched syndicated shows in America, second only to *Entertainment Tonight*, reaching an estimated eight million homes.

Figure 4 Making history: In 1975, the *Chicago Sun-Times'* Roger Ebert is the first to win a Pulitzer for film criticism. *Bettmann/Corbis*

Ebert's velocity as a writer is daunting, but his television presence made him the most influential critic in the country. He initially balked at the thought of hosting a program with a rival, only fearing that someone else might land the opportunity. That instinct served him well, as Siskel and Ebert's competitiveness was central to their popularity. Their arguments were eye-popping—at least as entertaining as many films they discussed—and the show's appeal was rooted in the authenticity of their battles. Their arguments were never staged. They didn't socialize apart from professional responsibilities, and their relationship was stamped by begrudging affection, and at times, genuine dislike. In the wake of their success, similar programs multiplied, but Siskel and Ebert's intellectual dexterity, lively chemistry, and unalloyed abilities to connect with audiences were unmatched.

Like seismic waves, Ebert and Siskel shifted the geography of power in the film industry. Historically, the axis had tilted between Los Angeles, where movies are made, and New York, where financial capital is consolidated. From James Agee in the 40s, to the inveterate influence of the *Times*, to Kael and Sarris in the 60s and 70s, New York writers had a hammerlock on critical influence. In the 1980s, however, Siskel and Ebert were the most recognized and trusted critics in the nation, bringing Chicago into the limelight. Each jockeyed for interviews with actors and directors. In kind, filmmakers wanted their ears. Even reclusive artists like Woody Allen sought out time with Ebert.

Two literate men discussing a range of topics, at once engaged and engaging—one slender and canny, the other cherubic and incisive. Sounds like another episode of *Siskel and Ebert*, but in this case it's Louis Malle's *My Dinner With André*, a cornerstone of American independent film. The movie is 89 minutes of two natural storytellers enjoying each other's company over a meal. Though the film was embraced at Telluride and the New York Film Festival, its release on October 11, 1981, at the Lincoln Plaza Cinema failed to attract much of an audience. After several lackluster weeks, the film seemed destined to fade away; it was, after all, a busy holiday season at the movies. Buoyed by a phalanx of stars, a massive budget, a movie star's directorial debut, and months of publicity, Warren Beatty's *Reds*, the long-awaited love story of Communists John Reed and Louise Bryant, debuted the first week of December. On their program, Siskel and Ebert recommended *Reds*, but their highest praise was reserved for *My Dinner*. Most agree their support placed this struggling film on the map, leading to wider distribution and exhibition. Paramount's $32 million investment in *Reds* never paid off, but *My Dinner*'s good fortune symbolized Ebert and Siskel's fiscal muscle. They could bring an unusual, perceptive film to the public eye and generate the necessary word of mouth to get people into theaters. The movie took care of the rest.

Physically and temperamentally, Gene Siskel was a skillful reporter, a nimble thinker, and a vibrant foil for Ebert. His approach was more sober, more skeptical, more pragmatic—"realism" mattered to him. Often saying he covered "the national dream beat," he wanted movies to reflect a country's hopes and fears. Ebert was too quick to cheer, he argued; in turn, Ebert believed Siskel was too pessimistic. Even their bodies—Siskel's tall, slim stature and balding head; Ebert's short, portly physique and mop of gray hair—were Don Quixote to Sancho Panza, Laurel to Hardy, Bert to Ernie. When disagreeing, their gestures were ritualized, Ebert throwing his hands outward and upward in exasperation, Siskel aiming his index finger at Ebert. At times, their theatrics overshadowed their criticism. "Is this the night Rog will finally bite the finger Gene is forever pushing in his face?" asked colleague Richard

Figure 5 Rough around the edges: Roger Ebert and Gene Siskel in the balcony of *Sneak Previews* (PBS), circa 1979. *Photofest*

Figure 6 Seasoned pros: Gene, Roger, and their iconic thumbs. The program is now *Siskel & Ebert* (Buena Vista Television), circa 1989. *Photofest*

T. Jameson. And "when will Gene call Rog on his tactic of shooting sidelong, what-am-I-to-do-with-this-nudnik? glances at the camera?"

Siskel's route to the movies had been the more circuitous. After studying philosophy at Yale, he served as a military reporter, began writing about real estate in the *Tribune*, and eventually landed the job as its head film critic, thus vying with Ebert's popularity at the *Sun-Times*. Although a quick-witted adversary, Siskel was never in the same league as Ebert. He loved words, and his bemused verbosity could be endearing, but there was always a restrained, perfunctory quality to his criticism. His grasp of film history was limited, confining the range and depth of his observations. He attended few film festivals, and he wrote less than his contemporaries. Reacting to the success of their television program, the *Tribune* sidelined Siskel in the 80s, cryptically describing him as "overextended." Thereafter, he was relegated to writing capsule reviews for the paper—hardly an opportunity for growth. Siskel was an adroit, adaptable reporter, someone who might be as comfortable writing from the Washington bureau as evaluating a movie. For him, film criticism was a job. But for Ebert, it was a calling.

Following ten months of health difficulties, Siskel passed away on February 20, 1999. It was the end of an era. That same year, Ebert dedicated his first Overlooked Film Festival to Gene Siskel, who liked to ask, "Is this film more interesting than a documentary of the same actors having lunch?" Ebert continued the program with rotating guest critics until selecting *Sun-Times* opinion columnist Richard Roeper as a permanent replacement—an unfortunate decision that's best left forgotten. It seemed both a pity and a sin to pass on guest critics as lively and incisive as David Ansen, Joyce Kulhawik, Janet Maslin, or Kenneth Turan. After years of arguing with Siskel, Ebert's desire for a less acrimonious partnership was understandable, but, in selecting Roeper, the tension between competitive writers of comparable insight and intellectual curiosity evaporated—and was possibly best summarized in an episode of *The Simpsons*. After Homer wins free movie tickets, he cries, "I feel like Roger Ebert or his kiss-ass new partner!" Still, Ebert worked with Roeper until his own battles with salivary cancer forced a leave of absence in July 2006. While negotiating a new contract with Disney-ABC Domestic Television in 2007, Ebert withheld the use of his "thumbs up" evaluation, the trademark he owns with Marlene Iglitzen, Siskel's widow. In July 2008, he parted ways with Disney, ending his more than three-decade association with the program. Disney continued to produce the show, in 2008 with the dismal pairing of entertainment reporters Ben Mankiewicz and Ben Lyons, and in 2009 with A. O. Scott of the *New York Times* and Michael Phillips of the *Chicago Tribune*. Scott, in particular, would have been a challenging partner to Ebert in his heyday, but his pairing with Phillips was canceled after one season.

Ebert proved resilient, though, when *Ebert Presents At the Movies* debuted in January 2011, returning the program to its public television roots. The format of two critics debating over the movies is the same, with Ignatiy Vishnevetsky of mubi.com and Christy Lemire of the Associated Press as hosts. Beyond their reviews, the show is sprinkled with DVD recommendations, reports from correspondents, and Ebert's own analysis, typically read by Bill Curtis or Werner Herzog. Ebert is the managing editor, his wife Chaz the executive producer, and *Ebert Presents* is easily the most promising post-Siskel incarnation of the program, with Vishnevetsky displaying real critical zest and a rich sense of film history. Like Ebert before him, he is hungry to make his points and convey his enthusiasms.

For twenty-four years, Ebert's collaboration with Siskel never overshadowed his own point of view. If anything, the pairing clarified his critical stances. Facing a longstanding rival can do that, and Ebert and

Siskel's competitive temperaments fit snugly with the Hecht-MacArthur image of Chicago newspapermen climbing over one another to secure the latest scoop. In actuality, however, Ebert was shaped by his mentors. After accepting the job of lead film critic for the *Sun-Times*, he bought the collected works of Dwight Macdonald, Pauline Kael, and Robert Warshaw—all of whom Ebert identifies as "Teachers" in the dedication of his *Great Movies*. "If Kael and Sarris were godmother and godfather to the Movie Generation," writes film historian David Bordwell, "Ebert became its voice from within." It's a useful family tree. Influenced by Sarris and Kael, Ebert inherited their better angels— from Sarris, a healthy respect for directorial expressiveness; from Kael, a willingness to consider a film on its own terms. It was Sarris who modeled the gifts of poring over a film and situating it within its historical context. For instance, Ebert—in reviews and his *Scorsese by Ebert*—describes awaiting the latest Scorsese film as a highlight of his job. When Scorsese directed the startlingly brilliant *Goodfellas*, Ebert declared it a great film, not only of its year, but also of its decade. When the director followed with a hellish mess like *Cape Fear*, Ebert gave a reluctant plug, then fired off another essay examining the tensions of writing for the public versus cinephiles. Like Sarris, he turns films of wide-ranging quality into occasions for thoughtful, if at times forgiving, critical analysis. More personally, he shares Sarris' large-heartedness and childlike awe of movies and their transcendent power.

In contrast, Kael modeled a lifetime of thinking and writing about movies in a robust vernacular that moved her readers and enraged her critics. Ebert's dedication to judging a movie on its own merits is an offshoot of her distinctions between trash and art—and the attendant pleasures of both. Yet Ebert's style is his alone. While sharing Kael's receptiveness to art, her unsystematic approach, and certainly her desire to be surprised, his ideas are communicated with a streamlined, Art Deco elegance. Writing for a daily keeps his enthusiasms and frustrations in check, providing built-in editorial discipline that would have benefitted Kael. So, although the length of their reviews differed, they still shared something invaluable: They could generally write what they pleased. That is, Ebert's reviews ran uncut and were never rewritten. "*Sun-Times* writers always felt it was our great advantage over the *Tribune*," Ebert recalls, "which sometimes subjected prose to three or four levels of writing." In the tradition of Kael and Sarris, then, Ebert possesses a formidable knowledge of film history, and his sagacious, snappy criticism complements Sarris' florid, demonstrative style and Kael's artfully colloquial, uninhibited approach.

The legacies of Kael and Sarris throw light on Ebert's. Their critical contentions affected a generation's thinking about the movies, but also carried the acrid stench of endless academic infighting. Ebert and Siskel's quarrels vibrated with moral outrage, yet they were less like jilted lovers than irritated brothers. Kael achieved recognition by criticizing Sarris, and, at first, his sensibilities were known to many through her judgment. In the long view, Sarris suffered more from the auteurist debate—and not because he was right or wrong. Kael moved on, but Sarris, continually glancing over his shoulder at her, collaborated in defining his ideas by her rejection of them.

Significantly, Ebert writes with affection for both. In fact, the manner in which he writes about colleagues conveys a great deal about his critical ethos and sense of self. Praising Paul Cox's *Innocence*, he observes, "This is the kind of film that makes critics want to reach out and shake their readers. Andrew Sarris, for example, who usually maintains a certain practiced objectivity, writes: 'The climax of the film is accompanied by a thrilling musical score that lifts the characters to a sublime metaphysical level such as is seldom attained in the cinema.' Then he goes on to call *Innocence* a 'film for the ages.' You see what I mean." Sarris is the go-to critic for describing movie passions that melt hearts. Here Ebert borrows his effusions to highlight their necessity, deepening respect for both the film and the critic. And in 1971, in a nod to Kael, Ebert wrote:

The Last Picture Show has been described as an evocation of the classic Hollywood narrative film. It is more than that; it is a belated entry in that age—the best film of 1951, you might say. Using period songs and decor to create nostalgia is familiar enough, but to tunnel down to the visual level and get that right, too, and in a way that will affect audiences even if they aren't aware how, is one hell of a directing accomplishment. Movies create our dreams as well as reflect them, and when we lose the movies we lose the dreams. I wonder if Bogdanovich's film doesn't at last explain what it was that Pauline Kael, and a lot of the rest of us, lost at the movies.

Like the film, his words evoke an earlier era—in this case, Pauline Kael's movie memories. Though a cliché, that "one hell of a" is Kael. And the final line effortlessly connects the film's motif of "paradise lost" with Kael's sensibilities. The words express Ebert's love for movies—and not only Bogdonovich's—and the ways they affect our present and past. He also reveals a love of criticism, allowing *The Last Picture Show* to interpret Kael's equivocal title, *I Lost It at the Movies*, demonstrating how criticism brings clarity to our lives. He extends the influence of her words by sharing and generalizing their import. Yet, Ebert seldom quotes other critics in his writings. When he does, the reference is usually an honorific. He's too assured to namedrop, but when he draws from teachers, he adds luster to their names. Given penchants among critics to don a Kael or Sarris jersey, this respect is especially resonant.

Kael and Ebert are both populists, but her voice was more enigmatic. In an episode of *Cheers*, lustful barkeep Sam Malone (Ted Danson) and the regulars film a documentary about life at the bar to assure Woody's (Woody Harrelson) Midwestern parents that he's cared for in Boston. Before the premiere, Sam tells love-interest Diane Chambers (Shelley Long), "You're just in time to see our masterpiece." "Should I alert Pauline Kael?" she asks. "Well if you want to," he replies, "But tell her to get her butt in gear. We're about to start." The joke turns on Kael's clout. Starved for a good time and refusing to fall for Hollywood formulas and mores, she often aligned herself with the audience. To boot, she's the only critic other than Ebert and Siskel likely to be mentioned on a popular sitcom. This was Pauline Kael, critic of the people—if only the people whose collars were white and who subscribed to *The New Yorker*. Hence the joke: Sam Malone watches Ebert and Siskel, but hoity-toity Diane, straining to fit in at the Boston bar, reads Kael.

Still, Kael liked the pronoun "we," and in her famous essay "Trash, Art, and the Movies" she was firmly one with the audience: "Movie art is not the opposite of what we have always enjoyed in movies, it is not to be found in a return to that official high culture, it is what we have always found good in movies only more so." Yet, when she disliked a film, moviegoers could be a discrete, credulous, even choleric group: "The wide movie audience appears to resent American pictures that aren't in a mainstream style. In some angry, instinctive way, the audience seems to be saying of the artists, 'How do *they* dare to be different?' The rewards for not being different have never been higher" (italics hers). Kael's alignment with the audience was fluid; she alternately defended and reprimanded the masses, depending on her purpose. As early as 1970 Charles Thomas Samuels pinpointed this contradiction, describing her as "the apostle of common feelings" who, at the same time, is suspicious of the audience. Kael's writing style—embodied in her use of "we"—"exonerates her readers." It "flatters people sharing her opinions," he wrote, "while those who don't may at least enjoy her spirited prose and encyclopedic knowledge of film history." In the face of such criticism, though, Kael never interrupted her style. In contrast, Ebert is more at ease with himself; his tone, steadier. He doesn't need to beget armies with words. For starters, his home is the *Sun-Times*, Chicago's working-class newspaper. In a profession where writers are constantly jockeying to land jobs at more prestigious publishing outlets, Ebert's loyalty to his city, to his paper, and to his readers recalls his father's lifelong membership in the International Brotherhood of Electrical Workers. He's more of a cultural broker of films who stands, personally and geographically, outside the entertainment industry. Although an expert in film criticism and history, he's no elitist. Having earned the trust and confidence of film producers and consumers, he occupies a rare middle ground between the two.

Ebert's visibility and fields of influence have nonetheless made him a lightning rod for criticism. In a 1988 issue of *Film Comment*, Richard Corliss charged Ebert and Siskel's abbreviated, give-and-take television reviews with having a deleterious effect on American film criticism. I remember holding this very issue in my hands in the Undergraduate Library at the University of Illinois. As a college freshman, I wondered, Was this the Kael-Sarris feud of my generation? It wasn't, but that's a compliment to Ebert's civility. In one camp, Corliss placed Agee, Sarris, Kael, and himself; in the other, philistines like Ebert, Siskel, Joel Siegel, and Gary Franklin. But Corliss' line of argument is a common fallacy among Ebert's critics: Entertainment reporters are more or less studio publicists; since Ebert is a popular television personality, his insights may seem, at first glance, to be on par with those of entertainment reporters. Siskel and Ebert's format of introducing and showing a film clip, then discussing and evaluating the movie for a few minutes prohibited in-depth scene analysis, Corliss complained. It's not criticism, Corliss argued; it's free publicity. Ebert replied in the following issue, agreeing with Corliss' frustrations regarding the program's time restrictions. He then leveled Corliss' claims, systematically emphasizing what everyone knew: Ebert's criticism is both insightful and prodigious, and he doesn't kowtow to studios and movie stars. True, studios supply free movie clips to television programs, believing any publicity is positive, but that's hardly grounds to accuse him of turning criticism into publicity. Besides, in his published criticism, Ebert has repeatedly acknowledged the lack of depth *Siskel and Ebert* permits. The depth of analysis disallowed on *Siskel and Ebert* is pervasive in Ebert's print criticism of movies, books, and festivals. When Corliss posits, "Nobody's publishing film books anymore," Ebert asks if he's read "David Bordwell on Ozu, Patrick McGilligan on Altman, or Linda Williams on pornography." With customary generosity, he defends himself and gives the nod to colleagues, who, along with him, write serious, detailed criticism in all venues of print. (This was, of course, well before the internet made everyone a film critic.)

The real enemy of well-informed criticism, Ebert argues, is the deference of the news media to movie stars, whose iconic capital fuels the industry that funds the publicity machines. Ebert's most telling example is a footnote that spotlights Corliss' swooning pen—"The hazel eyes that laser out of [Tom Cruise's] handsome face"— in his introduction of Cruise for a *Time* magazine cover story. In rebuttal to Ebert, Corliss claimed the Cruise essay was "vivid prose." Uh huh. As proof that a *Time* cover story was not an exchange for a positive review, Corliss cited Adrian Lyne's *Fatal Attraction*—a movie phenomenon that scored the magazine's cover *and* a half-hearted review. He's technically right, but what's more memorable? A milquetoast review of *Fatal Attraction* or the cover of Michael Douglas and Glenn Close in a white-knuckled embrace with the headline, "The Thriller Is Back"? And do the frames accompanying Corliss' essay, of Close attacking Douglas with a butcher knife and smearing blood on his face, along with the title "Killer!" have more integrity than the clips shown on *Siskel and Ebert*? Corliss writes, "I simply don't want people to think that what [Ebert and Siskel] have to do on TV is what I am supposed to do in print." We didn't. "I don't want junk food to be the only cuisine at the banquet," and, with this, Corliss loses on two counts. He fails to recognize that, for many, Ebert's television presence is a gateway to more in-depth criticism, and he fails to see the parallels between the consumerist mentality of review programs and his own writing venues. One example of Corliss' conflicting roles as critic and publicist was evidenced in his co-authored assessment of Jodie Foster's anemic *Little Man Tate*. The October 14, 1991, cover of *Time* was an 8 X 10 glossy of the director, nestled in a theater seat, backlit by a projection light, studiously examining the dailies. "Jodie Foster/A Director Is Born," the headline announced. "Stillborn" is more accurate. The essay read like a press release: "Not many people shine in or on every stage. Not many people are Jodie Foster." But Corliss' predictions were hollow. (Allowedly, Foster's *The Beaver* [2010] revealed a director and star with nerves of steel, but her near-two-decade gestation period to produce a provocative film is an unreasonable wait.) At the end of the day, here is the rub: If Corliss laments the influence of television reviewers who rarely write, then he should have stuck with Joel Siegel. Ebert simply confounds his critics. His television work whets the appetite for the sharp criticism he indefatigably supplies in newspapers, books, and websites.

On one point, however, both critics overgeneralize. Considering the loss of campus film societies, Ebert writes, "Serious discussion of good movies is no longer part of most students' undergraduate experience." "Go further," Corliss adds, "It's hardly part of anyone's experience."

Well, it was part of my experience—and plenty of my classmates, too. In my first year, I read David Bordwell and Kristin Thompson's *Film Art*, John Cawelti and Paul Schrader on film noir, Richard T. Jameson on Alan Pakula, Beth Genné on Vincente Minnelli, Donald Richie and David Desser on Kurosawa, Robin Wood and Laura Mulvey on Hitchcock, not to mention the weekly doses of Ebert, Kael, and David Ansen that arrived in my Oglesby Hall mailbox.

Serious discussions about movies were even integral to my high school years. Picture this. As a senior at Anna-Jonesboro Community High in Anna, Illinois (population 5000), I'm in Mrs. Kroeger's sixth-hour Advanced Debate Class, passionately arguing for the necessity of not an "X" but an "A" rating for intelligent, adult films inappropriate for those under 17. The prima facie evidence was Alan Parker's *Angel Heart*, a tenebrous, brooding New Orleans noir that raised eyebrows when the ratings board demanded cuts from a violent sex scene in exchange for an "R" rating. I brought along the movie poster: a coal-black image of Robert De Niro as Lucifer, his taloned fingernails clutching a cane, his hair slicked back and tightly bound. Beneath him, a frantic Mickey Rourke has sold his soul. At least it got my classmates' attention. (For my brother's sins, he traversed the full length of a mall, me dragging that linen-backed poster behind us. At home, against the soft yellow hue of my bedroom walls, it was nicknamed "Hell on Wheels." Eventually, I returned the print to the Chrisman Art Gallery in Cape Girardeau, Missouri. It's one thing to enjoy a frisson of terror in the theater; quite another to wake up with Old Scratch each morning.) I gave it my best shot, and the class applauded when my eight minutes were up. I knew I'd achieved my goal when Jason Holdman, a bright schoolmate whose family was Southern Baptist and dirt-poor—not the ideal audience for *Angel Heart*—said, "A legitimate need for movie directors and audiences." Best of all, the foundation of the speech was built upon generous quotes from Ebert's essay "A Case for the A Rating." My life attests to the truth that there was more intelligent talk of movies than critics believed, and Ebert was a crucial part of those conversations. His words matter, and I'm not alone. Reflecting on his love of film, director Jeff Nichols observed at Ebert's 2008 film festival, "I grew up with Ebert in my home." After receiving a congratulatory email from the critic regarding his first feature, *Shotgun Stories*, Nichols immediately phoned his parents and said, "Even if my movie's never released, know that Roger Ebert liked it." Fortunately the movie was exhibited, but Ebert's respect is all a mother needs to know.

This is not to imply that his influence is wholly salubrious. It isn't. Andrew Sarris warned that Ebert's wit and intelligence were being "steadily eroded by too calculating a deference to the banalities of a mass audience." Ebert argued that he remained sensitive to such concerns—yet at times, not nearly enough. I recall, in graduate school, surfing through channels late one night and stumbling upon Ebert and Siskel on *The Howard Stern Show*. I paused, but not for long. After the familiar exchange of Siskel needling Ebert about his weight, and Ebert ridiculing Siskel for purchasing John Travolta's white suit from *Saturday Night Fever* and allegedly needing to "take the crotch in," I turned it off. Their dog-and-pony show had grown stale and tiring, regardless of the venue. And why did they need to appear on Stern's program? How much visibility is compensation for that level of stupidity? The blame cannot be laid at the feet of shock journalism, either, as Ebert and Siskel collapsed into childishness in front of interviewers as civil as Lawrence Grobel. "My nature is to be antagonistic at times, especially with Gene," Ebert noted, "who brings out the antagonistic in me." That's well and good when the antagonism is rooted in passionate feelings about movie art, but when they personalized their bickering, on or off their program, it was just that: bickering. And it turned them into the caricatures they painted of one another; worse still, it diminished the profession of film criticism.

Fortunately, these moments were exceptions, not the rule. Aside from his low points with Siskel, Ebert generally engages his critics with fair-mindedness, and the respect he garners from colleagues affirms this. Writers as diverse as David Ansen, A. O. Scott, Andrew Sarris, Dave Eggers, Joyce Kulhawik, James Berardinelli, Janet Maslin, Kenneth Turan, Tom Shales, and Harry Knowles express admiration. Even the *Chicago Reader*'s exacting Jonathan Rosenbaum, who criticizes the economic constraints of film distribution and believes programs like Ebert's comply in keeping foreign films from the public, acknowledges Ebert's love of movies. And recognizing Ebert's popularity, Richard Schickel admits a measure of professional jealousy. (I sympathize. In high school, after sharing Ebert's droll review of *Motel Hell* with my best buddy Joey Collier, I remember a tinge of jealousy when he kept reading Ebert's reviews instead of going out to toss the football.) Ebert's mentors also vie with his influence, and the power of his perspective is glimpsed through its exaggeration. Discussing the production of *A Thousand Acres* and director Jocelyn Moorhouse's reported dissatisfaction with the final cut, Andrew Sarris observes: "Siskel and Ebert picked up on the industry buzz and gave it two thumbs down, and most every other critic lambasted it." This is sheer cock and bull. Ebert's critique of *A Thousand Acres* isn't his best, and we'll get to that, but implying that his opinion is molded by industry rumors is nonsense. Sarris cites no evidence because none exists. In the final analysis, Ebert's voice is one that even his teachers reckon with, however clumsily.

Less understood is Ebert's influence on filmmakers. Werner Herzog, Errol Morris, and Martin Scorsese all cite Ebert's encouragement as pivotal to their creative development and persistence. His impact spans generations. One need only attend Ebertfest, his annual film festival, to appreciate the directors he has energized over the years: Phil Morrison (*Junebug*), Henry Alex Rubin and Dana Adam Shapiro (*Murderball*),

Tarsen Singh (*The Cell*), Alex Proyas (*Dark City*), and Lodge Kerrigan (*Claire Dolan*). Newly hatched filmmakers like Kevin DiNovis (*Surrender Dorothy*), Jeff Nichols (*Shotgun Stories*), Hilary Birmingham (*Tully*), Jonathan Caouette (*Tarnation*), and Leah Mahan (*Sweet Old Song*) drink deeply from Ebert's reservoirs of confidence; they're visibly humbled by the opportunity to screen and discuss their films with him and fifteen-hundred audience members.

At times, Ebert is everywhere. "My web site and blog at the *Sun-Times* site have changed the way I work," he writes, "and even the way I think. When I lost my speech, I speeded up instead of slowing down." The *Sun-Times'* website offers a range of topics to click, including "Metro," "News," "Commentary," "Sports," "Business," and "Entertainment." And "Ebert." He's his own brand. The hits on his name far outpace the others, and each week he continues to write about the latest releases. Rogerebert.com provides access to a lifetime of his reviews, as well as his blog, where he ruminates on everything from Darwinism to the latest political developments. *Ebert Presents At the Movies* appears weekly on television and online. He's available on Facebook, his annual compendium of reviews is published each year, and his *Great Movies* series is a sustained effort to reconsider films from the past. He has an enormous following on Twitter, where his provocative tweets kindle debate, such as when he criticizes those who want to neuter the language in *Huckleberry Finn*, or when he writes, in reaction to *Jackass* star Ryan Dunn's reported death from drunk driving, "Friends don't let jackasses drink and drive." From the get-go, Ebert has developed a singular voice that illuminates movies with commonsensical wisdom and humor, and he's the first critic to adapt that voice to multiple social media and secure a mass following. All those years arguing with Siskel seem to have prepared him for a social networking landscape where feedback is instantaneous. Paired with a rival, he has demonstrated how one point of view can hone another. In marked contrast to the Kael-Sarris feud—an auteurist debate that has yielded an aesthetic stand-off—Ebert and Siskel have modeled a critical engagement that shows one can vehemently disagree about art while affirming the commitment to conversation and debate. And theirs was more than just entertainment. In the same way that Ebert's *Sun-Times* criticism introduced him to Chicago, and *Siskel and Ebert* introduced him to the nation, the web introduced him to the world. Along the way, his critical values have shaped a generation. Aesthetically, he's proved himself a worthy pupil of his teachers, a yardstick for his contemporaries, an inspiration to filmmakers, and a trusted confidant of readers and moviegoers. In America's cinematic lexicon, "Ebert" means more than "Film"; he's a metonymy for "Love of Film."

Chapter 2
Rule of Thumb

History demonstrates that power, authority, and mercy reside in the turn of a thumb. In portrayals of ancient Rome, a host of Hollywood films depict gladiatorial battles where victory is awarded by a sea of raised thumbs. Over and against these stock images, historian Anthony Corbeill argues that in fact the opposite was true: The raised thumb represented the death sentence for a warrior, while the thumb pressed against a closed fist was a symbol of mercy. Variations in meaning notwithstanding, the command of the opposable digit is an enduring one. Modern Western culture interprets a raised thumb as a hearty indicator of approval and a lowered one as a mark of disfavor. And in the American film industry, the future of a movie—its distribution, exhibition, and audience awareness—has hinged on the tilt of Roger Ebert's thumb. Millions of dollars are invested, earned, or lost based on its direction. Some criticize its simplicity. After all, what is more plebeian than reducing the evaluation of art to this sort of bottom-line? But Ebert has defended the symbol, saying that it mirrors the final judgments that punctuate people's street-level arguments about movies. It's the final word on his television program and more ubiquitously in print, where the coveted "'Thumbs Up!'—Roger Ebert" generates buzz and box-office. At the same time, the gesture follows more nuanced discussions of films in his televised critiques, and his reviews in the *Chicago Sun-Times* are accompanied by star ratings that translate into fast-and-dirty yeas or nays. For a moviegoer needing quick advice on Friday night or the cinephile craving analysis of De Palma's latest, Ebert's thumb allows Americans to enter a critical space from a range of entry points and a variety of depths.

Yet a thumb, however mighty, is but part of the man. With his trademark turtle-shell glasses, bookish sweater vest, and stocky build, Ebert is quintessentially Midwestern. He looks like America. If Americans are made anxious by hifalutin film analysis, Ebert is the sophisticated, critical mind who has never scared away audiences leery of intellectuals. Imagine, if you can, a film critic in France gaining popularity while offering a raised or lowered thumb at the end of a program dedicated to serious film analysis. This is why Ebert's criticism gains import within a distinctly American context. Backed up with a cogent, demanding, and, above all, trustworthy intellect, a sparkling sense of humor, and the unthreatening physical presence of a weekly guest in one's living room, Ebert is one of us—just smarter. And that thumb, with all its literal and iconic capital, is an indispensable aspect of his popularity and influence.

He is, in effect, the Robert Frost of American film criticism. Both men were late bloomers, though in different ways. Frost found love early in life and professional standing years later. Ebert achieved professional success early on but enduring love would wait for middle age. Both men's literary voices are distinctly regional—Frost the transplanted Northeasterner, Ebert the eternal Midwesterner. Both men are known for the deceptively simple surfaces of their prose and subject matter. As writers, both discovered freedom within the constraints of their genres: Frost with his rhymed verse, and Ebert with his newspaper reviews. Frost returns to nature, ever-present and available to all; Ebert to the movies, the most democratic and multi-sensory of arts. Both men primarily viewed themselves as teachers. Both spent time in, and cultivated lasting affections for, England. Both delighted in a naughty joke and maintained abiding, quiet respect for Darwin. Although neither were churchgoers, both maintained reverence for the roles of religious belief in everyday life. Paradoxically, both received the highest accolades within their professional guilds, yet their talents were also taken for granted—even resented by colleagues who envied their fame and the ease with which they maintained their professional productivity and influence. Finally, and again paradoxically, both men maintained the appearances of regionalism and special qualities of shyness while pursuing and securing positions of high visibility and puissance within literary circles and public life.

Frost firmly believed in the sound of the poem—the alchemy of a writer's voice finding the right subject matter and transforming the informal, vital rhythms of everyday conversation into lasting prose. Just as Frost's years as a New England farmer focused and deepened his poetic skills, Ebert's Midwestern roots molded his aesthetic sensibilities. He grew up in Urbana, Illinois, smack-dab in the middle of the state, and a critical, playful imagination permeates his criticism. Ebert has never shied away from mentioning his hometown in his writings, and it is always with warmth. He acknowledges how growing up in the Midwest informs his responses to movies:

> I have a friend who claims he only laughed real loud on five occasions during *Top Secret!* I laughed that much in the first ten minutes. It all depends on your sense of humor. My friend claims that I have a cornpone sense humor, because of my origins deep in central Illinois. I admit that is true. As a Gemini, however, I contain multitudes, and I also have a highly sophisticated, sharply intellectual sense of humor. Get me in the right mood, and I can laugh all over the map. That's why I liked *Top Secret!* This movie will cheerfully go for a laugh whenever one is even remotely likely to be found.

Ebert creatively embraces his beginnings while reinventing the Midwestern archetype. He accepts the "cornpone" label, pairs it with his Gemini status, and the immodest description undercuts any defensiveness. Basically, he assures his readers that it is okay to laugh at *Top Secret!* A critic with a cosmopolitan sense of humor can also have a great time at a goofy, bawdy comedy. To pretend otherwise is dishonest. *Top Secret!* is not great art, and it knows that. It's a non-stop giggle machine with zingers broad enough to engage the rustic and sophisticate in us all.

It is a truism that criticism is a form of autobiography, and Ebert's oeuvre provides a rich and singular self-portrait. Although he prizes his small-town roots, his memories are refreshingly free of sentimentality. Colorful personalities pop in from out of his past, like welcome character actors in classic movies. "Mrs. Seward, the draconian rhetoric teacher who drilled literacy into generations of Urbana (Ill.) High School Students, used to tell us we were having the best four years of our lives. We groaned. *Fame* is a movie that she might have enjoyed." He even permits her to do the dirty work. Assessing the ill-formed title of *The Opposite Sex and How to Live with Them*, Ebert notes that Mrs.

Seward "would have cracked director Matthew Meshekoff over the knuckles for that one. She would have gone on to describe his script as 'trite,' which was one of her favorite words, but which I have never used in a review, until now." Years later she cameos in his review of *The Chorus*, yet another story of a teacher inspiring an unlikely assortment of pupils. Ebert feels the movie is too prosaic, especially for a French film: "Where's the quirkiness, the nuance, the deeper levels?" Yet he finds those qualities in Mrs. Seward, who "gently suggested that the day would come when I would no longer find Thomas Wolfe readable." Here's a revealing difference: Pauline Kael loathed "the schoolmarm's approach" that defined art as the fulfillment of intentions; Ebert honored and humanized schoolmarms, placing them front and center. "Miss Fiske would have loved this movie," he writes of his hometown librarian at the onset of a review of *84 Charing Cross Road*. "And I would have loved seeing it with her, through her eyes ..." After cataloguing some of the film's disappointments, he concludes:

> Sigh. Miss Fiske, who you may remember from the first paragraph of this review, was the librarian at the Urbana Free-Library when I was growing up... [She] ran the book club and the Saturday morning puppet shows and the book fairs and the story readings. She never had to talk to me about the love of books because she simply exuded it and I absorbed it.
>
> She would have loved this movie. Sitting next to her, I suspect, I would have loved it, too. But Miss Fiske is gone now, and I found it pretty slow going on my own. And for that matter, Miss Fiske had a sharp critical intelligence, and I suspect that after seeing this movie she would have nodded and said she enjoyed it, but then she might have added, "Why didn't that silly woman get on the boat and go to London ten years sooner and save herself all that postage?"

Here, Ebert invites an old friend to the screening, and their varied reactions clarify the film. If one enjoys the movie, Miss Fiske is an ally. If it disappoints, her sensibility has the final word. Along the way, we're provided a snapshot of growing up with the riches of a good local library, and, of equal importance, a nurturing librarian. By mentioning Miss Fiske's critical mind, he challenges the image of the stoic, unsophisticated Midwesterner. In high school, I raced through Helene

Hanff's *84 Charing Cross Road*, and I remember liking the movie well enough, but Ebert's recollection of Miss Fiske is etched in my mind more clearly than the characters in the book and the film. This is a watermark of fine criticism—when the writing leaves an impression as indelible as the film itself.

Style is the man—so they also say—and never has this been more true than of Ebert's prose. It begins with words, and the one he returns to again and again is "cheerful," or its adverbial companion, "cheerfully." The word taps into Ebert's core as a critic: his innate humanism, his light touch, and his perennially fresh sense of humor. Regarding *Bad Dreams*, a dreary, assembly-line horror film aimed squarely at teenagers, he wonders longingly "if maybe there were some creative, cheerful and life-affirming screenplays around?" He disliked the jarring structure of *Pennies from Heaven*, a lavish film that interrupts unrelieved suffering among Depression-era misfits with joyful production numbers inspired by 1930s musicals. He concludes: "Just imagine if the creativity, energy, work, talent, and money that went into *Pennies from Heaven* had been devoted instead to a cheerful film on the same topic. Boy, would we need it now." For Ebert, a cheerful screenplay is an antidote to despair, a balm to ensure hope.

A cheerful sensibility can also convey a welcome knowingness. Self-possession, in life and art, is admirable. As Ebert observes of *8 Women*, "From the opening shot, the film cheerfully lets us know it's a spoof of overproduced Hollywood musicals." *Citizen Ruth* satirizes both sides of the abortion debate with "cheerful open-mindedness." *Quest for Fire* "cheerfully acknowledges" that we are comic beasts at heart. And recall that *Top Secret!* "cheerfully" goes for laughs in every nook and cranny. These movies understand their content and express it with invigorating directness. The same holds true for artists. Kenneth Branagh is "a director cheerfully willing to shoot for the moon, to pump up his scenes with melodrama and hyperbole." Branagh earns the ovation. The alternative is an artist without courage or the good sense to know that, quite often, great stylistic risk precedes great reward.

In Ebert's economy, a healthy attitude toward life and sex is essentially a cheerful one. The colorful characters in *Amarcord* are "bound together by their transparent simplicity and a strain of cheerful vulgarity." As the apple of Dudley Moore's eye in *10*, Bo Derek is "a pure and cheerful embodiment of carnal perfection." While vulgarity and carnality, in and of themselves, lead to unseemly vices, "cheerfulness" humanizes them. It implies an easy awareness of one's strengths and foibles. "Cheerful" carnality has a handle on sex in proportion to life's many pleasures. The adjective softens the vice, transforming vulgarity and carnality from mortal to venial sins. For Ebert, it's desirable to be a "cheerful embodiment" of just about anything.

Ebert's use of the phrase "free will" is also informative. It communicates his respect for movies that alter conventions and thwart expectations. The expression can praise a director and script: Eric Rohmer's characters "seem to retain free will. They aren't doomed, for example, to climb into the sack with each other at the end of the movie just because that's what usually happens." Or an entire movie. For Catherine Breillat's *Fat Girl*, it's an extraordinary commendation: "There is a jolting surprise in discovering that this film has free will, and can end as it wants, and that its director can make her point, however brutally." The theological aura of "free will" deepens the praise; it's as if the film were alive and capable of moral reasoning. Once again Ebert reveals himself a Gemini who contains multitudes. The author of *Ebert's Little Movie Glossary*, which pigoenholes movie clichés with ingenuity and affection, reserves his highest praise for unruly films that flout those conventions.

Beginning in the late 1990s, Ebert at times addressed his audience with a direct term of endearment: His playful salutation to his "Dear reader" has specific effects. In one way, it functions as a sort of open secret, a hush-hush revelation that Ebert firmly controls. In his review of *The Eyes of Tammy Faye*, a documentary exploring the life of fallen television evangelist Tammy Faye Baker, he admits fascination with *The Jim J. and Tammy Faye Show* in the 80s: "They were like two little puppets—Howdy Doody and Betty Boop made flesh. Tammy Faye cried on nearly every show and sang with the force of a Brenda Lee, and when she'd do her famous version of 'We're Blest,' yes, dear reader, I would sing along with her." Here, the "dear reader" is not patronizing, and Ebert's confession reverberates with the film's surprisingly empathetic tone toward its subject. In other contexts, the phrase addresses the cordial, enduring relationships among Ebert, his readers, and his most cherished films. A line from the time-traveling romance *Déjà Vu* reminds Ebert of his favorite dialogue in *Citizen Kane*, when Mr. Bernstein reflects on the memory of the girl on the Jersey ferry, dressed in white with a white parasol. He sees her for only a second, but remembers her every month of his long life. "Can you, dear reader, think of such a moment, too?" Ebert asks.

> Perfect love is almost always unrealized. It has to be. What makes those memories perfect is that they produce no history. The woman with the white parasol remains always frozen in an old man's memory. She never grows old, is never out of temper, never loses interest in him, never dies. She exists forever as a promise, like the green light at the end of Gatsby's pier.

In this case the motif of memory circles back on itself, and the review becomes a full-fledged reverie as he applauds one film by appreciating another. "Dear readers," all, are invited to reflect on the strength and limitations of unrealized love. As icing on the cake, he invokes Fitzgerald, inviting Gatsby to the soirée. These are not the ruminations of a novice critic. They are lessons from one who has suffered at the hands of romantic ideals and walked away the wiser for it. Ebert has lived to tell, revealing a critic in love with movies, literature, and love itself—not the perfect love of youth, but an abiding love that discovers the beauty of imperfection.

It's fitting, then, that Ebert is drawn to a cheerful script because he himself has a large spirit and magnanimous personality. He respects the dangerous notion of free will, because, without it, intelligent decisions in life and art are meaningless. And if he addresses his audience with affection, it is because his readership is loyal. That "dear reader" is more than a waggish greeting; it draws on the wholehearted, trustworthy relationships he's cultivated with countless readers in his ongoing role as elder statesman of American film criticism.

Philosophically, Ebert's aesthetics are rooted in his belief that the prevailing power of cinema is the ability to place oneself in the shoes of another: "We know we want it. We want to see through other people's eyes, have their experiences, stand in their shoes. That's the unspoken promise of the movies." Seeing *Citizen Kane* in high school in 1958, Ebert walked away convinced that movies have the potential to convey the truth of a human life. Great movies do just that, from Humphrey Bogart's disillusioned lover in Michael Curtiz's *Casablanca* (1942) to Peter Greene's desperate schizophrenic in Lodge Kerrigan's

Clean, Shaven (1995). Without question Ebert's empathy is central in his critical faculties, and his favorite films explore human behavior within the fabric of everyday life. Universal truths emerge, but only through the particulars. These values converge in Ramin Bahrani's *Man Push Cart* (2005), the story of a Pakistani immigrant's determination to survive in New York City by pushing a bagel cart. The film's force is its simplicity. The sparse editing, documentary-like camera, and unvarnished portrayal of endurance suggest to Ebert a theme of "human survival at a most fundamental economic level." Even the clipped title captures the mysterious unity of the singular and universal. Discussing the film at his festival, he asked, "How many times have I been to New York, ordered a cup of coffee, but not seen this man?" Bahrani's film encourages Ebert to live with his eyes open, and Ebert himself teaches us to see again, as well.

As a critic, Ebert exemplifies the empathy he demands from art. From this angle, his colleagues are useful counterpoints. At the risk of belaboring the obvious, John Simon has been a stringent critic of acting. He also criticized an actor's physical appearance—not necessarily for being wrong for a role, but simply for being wrong. About Glenda Jackson he complained, "In almost every play or film she inflicts her naked body on us, which, considering its quality, is the supreme insult flung at the spectators." Kathleen Turner was "competent by our screen standards and pretty from an angle or two—in repose and with ethereal lighting—but otherwise just another petty [*sic*] face." That "[*sic*]" is all his, and any writer who states and underlines a barb lacks confidence in his punch line. Criticism is, of course, subjective. Yet these women could never please Simon, whose arguments are as memorable for their partisanship as their sting. Never an inviting screen presence, Jackson always casts a difficult, mysterious spell. When I first saw her body in *Women in Love*, she seemed icily perfect. Cranking up the thermostat, Kathleen Turner was, to me, the last natural born movie star. The allure of her faux-European accent, honey-blonde hair, strapping height, and gusty personality transcended camera angles and lighting effects. When Kathleen Turner walked into a room, somebody walked into the room. Turner fared better with Pauline Kael, whose criticism, like a bonfire, was often all-consuming celebrations or denouncements. Kael treasured Marlon Brando, Debra Winger, and Jessica Lange, while Candice Bergen was flogged even in films in which she did not appear. Regarding Ali MacGraw in *The Getaway*, Kael wrote, "Last time I saw Candice Bergen, I thought she was a worse actress than MacGraw; now I think that I slandered Bergen. It must be that whichever you're seeing is worse." Or, in moments like this, whichever you're reading. For better or worse, these are defining sensibilities of New York film criticism in the 1970s and 80s: passionate, combative, factional. And actors weren't the only ones caught in the crossfire. When John Simon and Andrew Sarris criticized Barbra Streisand's looks or talent, they were also aiming at Kael's enthusiasm for Streisand, and, by extension, their critical nemesis.

In sharp contrast, Ebert's pen never sought to skewer the actor. As a guiding principle, he concentrates on the film. His writing is not a pretext to upbraid anyone. His empathy is manifest in myriad ways, and, with respect to acting, the impact on his criticism is two-fold: He rarely blames a film's shortcomings on actors, and when he critiques them, his words are observant and restrained. Both sensibilities are evident in his reaction to Fernando Trueba's *Two Much*, which he treats as an occasion to define the tricky, rarified genre of screwball comedy. After briefly criticizing a supporting player for overreaching, he concludes: "It's better to adopt the strategy used by [Melanie] Griffith, [Daryl] Hannah and [Danny] Aiello, who simply play their roles straight, and let the screenplay take care of the comedy. It doesn't, unfortunately, but that's not their fault." Time and again his point of view is judicious. In this case, the filmmakers are clearly giving it all they've got.

Ebert's attachment to the adjective "thankless" is another way of finding fault with a film while protecting the actor. It follows, then, that Renée Zellweger in *Me, Myself & Irene* is "asked to be loyal and sensible, lay down the law, pout, smile and be shocked. It's a thankless task; she's like the onscreen representative of the audience." Julia Louis-Dreyfus is also saddled with a "thankless" role in *Father's Day*, where her character misunderstands telephone messages. For Ebert, the subtext is clear: These are talented people, and the material is beneath them. A thankless role, in the end, excuses an actor from shouldering the blame. In more complicated films, it actually heightens accomplishment. Extolling *Working Girl*'s Sigourney Weaver, Ebert observes, "Supporting roles are crucial in movies like this. Weaver's role is a thankless one—she plays the pill who gets humiliated at the end—and yet it is an interesting assignment for an actor with Weaver's imagination. From her first frame on the screen, she has to say all the right things while subtly suggesting that she may not mean any of them." And Meryl Streep as the besieged Lindy Chamberlain in *A Cry in the Dark* is handed an equally "thankless assignment: to show us a woman who deliberately refused to allow insights into herself... Streep's performance is risky, and masterful." In each instance, the actors win, through amnesty (making the best of unworthy assignments) or triumph of imagination (bringing flair to a conventional role or performing a demanding duty with distinction). If a film fails to thank an actor, Ebert steps in.

Such a fixture of Ebert's critical sensibilities is his empathy toward actors that the exception proves the rule. It's not that he never takes an actor to task:

> You know me. I'm easy on actors. These are real people with real feelings. When I see a bad performance, I'm inclined to blame anyone but the actors. In the case of *Exit to Eden* I'm inclined to blame the actors. Starting with Rosie O'Donnell. I'm sorry, but I just don't get Rosie O'Donnell. I've seen her in three or four movies now, and she has generally had the same effect on me as fingernails on a blackboard. She's harsh and abrupt and staccato and doesn't seem to be having any fun. She looks mean... And of all the actresses I can imagine playing the role of the dominatrix, Dana Delaney is the last. She's a cute, merry-faced type—perfect for the dominatrix's best friend. For the lead, let's see. How about Faye Dunaway? Linda Fiorentino? Sigourney Weaver? See what I mean?

And Steve Martin's early film work, for instance, was every bit as grating to him as O'Donnell's. More often than not, however, Ebert's criticism of an actor is balanced with sardonic humor or a nod of appreciation for the actor's abilities. A trip to the Ebert woodshed might be a slow walk, but the belt never comes off. Case in point, he notes that Delaney is miscast *and* quickly describes her ideal role. His analysis of the acting in the airplane action film *Turbulence* is also typical: "In a performance that seems like an anthology of acting choices, [Ray] Liotta goes from charmer to intelligent negotiator to berserk slasher to demented madman. My favorite moment is when he's covered with blood, the plane is buckling through a Level 6 storm, bodies are littered everywhere, and he's singing 'Buffalo Gals, Won't You Come Out Tonight.'" Later, Ebert is more frank: "[Lauren] Holly's performance is the key to the movie, and it's not very good: She screams a lot and keeps shouting 'Ooohhh!' but doesn't generate much charisma, and frankly I wish the killer had strangled her and left the more likeable [Catherine] Hicks to land the plane." This is an act of goodwill. Ebert and I are two of a handful who saw *Turbulence* in theaters. (I enjoy Ray Liotta, and this movie was a test of stamina, intelligence, and loyalty.) So embarrassing was Holly's performance that it was difficult to watch. Ebert doesn't mollycoddle, but Holly's loss is Hicks' gain; in the face of serious acting incompetence, at least there's a supporting role to praise. Even with sitting ducks, his sense of humor and proportion leavens his criticism.

At other times his disappointment is genuinely instructive, taking into consideration the trajectory of an artist's career. Responding to Goldie Hawn's fish-out-of-water roles, he wrote, "*Wildcats* is clearly an attempt by Hawn to repeat a formula that was wonderfully successful in *Private Benjamin*: Wide-eyed Goldie copes with the real world. It was less successful in *Protocol*, and now it's worn out altogether." The sins of the mother visit the daughter in 2004's *Raising Helen*: "Kate Hudson, who stars, seems to be following in the footsteps of her mother, Goldie Hawn; both have genuine talent, but choose too often to bury themselves in commercial formulas." For Ebert, there's a perpetual tension between capable actors and ham-fisted conventions, but it's the latter that raises his hackles.

Figures 7–8 Ebert was tickled when a shot of Burt Reynolds passionately kissing Rachel Ward in *Sharky's Machine* dissolves into the Peachtree Plaza Hotel in Atlanta, Georgia. This stouthearted, stylish thriller—directed by and starring Reynolds—proves his talent. *Warner Bros.*

Similarly, his reviews of Burt Reynolds' movies in the 80s were a series of dire professional warnings. "Reynolds is so popular he can make money in almost anything," he lamented in 1981, "a maxim that *Cannonball Run* puts to the extreme test." Again in '81, reviewing *Sharky's Machine*: "As a director, Reynolds allows himself a few excesses (one howler is the dramatic cut from a sex scene to the phallic glory of the Peachtree Plaza Hotel). But he's put a lot of ambition in this movie, and it reminds us that there is a fine actor within the star of *Cannonball Run*." Yet Reynolds was an "assembly-line product" in the unspeakable *Stroker Ace* (1983), and, by the following year, Ebert was serving as triage consultant reviewing *Cannonball Run II*, the actor's sixth outing with stuntman-turned-director Hal Needham. Ebert's review could have been chiseled on marble: "Greater love hath no actor, than that he sacrifice his career on the altar of friendship." Signs of life were finally detected in Bill Forsyth's quiet character study, *Breaking In* (1989). After noting Reynolds' career slump, Ebert remarked, "This time, in the Forsyth universe, he shows the warmth and quirkiness that made him fun to watch in the first place"—an apt conclusion that neither overstates nor ignores the accomplishment. In times like this, Ebert is a cautious optimist. It is, after all, only one film. Over the long haul of an actor's career, Ebert is both critic and confidant—reminding him of missteps, as well as of his talent. Had Reynolds heeded the advice, the actor's celebrated return to mastery in *Boogie Nights* (1997) might have felt more like another notch in his belt than professional atonement.

Equal empathy was seen in Ebert's critiques of Vincent Gallo's road film, *The Brown Bunny*. To summarize, Ebert saw the film at Cannes and declared it the worst he'd sat through in his history of attending the festival. Gallo fired back, first by arguing that the film was a rough cut and then, bizarrely, by placing a hex on Ebert's colon. Ebert later met with Gallo, agreed to see the director's final cut, and gave the film a more positive review. No question the widely reported clash helped boost the film's meager visibility, yet few critics would be generous enough to meet a young director of modest gifts, not to mention rewatching the film. Ebert leaves the impression that it simply doesn't matter if the director is Vincent Gallo or Sidney Lumet. If the moment, no matter how awkward, provides an opportunity for artists—including himself—to grow, he rises to the occasion.

Figure 9 Marcello's expression says it all. His character in Federico Fellini's *La Dolce Vita* is the one that Ebert identifies with most closely. *KOCH Lorber*

Ebert's empathy—his thirst for stepping into the shoes of another—provides occasions for self-reflection. In 1984, he identified Marcello Mastroianni's gossip columnist in Fellini's *La Dolce Vita* as the movie character he relates most closely with, "not in terms of physical details but in terms of his spiritual dilemma: being torn between getting out the daily piece and writing that great novel that he knows he has in him." This identification would intensify over the years, and in 2002 he wrote:

> Movies do not change, but their viewers do. When I saw *La Dolce Vita* in 1961, I was an adolescent for whom "the sweet life" represented everything I dreamed of: sin, exotic European glamour, the weary romance of the cynical newspaperman. When I saw it again, around 1970, I was living in a version of Marcello's world; Chicago's North Avenue was not the Via Veneto, but at 3 A.M., the denizens were just as colorful, and I was about Marcello's age.
>
> When I saw the movie around 1980, Marcello was the same age, but I was ten years older, had stopped drinking, and saw him not as a role model, but as a victim, condemned to an endless search for happiness that could never be found, not that way. By 1991, when I analyzed the film a frame at a time at the University of Colorado, Marcello seemed younger still, and while I had once admired and then criticized him, now I pitied and loved him. And when I saw the movie right after Mastroianni died, I thought that Fellini and Marcello had taken a moment of discovery and made it immortal. There may be no such thing as the sweet life. But it is necessary to find that out for yourself.

In Ebert's hands, Fellini's film is more than a work of art; it is a mirror in which to measure our souls and the distances traveled. His critical humility is no repudiation of his first response. It's an honest reflection on how our relationship to art changes over time, how art helps us to see our lives with greater transparency and perspective. As such, it's a meaningful counterpoise to Pauline Kael's lack of interest in seeing a movie twice and Andrew Sarris' shifting opinions of a director's reputation. For Ebert, movies are opportunities for self-reflection as well as entertainment, and, as part and parcel of a critic's calling, they demand that one eternally learn. His writing is also generous. Somehow by the end of that second paragraph, I appreciate Fellini's achievement as clearly as Ebert's journey.

As the Fellini review suggests, Ebert has had his own complicated relationship with alcohol. His struggles are just beneath the surface of his scathing review of *Only When I Laugh* (1981), based on a play by Neil Simon and starring Marsha Mason, who was married to Simon at the time: "Simon and Mason must not drink, know little about drinking, and less about how to stop drinking." His anger toward the film's shallow view of recovery is understandable. Two years earlier, in August of 1979, Ebert had poured his last scotch and soda. In 2005, he discussed his battles with alcohol for the first time in a balanced interview in *Chicago* magazine; on August 25, 2009, his blog entry—titled "My Name Is Roger. And I'm an Alcoholic"—detailed his partnership with Alcoholics Anonymous. He hasn't taken a drink for more than thirty years and his physical condition makes it unlikely that he will. "Since surgery in July of 2006 I have literally not been able to drink at all," he wrote. "Unless I go insane and start pouring booze into my g-tube, I believe I'm reasonably safe." After decades of success, his intentions in talking about AA were clear: "There's a chance somebody will read this and take the steps toward sobriety." What's striking is how Ebert frames his personal difficulties as opportunities for empathy. "I began to realize that I had tended to avoid some people because of my instant conclusions about who they were and what they would have to say," he wrote. "I discovered that everyone [in AA], speaking honestly and openly, had important things to tell me."

So Ebert knows what he's talking about when he rises to Mel Gibson's defense, even when few have kind words to say about him—when, indeed, Gibson's widely publicized rants make it difficult to defend him. In his review of *The Beaver*, Ebert observes that Gibson "is after all a superb actor." With characteristic neutrality, Ebert writes:

> His personal life is in ruins because of the disease of alcoholism, which he is still struggling with. Though he's responsible for his outrageous acts and statements, I think this is not the good man I have met many times. From what I know about alcoholism, I believe he goes through personality changes, that he is content on some days and consumed by rage and madness on others, and that such changes are symptoms of the disease. Make your own diagnosis.

I respect Ebert's final sentence, which reflects his general attitude toward Alcoholics Anonymous. "If you want AA," he writes, "it is there. That's how I feel. If you have problems with it, don't come." He isn't interested in forcing his views on others, but he's humble enough to share his story with the expectation that someone might be helped.

So Ebert, as well, has weathered life's vicissitudes to become the symbol of his craft. Like Frost, who regularly lectured on the role of poetry in everyday life, and who relished holding court through public engagements, Ebert, too, is a writer of the people. His critical platform also involves the dual roles of practitioner and instructor. With a nurturing spirit, he imparts his aesthetics by tirelessly sharing his enthusiasms. And his influence is ever-present.

Take Linda Dillow, a childhood friend of mine and kindred spirit. Uncommonly smart, Linda could play the piano for days, had a cute, toothy grin, and was raised in a Nazarene congregation that frowned on movies. So films were forbidden, but she could watch television, including *Siskel and Ebert*. "They don't like anything that's good," she complained to me one day. "'We can't recommend *Aliens*, but don't miss *The Peanut Butter Man*!'" — *The Peanut Butter Man* being her *nom de plume* for every obscure art film championed by Ebert and Siskel. (Of course, Ebert loved *Aliens*; not all who confront him have their facts straight.) So Ebert remains a paradox. For Linda, he and Siskel were lovers of highbrow entertainment far removed from popular tastes; yet her access to them was contingent on their popularity that extended to non-moviegoers like her. Over time, Linda became a sophisticated film connoisseur ("Movies do not change, but their viewers do"), and we had even more to talk about. All told, Ebert's sphere of influence is grand. Brian De Palma and Martin Scorsese seek him out for feedback, but his impact has reached Linda Dillow too. From elite New York filmmakers to fresh Southern Illinois youth, everyone contends with Ebert, whose ongoing master class comprises the largest, most beloved extension course in American film criticism.

Chapter 3
Close to Ebert

On the relationship between style and content, Ebert's Law remains: A movie isn't just what it's about; it's *how* it is what it's about. It's what makes a trifle like *Lassiter* enjoyable ("Here's a basic rule about thrillers: Style is a lot more important than plot") and an earnest adaptation like *Agnes of God* confusing and portentous ("The movie uses each half of its story to avoid dealing with the other"). Without sounding overrefined or academic, Ebert consistently and gracefully hones in on the cross roads between a movie's style and content. His meditations on a decade of Adrian Lyne's films illuminate these values. Lyne has always been a director drawn to tortured psychosexual tragedies, and his films are marked with a distinctive, sensual pallet. In 1980, Ebert was impressed with *Foxes*, Lyne's coming-of-age depiction of Los Angeles teens in search of drugs, family, and identity. "It's a loosely structured film," Ebert observes, "deliberately episodic to suggest the shapeless form of these teen-agers' typical days and nights." He notes the movie's parallels between one teenager and her mother, who married young and also needs guidance. "*Foxes* is an ambitious movie, not an exploitation picture," he concludes:

> It's a lot more serious, for example, than the hit *Little Darlings*. It contains the sounds and rhythms of real teen-age lives; it was written and directed after a lot of research, and is acted by kids who are to one degree or another playing themselves. The movie's a rare attempt to provide a portrait of the way teen-agers really do live today in some suburban cultures.

Ambitious, serious, and rare. Admiring a stylistic approach that deepens the movie's subject matter, Ebert offers a candid assessment of a first effort that was largely overlooked by audiences and critics.

Anything but overlooked, Lyne's *Flashdance* (1983) was a summer box-office sensation, whose critical derision was outweighed only by its popularity. The script borrows more than a page from Warner Brothers' *Gold Diggers* movies of the 30s: A welder by day and go-go dancer by night, Alex (Jennifer Beals) dreams of making it as a professional ballerina and falls in love with a handsome benefactor. Ebert's review is a model of restraint. In one fell swoop, he rejects the movie's structure, obliquely defends its director (by mentioning sunnier days), and protects its ingenue. In his final one-and-one-half-star admonishment, he invokes both *Urban Cowboy* and the Bard:

> *Flashdance* is like a movie that won a free ninety-minute shopping spree in the Hollywood supermarket. The director (Adrian Lyne, of the much better *Foxes*) and his collaborators race crazily down the aisles, grabbing a piece of *Saturday Night Fever*, a slice of *Urban Cowboy*, a quart of *Marty*, and a two-pound box of "Archie Bunker's Place." The result is great sound and flashdance, signifying nothing. But Jennifer Beals shouldn't feel bad. She is a natural talent, she is fresh and engaging here, and only needs to find an agent with a natural talent for turning down scripts.

It's charity disguised as humor. Nobody walks away hurt (except possibly that anonymous agent—another critical stratagem that deflects responsibility from director and actor), largely due to a bonhomous tone that affirms talent while gently rapping the director's knuckles. At this career juncture, Lyne's misfires are noted but forgiven.

Flashdance's astonishing commercial success established Lyne as a bankable director, and he followed his rock-and-roll fairy tale with an adaptation of Elizabeth McNeill's pseudonymous *9½ Weeks* (1986), a memoir of a sadomasochistic affair that lasted the length of its title. No film of the 80s received more advance publicity. The steamy source material invited comparisons with *Last Tango in Paris*, and Lyne spent months with his editors paring the movie into R-rated shape. Though a hit in France and Italy, the movie opened to audience apathy and critical disdain in the States—with the noteworthy exception of Roger Ebert.

(The film's release in February '86 coincided with my first trip to New York City. I was sixteen. The whirlwind weekend was overwhelming, as was the advertising blitz for *9½ Weeks*. The poster art—splashed across every billboard and alleyway within view—consisted of an atmospheric black-and-white close-up of Kim Basinger and Mickey Rourke on the verge of a very deep kiss, with intense orange light emanating behind them, and floating above their heads: "THEY BROKE EVERY RULE." *What* rules? I just wanted Dawn Cates—future Prom Queen with intense orange hair—to like me.)

While quickly acknowledging the fanfare encircling the film, Ebert's review reaches an unexpected conclusion: "I went expecting erotic brinksmanship (how far *will* its famous stars go in the name of their art?) and came away surprised by how thoughtful the movie is, how clearly it sees exactly what really happens between its characters." Clocking in at thirteen paragraphs, this is one of Ebert's most expansive critiques. He unpacks the initial meeting of John and Elizabeth with an eye for detail:

> Their first meeting is crucial to the entire film, and it is a quiet master-piece of implication. She waits by a counter. Senses someone is standing behind her. Turns, and meets his eyes. He smiles. She turns away. Is obviously surprised by how much power was in their exchange of glances. She hesitates, turns back, meets his eyes again, almost boldly, and then turns away again. And a few minutes later looks at him very curiously as he walks away along the street.

For a newspaperman, this is a rare, voluptuous description. The varied lengths of his sentences mimic the motion of the couple's furtive, darting glances. He soon pulls focus from a close analysis of a key scene to a wider respect for the film's structure, which contrasts Elizabeth's familiar, daily routines and her illicit couplings with John. "This everyday material is an interesting strategy," Ebert writes. "It makes it clear that the private life of Elizabeth and John is a conscious game they're playing outside of the real world, and not just a fantasy in a movie where reality has been placed on hold." Hence the movie's style—beyond Lyne's passion for chiaroscuro and smooth, shiny surfaces—amplifies the mysterious essence of the affair. Ebert pushes further. In response to Elizabeth's decision to end the affair, he argues:

That's what makes the movie fascinating: Not that it shows these two people entering a bizarre sexual relationship, but because it shows the woman deciding for herself what she will, and will not, agree to. At the end of *9½ Weeks*, there is an argument, not for sexual liberation, but for sexual responsibility.

This is a bold, provocative claim. The argument is debatable, but Ebert builds his case with logic and care.

But then, a couple of reservations. Ever the realist, Ebert feels that one frenzied sexual interlude "owes more to improbable gymnastic events than to the actual capabilities of the human body." Another scene shows John purchasing a riding whip, with no follow-through at any point in the film. "To buy a whip and not use it," Ebert quips, "is like Camille coughing in the first reel and not dying in the last." Again, the ribbing momentarily relieves the straight-faced tone of the film and critique. For Ebert, even in the realm of sexual obsession, practicalities intrude.

This droll intermission is but a warm-up for closing arguments. He goes on to praise the actors and the risks they take, especially Basinger. By the end, he brings it all home:

The Hitcher is also about a sadomasochistic relationship between a stronger personality and a weaker one. Because it lacks the honesty to declare what it is really about, and because it romanticizes the cruel acts of its characters, it left me feeling only disgust and

Figure 10 Adrian Lyne's *9½ Weeks* illustrates the power of close-ups: Elizabeth (Kim Basinger) senses that someone is behind her. She turns, makes eye contact with John (Mickey Rourke) ...

Figure 11 ... and he returns her gaze with a knowing smile. To Ebert, their first encounter is "a quiet masterpiece of implication." *M-G-M* and *PSO*

disquiet. *9½ Weeks* is not only a better film, but a more humanistic one, in which it is argued that sexual experimentation is one thing, but the real human personality is something else, something incomparably deeper and more valuable—and more erotic.

As in his review of *Foxes*, creating closure by comparing a film to a related—and, in this case, lesser one—is a common critical ploy. Yet Ebert raises the stakes in the final sentence, leveling his own *pièce de résistance*. He elegantly relates the film to the ineffable realms of human nature, psychology, and sexuality. There is a hint of lavishness here. Although few may feel that *9½ Weeks* stimulates invigorating debate or offers take-home insights into human nature, Ebert proves his mettle by analyzing the style and implications of the movie with the dedication of an explorer. In a later interview with Basinger, he observes: "If she is not yet considered to be a Great American Actress, maybe it's because she's so great-looking, so frankly sexy. And yet no other actress has had a more interesting run of major roles in the last few years than Kim Basinger." His respect for her is laced with the same critical sensitivity that governs his review of *9½ Weeks*: an unyielding determination to see beyond appearances.

And notice what he does not do. Writing for the *Wall Street Journal*, Julie Salamon describes Lyne as "a former director of fashion commercials" and compares *9½ Weeks* to a Calvin Klein perfume ad. "[H]is first feature film was, for better or worse, *Flashdance* [*sic*]," she writes, "the movie musical for the video generation that engendered a new fashion style." "Mr. Lyne knows how to create a striking look," she observes. "But movies last so much longer than perfume ads." This is an easy dismissal. For Salamon, Lyne's past is prologue; the director of sleek commercials makes sleek, empty films. Though Ebert thinks less of *Flashdance* than she does of *9½ Weeks*, none of his reviews mentions Lyne's earlier work in commercials. Not that it's off-limits to critics, and no doubt some believe Lyne is an adman at heart. But this is my point. Although Ebert is ever-attentive to style, his evaluation is first and foremost anchored in what's on the screen. Lyne's films may signify nothing or they may communicate complex truths about human nature, but it's a careful scouring of the movie, not the director's resume that governs Ebert's conclusion. It is also revealing that when Ebert mentions Lyne's previous work—in film, not in commercials—he does so to *defend* Lyne. If *Flashdance* disappoints, it is worth remembering that *Foxes* is a lot better. Above all, Ebert remains the tough-minded *and* generous critic.

If *Foxes* announced Lyne's talent, if *Flashdance* lined his pocketbooks, and *9½ Weeks* raised eyebrows and temperatures, his next movie was a full-fledged cultural phenomenon. The characters' names alone elicit unsettling memories and goosebumps. Dan Gallagher. Hardworking lawyer and comfortable family man who lives to regret a weekend liaison. Alex Forrest. Striking, successful book editor who is discarded by love, and who, with plain language and implacable logic, refuses to be ignored. Beth Gallagher. Faithful, nurturing wife who protects her clan with fierce tenacity. In Adrian Lyne's *Fatal Attraction*, Michael Douglas, Glenn Close, and Anne Archer created an unforgettable, lubricious, and tragic love triangle. I saw the film (with Dawn Cates on my arm, I might add) the day it opened, September 18, 1987, and it remains the only movie I have seen four times in the theater. My fascination was threefold. First, the audience's wild, uninhibited reactions were unlike any I had experienced at the movies. Watching *Fatal Attraction* in a packed theater was like riding a rickety roller coaster replete with gasps, screams, and, at moments, bloodthirsty instructions from the audience to take out Alex. Second, the film's tremendous popularity encouraged multiple viewings; it was still playing in first-run theaters the following spring. In fact, theater owners exploited its appeal to enhance the box-office of other movies: "Buy a ticket for *Switching Channels* and stay for a free screening of *Fatal Attraction*!" And then, third, there was Glenn Close's scorching, otherworldly sexuality. And her burnt blonde locks. Did I mention she's briefly nude in the film? Make that fivefold.

As audiences queued up, critics were split. Ebert's attention to style guides his assessment of the film, never more clearly than in the opening sentence: "*Fatal Attraction* is a spellbinding psychological thriller, and could have been a great movie if the filmmakers had not thrown character and plausibility to the winds in the last act to give us their version of a grown-up *Friday the 13th*"—this in reference to *Fatal Attraction*'s bloody climax when Alex, pregnant with Dan's child, extends her campaign of terror by breaking into the family's pastoral home and attacking Beth with a butcher knife. Dan races to the rescue, and, in homage to *Les Diaboliques*, appears to drown Alex in the family bathtub. But, like a phoenix from its ashes, Alex rises from the water, only to be shot in the heart by Beth.

On several levels, Ebert's distaste for the film is motivated by Midwestern pragmatism and a healthy dose of compassion for its forlorn antagonist. Just as in *9½ Weeks*, he takes issue with the movie's giddy, reckless sex scenes, declaring Lyne a director "whose ideas of love and genital acrobatics seem more or less equivalent." That misstep, however, is minor compared to the grisly finale, "complete with the unforgivable *Friday the 13th* cliché that the villain is never *really* dead. The conclusion, by the way, operates on the premise that Douglas cares absolutely nothing for his unborn child." I respect that "by the way," which underscores concern for the moral implications of style. Yes, the movie interrupts gripping melodrama with tired horror conventions. Worse still, the moral consequences of the climax and *dénouement* are disturbing and unacknowledged. Despite the negative reaction, however, Ebert's regard for the filmmaker's talents is high. The movie is deeply offensive because everything—that is, style in proportion to content—is so right for so long. But not long enough. His verdict: "*Fatal Attraction* clearly had the potential to be a great movie." Like Alex Forrest herself, Ebert walked out feeling cheated and betrayed.

As *Fatal Attraction* moved from "movie" to "zeitgeist," Adrian Lyne revealed that the violent ending shown in theaters was not in James Dearden's original script. The first draft ended with Alex Forrest's suicide, an action that remained true to her desperate mental state while bringing closure to the film's *Madame Butterfly* motif. For example, during Dan and Alex's weekend fling, they discuss their mutual affection for the opera, which culminates in the rebuffed lover's suicide. When Alex drops by Dan's office unawares, she presents a peace offering of two tickets to *Madame Butterfly*, which he politely refuses. From a structural point of view, Alex's suicide would have created unity and made good dramatic sense. Nonetheless, this ending reportedly left test audiences lukewarm, salivating for revenge. In a follow-up essay to his review, Ebert addresses the movie's popularity in response to Lyne's comments about the re-editing. He quotes Lyne:

"All sorts of endings had been considered for this film," Lyne told *New York Post* writer Nina Darnton. "We thought of just about everything, apart from the dog doing it. Maybe if we were making a French movie, which, in truth, most of the films I like best tend to be, we wouldn't have taken this route. We had shot it the other way, but when we screened it in the previews, the audiences hated her (Close) so much. People were unsatisfied by an off-camera resolution."

After describing the revised ending, Ebert returns to Lyne's ideas:

[Lyne] prefers "French films," by which I guess he means films told with an adult and thoughtful sensibility. In his system, "American films" are films that aim cheerfully for the lowest common denominator. Lyne boasted to *Chicago Sun-Times* writer Peter Keough that with the current ending, audiences "go nuts! They go potty! ... They sing along!"

Well, terrific. But I remember one of the movie's best scenes, in which Glenn Close is all alone in her apartment, lonely and isolated, and she compulsively flicks a light on and off. Lyne says that is his own favorite scene in the movie. I have a question. Why couldn't the movie have ended with that scene? Play it through in your head. At the end, but before the bloodshed and carnage, Close achieves some sort of insight into herself—some glimmer of sanity, some brief window in which she can see her madness from the outside. And then she is really alone.

That's one possible ending. Another one would be to replace the "unsatisfactory" off-screen suicide with an on-screen suicide death scene for Close. Early in the film, she and Douglas have a scene where they discuss their love of opera and the plot of *Madame Butterfly*, in which the Japanese heroine commits suicide after her American lover abandons her and goes back to his wife. The conversation is obviously there to set up a suicide. Why not let it happen, poignantly, tragically, and then supply a closing scene in which Douglas surveys the emotional fallout of his one-night stand?

Would such an ending affect the movie's box-office? How will we ever know? My notion is that *Fatal Attraction* tells such a compelling story and creates such unforgettable characters that audiences would be more moved by an honest ending than by the fraudulent cop-out of the bathtub scene.

What's so bad about French movies, anyway?

And more to the point, why is it assumed that the American audience is so stupid that it should get the weirdo ending it deserves?

Ebert exceeds the critic's imaginative task of analyzing a film, in this case by editing a more compelling final cut. Implicit in Lyne's comments is the belief that the original ending would have been a blow to the movie's popularity. Ebert questions this assumption, again grounding his arguments in a consideration of the movie's structure and style. On its own terms, the film asks for its length to be taken seriously. But the two hypothetical endings that Ebert posits display his preternatural instinct for understanding what makes a movie intelligent and effective. Consider his first suggestion of ending with the eerie scene of Alex Forrest alone in her apartment, turning a light on and off while listening to *Madame Butterfly*, coming to terms with her isolation.

In time, more was revealed regarding the nature and function of that scene. The following year, Ebert interviewed Glenn Close and inquired about the re-editing of *Fatal Attraction*:

"That movie was compromised at the end," Close said, bitterly. "It's not cool for me to talk about it; I have to be a member of the team.

Figure 12 In Adrian Lyne's *Fatal Attraction*, Alex Forrest (Glenn Close) sits alone in her apartment, turning a light on and off while listening to *Madame Butterfly*. "Why couldn't the movie have ended with that scene?" Ebert asked. In fact, it originally did. *Paramount*

But it's difficult for me to keep my mouth shut about something I felt very strongly about. For two and a half weeks I was up against everyone. They wanted to change the ending, to put in that violent scene. It was deeply disturbing to me, and yet the movie made all that money. It's not a clear-cut situation, except from the artistic point of view. Artistically, they were wrong. But I understand their reasons and for those reasons they were right. They sold a lot of tickets.

"What compromised the ending was, until those last moments the movie was so true. That woman was suicidal. What they asked me to do—entering the house, getting involved in all that violence—was a total betrayal of the character. Remember the scene where she switches the lamp on and off? It was going to be at the end of the movie. You needed something near the end where the audience is reminded that this is a creature in dire distress. But they never filmed the scene setting up the fact that Madame Butterfly kills herself—the scene that would have set up my suicide. So instead of using the scene with the lamp at the end of the movie, where it would have shown my devastation and helped the character not be a monster, they put it at the beginning, to make her look crazy. What can you do?"

Sometimes compelling criticism is like old-fashioned detective work. Ebert thoroughly analyzes the film, listens carefully to the director's point of view, and offers his own perspective. Now consider Ebert's resolutions in light of Close's position; his proposed endings are mirror images of the logic and consistency of Dearden's original script. The scene of Alex alone at home, flipping the light on and off, was the intended harbinger of her suicide. The version shown to test audiences may very well have contained an "off-camera resolution," as Lyne stated. What is not debatable is that an on-screen suicide of Alex slicing her throat on her bathroom floor was actually filmed, albeit in long shot. (She wears the same costume in both scenes—a large white t-shirt. This ending can be viewed on the film's DVD.) All of this information is part of *Fatal Attraction*'s folklore, and the movie's multiple endings are now selling points for the film's life on home video and DVD. What's extraordinary is that Ebert, without being privy to such details and machination, was essentially an advocate for a movie that everyone made and was presumably proud of, prior to audience feedback. Many critics noted *Fatal Attraction*'s narrative inconsistencies, but no critics approached Ebert's intuition for analyzing and diagnosing how and where this bewitching film went so very wrong.

Post-script: In 1990, Michael Douglas discussed *Fatal Attraction*'s ending with David Thomson in *Film Comment*:

> You can talk about [Dan Gallagher's] weakness—or you can talk about realities. You're talking now more about the script, or which way the story goes. I think you hope that they're going to get back together again. The picture was about a disturbed woman— whether this was the married man that broke the camel's back, or it was a long process. It was a woman who handled and liked the arrangement, as a lot of women do, of dealing with the security of a married man, and all of a sudden—the floodgates opened. And then it became a story about getting back. Then, once the family was *attacked*—I know the debate about the ending.

> *Which started among the filmmakers?*

> Yeah. It was, and then fanned by Glenn and some other people. I found it preposterous. When you take a play out of town, based on the audience response you rewrite the endings, you change characters. Everything! Ultimately for the most rewarding benefit of the audience—and to make a picture work! The ending we had before, we underestimated how strongly the audience felt against her attack on the family. So one character does not make a movie work.

Nor does screenwriting by committee. There are ironies here. Close is an actor who moves effortlessly from stage to screen. She understands the demands of the theater and the playwriting process. In essence, Douglas sets up a straw man; Close does not object to editing per se—only editing that betrays the character. More irony. At the time of the interview, Douglas was promoting *The War of the Roses*, a movie that ends with a husband and wife splitting their home in two, and, further down the road, killing each other. The film's director was repeatedly praised for standing by his artistic vision and not kowtowing to the desires of studio executives for a more humane resolution. In the end, the movie was a critical and commercial success. As a producer and actor, Douglas knows firsthand the pressures involved in making movies, and film editing involves complex and risky decisions. In the context of *Fatal Attraction*, I return to Douglas' words: the discussion was initiated by the filmmakers "and then fanned by Glenn and some other people." More influential than Close is Ebert, who provides the forum for a national debate about the nature of art as well as filmmakers' assumptions regarding audiences. In turn, he provides a platform for Close's minority position.

In the midst of artistic contretemps, Ebert is very much one of the "other people" who initiates public debate and advocates an understanding of art that affirms the intelligence of its creators and audiences. Springing from an analysis of a film's content and style, Ebert has expertly opened the movies up to a broader discussion of the relationships between art and commerce, between filmmakers and audiences. What is finally at stake in arguments about movies like *Fatal Attraction* is not simply how a film concludes or whether an actor, director, or critic is pleased with the final product. What is at stake is the nature of the relationship between art, its creators, and its audiences. And there is Ebert, at the critical forefront, his hand patiently raised: "I have a question."

Chapter 4
The Total Effect

Roger Ebert eats films whole. He is particularly skilled at conveying the total effect, the sum of the parts. This knack is often evidenced in indelible summations. Regarding Tony Scott's *The Hunger*, a vampire film in which style not only overwhelms but digests its substance, Ebert writes, "In Herzog's *Nosferatu*, we felt some of the blood-scented lure of eternal death-in-life. Here, it's just—how would an ad put it?—Catherine Deneuve for Dracula." Cataloguing the shortcomings of Michael Cimino's *Heaven's Gate*, he concludes, "There is more. There is much more. It all adds up to a great deal less. This movie is $36 million thrown to the winds. It is the most scandalous cinematic waste I have ever seen, and remember, I've seen *Paint Your Wagon*." The same discerning wit that takes the edge off negative reviews engenders respect for sturdier films. Pondering *The Exorcist*, he concludes: "Even in the extremes of [William] Friedkin's vision there is still a feeling that this is, after all, cinematic escapism and not a confrontation with real life. There is a fine line to be drawn there, and *The Exorcist* finds it and stays a millimeter on this side." Ebert's "millimeter" captures the tone of a film that leaves some mesmerized, others physically ill. And he creates memorable closure. Tim Robbins' *Dead Man Walking* "ennobles filmmaking." "This is the kind of movie," he later argues, "that spoils us for other films, because it reveals so starkly how most movies fall into conventional routine, and lull us with the reassurance that they will not look too hard, or probe too deeply, or make us think beyond the boundaries of what is comfortable." So a reflection on "most movies" illuminates the spiritual and intellectual integrity of another. Ebert's dexterity—his creativity with words and comparisons, his trenchant sense of humor, his storehouse knowledge of film history—all of this spoils us for other critics. His pungent summaries launch analyses, too. Consider the forthright opening of his review of Frank Perry's *Mommie Dearest*:

> I can't imagine who would want to subject themselves to this movie. *Mommie Dearest* is a painful experience that drones on endlessly, as Joan Crawford's relationship with her daughter, Christina, disintegrates from cruelty through jealousy into pathos. It is unremittingly depressing, not to any purpose of drama or entertainment, but just to depress. It left me feeling creepy. The movie was inspired, of course, by a best-selling memoir in which adopted daughter Christina Crawford portrayed her movie-star mother as a grasping, sadistic, alcoholic wretch whose own insecurities and monstrous ego made life miserable for everyone around her. I have no idea if the book's portrait is an accurate one, but the movie is faithful to it in one key sense: It made life miserable for me.

Framing the film as an unnerving emotional experience, the paragraph is brimming with telling detail. The opening sentence shatters any mystery regarding where he stands; this is a one-star review, minus the trademark good humor. In a way, that first sentence mirrors the movie: the intentions are serious, and, for effect, conveyed in an aggressive, even jarring style. But if a film is unsettling, it had better be in the service of a larger or higher purpose. And in a move that reflects his fair-mindedness, he recognizes the subjectivity of the source material, leading to his stinging conclusion: "It made life miserable for me." Probably no modern autobiography has been more carefully scrutinized and found wanting than Christina Crawford's. Yet, in 1981, just three years after its publication, the account was generally accepted as a final, bruising obituary. In this context, Ebert's disinterested, journalistic tone is all the more welcome.

Not surprisingly, his disappointment is rooted not in the film's content, but in its style. The sensationalism of *Mommie Dearest* trumps psychological insight. Adding insult to injury, "the movie doesn't even make narrative sense. Success follows crisis without any pattern... The scenes don't build, they just happen." Sifting through the ashes, very late in the game (halfway through his fifth and final paragraph), Ebert acknowledges some strengths: "The sets look absolutely great, Faye Dunaway's impersonation of Crawford is stunningly suggestive and convincing, and little Mara Hobel, as Baby Christina, handles several difficult moments very well. But to what end? *Mommie Dearest* is a movie that knows exactly how it wants to look, but has no idea what it wants to make us feel." The point is the means must justify the end. A striking star turn and lavish production values are insufficient when the overarching purpose is exploitive. A movie with no sense of itself, with no clear grasp of what it wants from or how it hopes to affect its audience, is a waste of time.

Now compare Ebert's critique with the opening of Pauline Kael's review:

> Faye Dunaway gives a startling, ferocious performance in *Mommie Dearest*. It's deeper than an impersonation; she turns herself into Joan Crawford, all right, but she's more Faye Dunaway than ever. She digs into herself and gets inside "Joan Crawford" in a way that only another torn, driven actress could. (She may have created a new form of *folie à deux*.) With her icy features, her nervous affectations, her honeyed emotionalism, Dunaway has been a vividly neurotic star; she has always seemed to be racing—breathless and flustered—right on the edge of collapse. In *Mommie Dearest*, she slows herself down in order to incarnate the bulldozer styles in neurosis of an earlier movie era; her Joan Crawford is more deliberate and calculating—and much stronger—than other Dunaway characters. As Joan the martinet, a fanatical believer in discipline, cleanliness, order, Dunaway lets loose with a fury that she may not have known was in her. She goes over the top, discovers higher peaks waiting, and shoots over them, too. Has any movie queen ever gone this far before? Alone and self-mesmerized, she plays the entire film on emotion. Her performance is extravagant—it's operatic and full of primal anger; she's grabbing the world by the short hairs...

And the paragraph is not over. Beyond the stylistic differences in Ebert's lean, distilled prose and Kael's exhaustive, sinuous paean, Kael begins and ends her analysis with Dunaway. She sketches an evocative description of Dunaway's performance and the role's significance within the arc of her career. Kael's review is one of her most apocalyptic; it accentuates her analytic prowess, as well as her Achilles heel. For one thing, her analysis of the acting is as precise and sweeping as Dunaway's portrayal. When asked, "Does Faye Dunaway really have the skirt taken in in sixteen different places?" director Sidney Lumet replied, "She does. And she's right." Like Dunaway, Kael takes the movie in in sixteen different places too, surveying Dunaway's performance with anthropological detail and finding her "Crawford" to be oddly rational, even "frighteningly human." She sees purpose and symbolic import where Ebert does not; some of the disturbing scenes of abuse suggest "a great subject: the horrifying misunderstanding between all parents and children." Like Ebert, she also notes the film's gaffes in continuity and a host of other distractions, but nothing overshadows Dunaway's towering accomplishment of channeling and humanizing Crawford.

There is an undeniable sense of discovery and vitality here. Kael is side-swiped by Dunaway's dedication—by the grandeur and tragedy she brings to the role, by the way she dominates the film and alters

Figure 13 If only she'd chosen him: Joan Crawford is pitch-perfect in her signature role of Mildred Pierce. Here, she shares the stage with Jack Carson as Wally Fay, a business partner with romance on his mind. *Warner Bros.*

its tone. As a scrupulous analysis of a performance, Kael's review is a bulls-eye. Effective though it is, it's not without flaws. She pushes too far at times and undermines her core arguments. Of Crawford she writes, "In the obit that George Cukor wrote, he said, 'Whatever she did, she did whole-heartedly.' Strenuously, rather; she was incapable of lightness, of delicacy. In a scene in which Joan is rehearsing for *Mildred Pierce*, Dunaway looks like her, but you're aware of an enormous difference: This is *Mildred Pierce* with a real actress in the part." This quick swipe points to a larger, regrettable weakness: a failure to resist expressing a familiar prejudice. What's more, it's wrong—or, at the very least, unsupported by argument. Kael mentions Crawford's movies in the 40s and 50s, "when her falseness was so regal that you couldn't cut through it." But the criticism is directed at *Mildred Pierce*, not *Johnny Guitar*, so even this statement requires greater precision. The glory of Crawford's Mildred Pierce is the melding of her M-G-M glamour with the gutsy determination and worldweariness that marked her arrival at Warner Brothers. *Mildred Pierce* heralded Crawford's hard-earned confidence as an actor, and her stylish intensity is all the more vivid because of her *underplaying*—exactly what Kael misses. In one classic confrontation after another, Crawford pulls back and shares the stage with the game, lusty supporting players: Jack Carson, Eve Arden, Ann Blyth, and Zachary Scott. It goes without saying that Crawford's talent was not rooted in range, but did Kael ever see her brief, delightful self-parody in *It's a Great Feeling*? Truth be told, Crawford is pitch-perfect as Mildred, and Kael's comparison inadvertently suggests that if Michael Curtiz had directed *Mommie Dearest*, Dunaway's work might have received the point of view and modulation it needed. In one line, a Kaelian broadside vitiates her unstinting, justified praise of Dunaway.

Still, other reviews show just how effective are Ebert's gift for bottom-lining and Kael's ability to bring a performance to life. In *Time*, Richard Schickel dismissed *Mommie Dearest*. His first, larger paragraph is more a defense of Crawford than a review of the movie. Central to Schickel's argument is his belief that the autobiography and film are sensational and unwarranted. After astutely questioning the film's premise, he argues the film lacks both "psychological intelligence" and "an awareness of Hollywood sociology." "Confronted by a movie without narrative or human interest, one is finally reduced to watching the paint dry—on Dunaway's face." This final turn of the knife is anticlimactic, even cruel, given Dunaway's obvious physical and emotional investment in the role. Schickel's vivid closing line arrives at the expense of analysis and illustrates one of Renata Adler's chief criticisms of Kael: "taking, that is, something from *within* the film and, with an air of intellectual triumph, turning it pointlessly *against* the film or a performer" (italics hers). The strategy is just as unpleasant when Schickel employs it. (Given his achievements in film biography and history, he's excused. Schickel is more than capable of supporting these arguments; here, he's managing *Time* constraints.) All the same, the clipped ending is instructive, as some found the film too preposterous to merit serious and lengthier discussion. Janet Maslin in the *New York Times* offered a more well-rounded assessment, arguing that Dunaway's performance "amounts to a small miracle, as one movie queen transforms herself passionately and wholeheartedly into another." Like Kael, Maslin draws attention to the film's opening montage that details Crawford's arduous morning rituals. Yet, by the end, Maslin feels the movie's treatment of mother and daughter is imbalanced and superficial. Joan Crawford "needn't have been lionized here," she concludes, "but she did need more humanity than Mr. Perry allows her in order for 'Mommie Dearest' to have any claim to coherence or continuity." These critical approaches are revealing. Everyone is disappointed in the movie as a narrative with a clear, cause-and-effect structure. Like Ebert and Kael, Schickel catches the film's intensity, but his passion is too quickly extinguished. Maslin (like Kael) brings the texture of the movie to life more gracefully than Ebert and Schickel, but her measured tone is no match for Ebert's and Kael's gut-level reactions.

Released on September 18, 1981, the reception of *Mommie Dearest* was as schizophrenic as its editing. Dunaway's work, often discussed separately from the movie, has entered the pantheon of unforgettable screen performances. At the time, she ran a close second in the New York Film Critics' Best Actress race—more evidence, I think, of Kael's prestige and influence. In spite of this, many audiences shared Ebert's misery, while others snickered, characterizing the movie's heightened emotional violence as camp. In classic helter-skelter fashion, Kael's review restores faith in her sensibilities with final remarks that proved eerily prophetic: "After Michael Redgrave played the insane ventriloquist in *Dead of Night*, bits of the character's paranoia kept turning up in his other performances; it

Figure 14 Faye Dunaway's impersonation of Joan Crawford in *Mommie Dearest* is spellbinding. Her commitment is total, urging Pauline Kael to ask: "Has any movie queen ever gone this far before?" *Paramount*

could be hair-raising if Faye Dunaway were to have trouble shaking off the gorgon Joan."

Hair-raising, indeed. Dunaway's follow-up was a remake of *The Wicked Lady*—hardly a title or role she needed after *Mommie Dearest*. Next, Dunaway was one of the villainesses in *Supergirl*. To Ebert, Dunaway and sidekick Brenda Vaccaro had a creepy relationship: "Their roles reminded me of *Mommie Dearest* in search of daughters." Had he read Kael's review? Did it affect his perception of Dunaway? I attribute his remark more to Kael's clairvoyance than to her sway. In the history of film criticism, never have the closing lines of a review proved more prescient than Kael's. She also noted, "The emotional violence in this film is potent; you can't get it out of your mind," and moviegoers suffered the same malady. For the next seven years, Dunaway labored diligently to escape the shadow of her uncanny impersonation. Her career became a case study in how a performance can be so resonant that the general tenor of a body of work is affected. Dunaway speaks of having felt "frozen" in a face, and it was Kael the diviner who predicted as much.

Ebert's and Kael's reflections on *Mommie Dearest* present a rousing dialectic. Echoing Kael's praise of Dunaway, both play their reviews on emotion—Kael, through her ecstatic, gushing appreciation of

Dunaway; Ebert, by conveying the misery of an experience that even a tour-de-force cannot redeem. And, as already hinted, there's a curious parallel between Kael's analysis and Dunaway's acting. Dunaway's long, sustained arias match Kael's extravagant prose. "The best that can be said about the movie itself," writes Kael, "is that it doesn't seem to get in the way of its star," which might well be said of her own relationship with editor Wallace Shawn at *The New Yorker*, which provided her with copious space. And the *Mommie Dearest* review demonstrates her Olympian ability to scrutinize a dazzling performance, as well as a film's shortcomings. On that same canvas, she also chases rabbit trails and succumbs to predictable attacks that hint of self-satisfaction. Once again, her analysis arrives at the same conclusions: Dunaway is amazing, Crawford is untalented, and Kael is the one who points it all out. On such occasions, she shows conviction without the messiness of persuasion. In contrast, Ebert's strength is his single-minded intensity and unflinching directness; the economy of both his ideas and his newspaper venue does not permit him to veer off track. And his arguments are cogent—he consistently provides evidence to support his claims. If Kael's review is an uninhibited commemoration, Ebert's is a primal moan, and it shows how central the total effect is to his aesthetic: "The scenes don't build, they just happen." Ebert does not pen the crystalline descriptions that are Kael's crowning achievement, and this is a loss. (I've always wanted him to unpack that brief reference to Dunaway's "stunningly suggestive and convincing" performance.) All the same, his focus remains on the movie *as a movie*, and his writing nails the film as an emotional experience. True, the sets and the lead are great, but the movie fails to cohere on the most basic narrative and psychological levels. Although Ebert admired Dunaway, his critique illustrates how, for him, a performance is only one of many factors that shape a film.

So, in the realm of sizing up acting—considering an actor's strengths and weaknesses, weighing the worth of a performance in relationship to a movie—nobody could touch Kael. And I'll always be grateful to her because she taught me that it's okay to hate Meryl Streep. Now that's a bit strong. Nobody hates Meryl Streep, the merriest and most self-effacing of movie stars. What I mean is, she taught me that it's okay to trust my instincts, to argue an opinion that goes against the grain. Kael was indisputably Streep's toughest critic, and although Streep once claimed that she would like to slug Kael, I'm sure she understood that Kael didn't hate her. Throughout five decades of screen acting, Streep long ago solidified her reputation as one of the most versatile of American actresses. Yet, in the 1980s, she was already being venerated by critics and audiences, and Kael was a voice in the wilderness, arguing that, in fact, Streep was consistently miscast.

Ebert, on the other hand, championed Streep during this period. Take his review of *Silkwood* (1983), where Streep is Karen Silkwood, the whistle-blower who called attention to safety risks and compromises at the Kerr-McGee nuclear plant in Oklahoma:

> [T]here's a tiny detail in the first moments of the movie that reveals how completely Streep has thought through the role. Silkwood walks into the factory, punches her time card, automatically looks at her own wristwatch, and then shakes her wrist: It's a self-winding watch, I guess. That little shake of the wrist is an actor's choice. There are a lot of them in this movie, all almost as invisible as the first one; little by little, Streep and her coactors build characters so convincing that we become witnesses instead of merely viewers.

Noticing a shake of a wrist is a nice touch, and Ebert is correct in arguing that the details—or "goodies," as James Cagney called them—reflect Streep's punctilious attention to her craft. Yet bountiful choices mean little if they feel unnatural or distracting, or if an actor simply isn't right for a role. In this instance, Ebert sees details, which suggest verisimilitude and "another of [Streep's] great performances." But his bar for great acting is rather low here; surely it's possible for an actor to think deeply about a role and still be unconvincing. And if one accepts Ebert's reasoning, providing a single example isn't enough to settle the argument. He needs to cite more of those "invisible" details to be persuasive.

Now look at Kael's review of *Silkwood*, where she too zeros in on the details of Streep's performance. In one scene, Silkwood playfully teases some co-workers in the break room of the Kerr-McGee plant, nearly taking a bite out of somebody's sandwich. "Meryl Streep imitates raunchiness meticulously—exquisitely," Kael observes. "But she hasn't got the craving to take that bite." She then contrasts Streep's approach with other film stars, past and present. "If the young Barbara Stanwyck had grabbed the sandwich," she writes, "we'd have registered that her appetite made her break the rules." "[I]f Debra Winger had chomped on it, we'd have felt her sensual greed. With Streep," she argues, "we just observe how accomplished she is." There's insight here, as well as passion and a feeling for film history; the comparisons clarify her point and trade on positive associations with Stanwyck and Winger. Both actresses, of course, easily convey sexual hunger, and this is another contrast with Streep. In fact, the subtext of Kael's complaint is that Streep isn't believably sexy on screen. She's mastered "the external details of 'Okie bad girl,'" but the full-blooded acting and palpable fleshiness of a Stanwyck or Winger are missing.

But, on this much, Ebert and Kael agree: They're fascinated with Streep. Yet Ebert's argument yields less. The detail he cites isn't fresh or telling enough to suggest dynamic acting. Kael absorbs the same details (Streep "does a whole lot of little things with her hands and her body; she's certainly out to prove that she's physical"), but arrives at a different conclusion: "She has no natural vitality; she's like a replicant—all shtick." This is a bit much, and I question the pairing of "replicant," which invokes those freakish lost souls from *Blade Runner* who desperately want to be human, and "shtick," which suggests weathered, unimaginative vaudevillians. Still, it underscores a critical difference. When it comes to acting, Ebert treats performance details as positive criteria: Streep triumphs because the nuances are there. In a sense, her commitment to detail *makes* her an effective performer. As in her *Mommie Dearest* critique, Kael is more concerned about the liveliness and believability of the nuances, and she's equally interested in the function of a performance within the movie and the actor's career. "Since [Streep] has reached great heights of prestige, and many projects are offered to her," she argues, "she's the one who's making the wrong choices—she's miscasting herself." Kael is more personal and pointed; in both cases, it's as if she's giving Dunaway and Streep candid career advice.

No matter, Kael's closing is the most honest, potent appeal from a critic to a major artist since James Agee pleaded with Bette Davis to rethink her career trajectory in the 40s:

Meryl Streep has been quoted as saying, "I've always felt that I can do anything." No doubt that's a wonderful feeling, and I don't think she should abandon it, but she shouldn't take it too literally, either. It *may* be true for her on the stage, but in movies even the greatest stars have been successes only within a certain range of roles. Katharine Hepburn didn't play Sadie Thompson or Mildred Pierce, and Ginger Rogers didn't appear in *The Swan*. Anna Magnani didn't try out for Scarlet O'Hara, Bette Davis wasn't cast as the second wife in *Rebecca*, and Garbo didn't break her heart over not doing *Stella Dallas*. Part of being a good movie actress is in knowing what you come across as. My guess is that Meryl Streep could be a hell-raising romantic comedienne. (A tiny dirty laugh comes out of her just once in *Silkwood* and it's funkier and more expressive than any of her line readings.) She has the singing voice for musical comedy, and the agility and crazy daring for knockabout farce. And maybe she can play certain serious and tragic roles, too—she was unusually effective in her supporting role in *The Deer Hunter*. But in her starring performances she has been giving us artificial creations. She doesn't seem to know how to draw on herself; she hasn't yet released an innate personality on the screen.

Kael moves from hyperbole (Streep as alien) to counseling (Know thyself), and her quoting of Streep, though corrective, is not uncaring. She places Streep in the same league as Hepburn, Davis, and Garbo—and, even if the example is negative, what a roll call! When Streep finally got a crack at comedic roles in the late 80s and early 90s, Kael rightfully returned *Postcards from the Edge* to sender. It's too bad, though, that she didn't weigh in on Streep's craven, hyper-feminine romance novelist in *She-Devil*, one of Streep's most wickedly inspired performances and worst movies. Beyond comedy, Kael didn't live long enough to see Streep's perfectly controlled turn as a sly, unbending nun in *Doubt*—a crowning achievement of her, or any actor's, career; or her impersonation of Julia Child in *Julie & Julia*, a role that joyfully combined her gifts for physical comedy, drama, and mimicry.

Full disclosure: I've always enjoyed Meryl Streep, but often felt that she was wrong in her movie roles—*Silkwood*, *Falling In Love*, *Out of Africa*, *Heartburn*, *Marvin's Room*. Yes, even her effort in *Sophie's Choice* fell victim to William Styron's pretentious prose. The same quality that irked James Agee about Bette Davis—that her acting was too affected, her mannerisms too "first-ladyish"—is what distanced me from Streep. In the mid-80s, I recall Gene Shalit interviewing Streep on the *Today* show. At one point he asked if she felt that she'd ever given a bad performance. She paused and said, "Yes, I wasn't pleased with my performance in *Stab*." This is extraordinary, since she is flawless in *Stab* (whose title was sadly changed to *Still of the Night*). As an heiress who may have killed her lover, Streep unquestionably unleashes an "innate personality": neurotic, mysterious, wealthy, educated, and sensual. Her cool, clinical elegance sets the film's tone, and, at the climax, she breathlessly unpacks her complicated relationship to an abusive, deceased father. It's a heart-stopper that ranks among her finest moments on screen. Fluttering about in this film, she's constantly lighting cigarettes, pulling back her hair, wringing her hands. Gestures that Kael viewed as window-dressing are used to impeccable effect— they convey her conflicted, jagged emotions and shield her from intimacy. She's simultaneously controlled and effusive: she maintains appearances but her emotions keep rising, flooding the character with sexual energy. In fact, her sexuality is surprisingly dangerous—she's always knocking over valuables, leaning against balconies, collapsing into a lover's arms. Rex Reed complained that Streep whispers her dialogue, but I sensed that if she raised her voice she might detonate. *Still of the Night* is a conventional thriller steeped in Freudian lore, but Streep's splendid unease is magnetizing. "Part of being a good movie actress is in knowing what you come across as," and, here, Streep is physically perfect. Beautifully lit by Nestor Almendros, her face is a pool of light, curtained by icy-blonde bangs. In fact, that pageboy haircut is as shiny and sharp as the knives darting around her in dark closets and alleyways.

In short, Streep's words remind me that an actor isn't always her best critic. Her point of view deepened my trust not only in Kael's, but in my own responses. Even if one disagreed with Kael—and legions did, not to mention Streep herself—her comments ushered in fresh thinking about Streep and, consequently, American screen acting. In terms of acting, Ebert's standards are less exacting. In *Silkwood*, he believes the performances are true to form, and he pursues the bottom line. "The movie isn't about plutonium," he writes; "it's about the American working class." From Kael's point of view, however, the whole enterprise is a sham if the lead isn't convincing as a member of the proletariat. Kael sees Streep, and she begins and ends with the actress. Ebert sees the whole and pays attention to the acting, but his claims aren't as provocative. Unlike Kael, nobody's going to haggle with him into the night over his thoughts on *Silkwood*.

Writing about other movies, their approaches have reverse effects. Ebert and Kael responded strongly to the emotional undercurrents in Francis Ford Coppola's *Peggy Sue Got Married* (1986), where, at a twenty-fifth high school reunion, Peggy Sue (Kathleen Turner) is magically transported from middle age to adolescence. As she's reunited with loved ones—including her long-deceased mother—the movie generates, for Kael, tangled feelings and perhaps "our own longings for the mother we've lost." Ebert also shares a sense of awe at the movie's premise. "Certain times and places can re-create, with a headstrong rush, what it felt like to be seventeen years old—" he observes, "and we are sometimes more in touch with ourselves at that age than the way we felt a year ago." The movie clearly captures their imaginations, but they part ways regarding its value.

More than Peggy Sue is transplanted in Ebert's openings words:

> We walk like ghosts through the spaces of our adolescence. We've all done it. We stroll unseen across the high school football field. We go back to the drive-in restaurants where we all hung out, all those years ago. We walk into a drugstore for some aspirin, and the magazine rack brings back a memory of sneaking a peek at a Playmate in 1959.

For Ebert, the movie becomes a scrapbook. High-school football, drive-ins, local drugstores, *Playboy*—all that's missing is a first kiss. *Peggy Sue* opens up the past as well as the present, and, unlike Kael's more guarded stance toward sentimentality, Ebert enjoys reflecting on both. But, aside from the film's delightful temporal predicaments ("Imagine kissing someone for the first time," he posits, "after you have already kissed them for the last time"), the film stands on the shoulders of Kathleen Turner, and he dedicates a paragraph to her. "How does she play a seventeen-year-old?" he asks, and answers:

> Not by trying to actually look seventeen, because the movie doesn't try to pull off that stunt (the convention is that the heroine looks adult to us, but like a teen-ager to the other characters). Turner, who is

actually thirty-two, plays a teen-ager by making certain changes in her speech and movement: She talks more impetuously, not waiting for other people to reply, and she walks in that heedless teen-age way of those who have not yet stumbled often enough to step carefully. There is a moment when she throws herself down on her bed, and never mind what she looks like, it feels like a seventeen-year old sprawled there. Her performance is a textbook study in body language; she knows that one of the symptoms of growing older is that you arrange your limbs more thoughtfully in repose.

Ebert drinks in Turner's artfulness. When it comes to acting, he's interested in feelings over appearance. And his review of *Peggy Sue* is one of his finest. In the opening, he forges an emotional connection with his readers, pulling them back to his and their adolescence. In praising Turner, he describes her skillfulness in detail, and, by doing so, brings her performance to life. (If you only read Ebert's review, you still walk away with a feeling for her accomplishment.) That would be enough, but, no, there's more: Notice how Ebert announces himself in his description of the acting. Here's a critic who *has* stumbled enough to step carefully, who arranges his limbs—and words—more thoughtfully in repose. This is a paragraph about Turner *and* Ebert.

Figure 15 Through body language and a youthful sensibility, Kathleen Turner transforms herself into a seventeen year old in Francis Ford Coppola's *Peggy Sue Got Married*. *Tri-Star* and *Rastar*

Kael, on the other hand, is less impressed. For her, Turner telegraphs her acting and her body presents a problem:

> For most of the movie, she's supposed to be not quite eighteen, and she's trying to act young—one of the toughest things to do on camera. It's especially tough for her, because she's a womanly big woman poured into tight teen-age-schoolgirl dresses. I don't know why Coppola or the writers didn't slip in a few lines of dialogue to turn her height and fleshiness to a sexy, comic advantage. Couldn't her boyfriend have contrasted her with her petite-little-nothing schoolmates? The movie never acknowledges that she looks different from the other girls, and so we're acutely aware of it.

Kael is onto something; it *would* be a kick to hear her boyfriend Charlie (Nicolas Cage) discuss his physical attraction to her. And since Charlie is so gaunt and his voice so cracked, it's plausible that he sees her fleshiness as a counterbalance to his weightlessness. At the same time, does Kael (and, to a certain extent, Ebert) not understand that a womanly big woman is sometimes a womanly big teenager? My high school was filled with both petite-little-nothings and full-figures. There were busts, hips, and shoulders of all sizes—and among the big-boned, nothing light years removed from Kathleen Turner's Peggy Sue. From this angle, Ebert's reading is more creative than Kael's more literal take. By characterizing the film's ease with Turner's physique as a convention, he's free to fully absorb her performance.

Above all, their final comments, which return to the director, illustrate their temperaments. Ebert earnestly describes Coppola's recent movies as stylistic experimentations with "honorable but uneven results," as if the failures of *One From the Heart* and *Rumble Fish* are best attributed to unevenness. He's a master of euphemism, excepting his final assessment of *Peggy Sue*, where he's a prince of exaggeration: "This was one of the best movies of 1986." In the meanwhile, Kael wraps it up with obdurate singularity. "I came away with the feeling that Coppola took on a piece of crap thinking he could do something with it," she writes, "and when he discovered he couldn't it turned into sad crap." Here, she combines straight talk, apathy toward a celebrated director, and—as John Simon might put it—crowd-pleasing vulgarity. But, following this, her abrupt closing line is dead-on: "The tone at the end is maudlin and baffled." For the resolution of *Peggy Sue*—which involves both a Shriner's-like gathering of old men who attempt to return her to the present, as well as a reunion with husband and daughter—is hopeless. Turner is a lovely, no-nonsense Peggy Sue, but *Peggy Sue's* ending is flabby and mawkish.

If Kael is wrong-headed in her focus on Turner, she balances this with a final verdict that counts. For Ebert, everything in the movie comes together, but he exaggerates in the bottom of the ninth; *Peggy Sue* contains a great performance, but isn't a great film. His final declaration, that it's one of the year's best, underscores a tendency to be so excited about some qualities (Turner's acting, Coppola's comeback) that he turns a blind eye to others (an embarrassing wrap-up). In the case of *Peggy Sue*, Kael closely analyzes the acting but misses the spirit of Turner's accomplishment. And her return to high school isn't as flattering; all that "crap" suggests a jejune posture. Ebert, on the other hand, illuminates Turner's performance by scrutinizing its total effect. What remains is a writer's seasoned humility.

And one last example. Ebert and Kael both identified narrative conventions as weaknesses in Costa-Gavras' *Music Box*, but, in this case, Ebert's focus on narrative ignores the movie's raison d'être. The film explores tense relations between father and daughter. Jessica Lange is Ann Talbot, a Chicago attorney whose Hungarian refugee father, Michael Laszlo (Armin Mueller-Stahl), is accused of Nazi war crimes and threatened with extradition. Ann agrees to defend her father, and, as the trial unfolds, she confronts many disquieting questions about what is and is not knowable regarding family and loved ones. The title derives from a scene in which photographs emerge, one-by-one, from an old music box. For Ebert, the scene symbolizes the movie's shortcomings: "It is intended as a dramatic moment, but it is all too neat, the clockwork machinery operating right on time for the requirements of the plot. The entire movie is like that. It is put together out of pieces taken off the shelf, and although it is about suffering, trust, and family love, it has no heart." Ebert essentially sees the film as a failed thriller, its strong performances overshadowed by rote plot devices. As is often the case, the focus of Ebert's analysis is on the film's narrative structure. He considers the movie's plot possibilities, argues there is no market for a film about Nazi hunters who falsely accuse, and determines the father to be guilty. The result, for him, is an obvious, unsatisfying mystery.

Furthermore, he compares Joe Eszterhas' script to two of the writer's earlier efforts (*Jagged Edge* and *Betrayed*), and argues they are played out variations on the same theme: Woman loves and trusts a man who may be a heinous murderer. This is a fair comparison, and the parallels certainly suggest Eszterhas' lack of imagination. Yet, applying Ebert's Law to the trio of scripts provides further insights. *Jagged Edge* is a crackerjack thriller that delivers real chills as a lawyer discovers that her client and lover is a murderer. Aspiring to be an acting showcase and romantic thriller, it excels at both. *Betrayed*, also directed by Costa-Gavras, is a bizarre political potboiler in which an undercover FBI agent falls in love with a man who may be a member of a white supremist organization. Here, the melodrama is so heightened and unlikely that it overwhelms the attempts at suspense and social critique. *Music Box* follows the Eszterhas outline, but with a decisive difference: the leads are now father and daughter, which opens a pandora's box of philo-sophical and theological perplexities unavailable to the other films.

Thematically, *Music Box* is more than a thriller. Though its themes are raised indirectly, the movie is essentially about the limits of anyone's ability to exhaustively know or be known. When Ann cries out to her father, "Papa, what are we gonna do?" the operative word is "we." Ann's beliefs, fortitude, and temperament are inherited and molded by her father; if he engaged in unspeakable acts, then it is a lineage she shares. Her determination to understand presents all sorts of complex dilemmas, from a child's unease when considering a parent's sexuality

Figure 16 In Costa-Gavras' *Music Box*, Jessica Lange portrays Ann Talbot, whose searching eyes implore her father, Mike Laszlo (Armin Mueller-Stahl), to discuss his past ...

Figure 17 ... While low-key lighting blankets Laszlo in mystery. *Carolco Pictures*

to larger questions about the boundaries of knowing and the moral responsibilities that accompany family bonds. *Music Box* touches on all these issues, and in doing so, becomes spiritually larger than its parts. By framing the movie principally as a thriller, where a character is either guilty or not, Ebert limits the film's scope, and by extension, his perceptions. Kael describes it as a melodrama "with the pull of a thriller" and this is helpful; it allows her to appreciate the movie's deeper dimensions. While acknowledging the constraints of the genre, she emphasizes the movie's accomplishments in light of them. With the right actors and material, she argues, Costa-Gavras "has the knack of giving tempo and urgency to courtroom scenes. Others try for it; he really does it." While Ebert is disappointed that the film contains courtroom conventions, like the arrival of eleventh-hour witnesses and evidence, Kael admires the film's style and the director's gift for bringing vitality to such familiar terrain.

Predictably, Ebert faults not the actors but the filmmakers. In particular, the hazy characterization of Mike Laszlo ruffles his brow; he argues the role should be the lead rather than a secondary pawn. Praising Lange, he holds Costa-Gavras and Eszterhas responsible for the film's failings: "They have put her into a thriller in which there can be no real suspense, and provided her with a lot of emotional scenes that we look at in a detached way because we have figured out the plot and her character has not." Contrastingly, Kael reads Laszlo's ambiguity as an asset, arguing that Mueller-Stahl "keeps the father from becoming too easy for the audience to decipher: he's a formal, Old World father—you never feel you know him. (So you understand his daughter's not knowing him.)" For Kael, the acting lifts the film above its genre. She quotes Lange as saying, "I love the sound of the cello" and finds a metaphor here: "That's her emotional sound in this role: intelligent, searching, womanly." Which inspires Kael's elegant finish: "What counts is the Old World, New World texture that Jessica Lange brings to toughness. Her beautiful throatiness counts. She has the will and the technique to take a role that's really no more than a function of melodrama and turn this movie into a cello concerto." Kael's words reignite Lange's performance, and the spotlight becomes both of them.

Music Box, finally, is a movie of textures, from the chiaroscuro lighting that envelopes Mueller-Stahl in ambiguity to the motif of pounding drums that punctuates rising tensions. The opening credits foreground this, as the titles appear over a close-up of the revolving cylinder in a music box, its pins plucking out a haunting ballad on the metal comb. The studs of pins are even apparent within the font of the filmmakers' names, layering texture upon texture. Ebert's emphasis on genre addresses the film as a whodunit, and, on this level, he's on target: the movie will not be remembered for its suspense. Kael agrees, but sees more. Again, their varied sensibilities are evident, each producing hits and misses. Ebert specializes in a thorough, well-reasoned vetting: Does the film succeed on its own terms? Kael appraises everything: the demands of genre, the lead performances, even the wardrobe of supporting players. Ebert breaks down the film's structure and rebuffs its predictability; Kael's tactile language brings great acting to life—in this case, even the timbre of Lange's voice. Ebert's gift is his impeccable concentration, his skillful way of sizing up a work of art. Yet his attention to narrative can eclipse a movie's soul. Kael's éclat is her ability to capture the texture of movies through words, but her digressions can distract. Like the meticulously arranged teeth in a music box, Ebert and Kael strike distinct chords, harmonizing their talents. In unison, her flourish complements his focus, and reading one elicits gratitude for the other.

Chapter 5
Lit Crit

A love of words precedes and ushers in a love of images, and Ebert's deep-seated empathy was honed from reading books, as well as watching movies. In fact, Ebert's childhood memories are peppered with affection for literature. His mother was a bookkeeper and his father, Walter H. Ebert, an electrician for the University of Illinois. Doubtlessly, growing up in the shadow of a major research institution fertilized his intellectual curiosity from an early age, and his father recognized this. One afternoon Walter was summoned to campus for some electrical work, where he strolled past a row of professors' offices. That night he told his son, "I saw the professors there, smoking their pipes, reading in their offices with their feet up on their desks, and I say, 'Boy, that's for you.'" Roger's recollections, too, evoke the quintessential portrait of an only child finding sustenance and companionship in books. Reviewing *Greystoke*, he writes: "I think it helps, in seeing this movie, to draw on a background of rainy Saturday afternoons when you were ten and had your nose buried in *Tarzan* books." The ten-year-old who snuggles up with books on a rainy day becomes the critic who discerns and elucidates the pleasures of pulp and art.

Then and now, Ebert is content to be alone with books, and books serve as chapters to his life. In childhood, he pored over Elizabeth Enright's Melendy Family series; he still combs used bookstores searching for first editions. He devoured Thomas Wolfe in adolescence, when, according to Mrs. Seward, he still had a chance. And in college he graduated to Henry James and Franz Kafka. As an adult, his tastes range from Philip Roth to Patrick Süskind, from John Le Carré to

Charles Palliser. Since reading naturally prompts introspection, books are conduits of healing for Ebert. In his 60s and recovering from radiation treatments for salivary cancer, he found consolation in Willa Cather. In fact, Ebert originally aspired to be an English professor: "Reading Shakespeare, Milton and Chaucer and talking about them in afternoon seminars with cups of tea seems to me to be the most pleasant lifestyle imaginable." Rotogravure images of academia notwithstanding, his has been a lifelong romance with books. When the *Sun-Times* offered him the job as lead film critic in 1967, Ebert was already enrolled as a graduate student in English at the University of Chicago. Luckily, he never had to choose between the classroom and film. He left higher education for journalism, but would later teach extension courses in film for the University of Chicago, somehow squeezing in frame-by-frame analyses with students alongside full-time reviewing. It appears Walter knew his son after all.

Ebert's critical and literary prowess is governed by a healthy Midwestern pragmatism. He understands the symbiotic relationship between books and movies. For Ebert, a literary adaptation is not a mirror of a novel; a film must be evaluated on its own merits. At the same time, an adaptation needs to convey the spirit of its source in fresh, imaginative ways. Thoughtful reader as he is, he engages words as they are, discerns meanings, and expects filmmakers to marry the effect of the work with perspective and inventiveness. There are countless ways of doing this. Take John Knowles' *A Separate Peace*. Ebert recommends Larry Peerce's film, but argues its literalness is both boon and bane: "The movie's very faithfulness to the novel, its unwillingness to expand or analyze Knowles' vision, makes it dependent on its source." More cinematically daring is Karl Reisz's adaptation of John Fowles' *The French Lieutenant's Woman*. Eschewing the novel's multiple narrative lines, the film divides the story into two tracks: The Victorian melodrama is portrayed by modern actors having an affair of their own, and the film's force is the comparative value of these parallel worlds. For Ebert, the device is ingenious: "The movie's a challenge to our intelligence, takes delight in playing with our expectations, and has one other considerable achievement as well: It entertains admirers of Fowles' novel, but does not reveal the book's secrets. If you see the movie, the book will still surprise you, and that's as it should be." The movie excels because its structure captures and amplifies the

novel's inner rhythms and complicated construction. These films illustrate the diversity of approaches Ebert responds to. Peerce directs an
adaptation that communicates no more or less than the straightforward
book; Reisz's adaptation is a work of art in its own right, related and
faithful to Fowles' vision, but distinct in design and expression. Ebert
respects both, but not with equal enthusiasm.

Ebert's pragmatism is seen in his reactions to movies depicting
characters putatively transformed by literature. Simply put, he refuses
to be conned by phony sentiment. He rejects *Educating Rita* and
Dead Poets Society for failing to convince us that the characters are
truly reading the books that are changing them. These movies recall
Mark Twain's description of a woman swearing, oft-repeated by Ebert:
"She knows the words, but not the music." In particular, *Dead Poets*
is a grossly manipulative film, and the best thing to emerge from it is
Ebert's closing advice, where a quote from Henry David Thoreau's
Walden is recommended "for serious study by the authors of this film:
'... instead of studying how to make it worth men's while to buy my
baskets, I studied rather how to avoid the necessity of selling them.'
Think about it." In the end, he holds these films to their own standards,
and screenwriters can benefit from his peroration. The curative is *La
Lectrice*, where a young Frenchwoman employs herself as a reader,
subtly channeling the characters in the books—and, by extension, the
fantasies of her clients. For a bibliophile like Ebert, this film compre-
hends the sensual, transformative possibilities of entering into the
experience of another through literature, prompting this confession:
"When the movie was over, I wanted to go out and find the novel by
Raymond Jean that the screenplay is based on. I didn't want to read
it. I wanted someone to read it to me." Ebert distinguishes intuitively
among films that use books as plot devices and ones that convey
soulful affection for language and words.

Ebert's pragmatism further extends to the way he engages his
readers. While discussing Volkner Schlondorf's *Swann in Love*,
he acknowledges that most moviegoers will not be familiar with
Proust's writing, and consequently dispenses with the novel-to-screen
discussion in favor of enumerating the film's merits. Ebert also freely
admits to not having read a book, and his candid "unread by me" is
a bracing reminder that even voracious readers cannot get to every
book. Nor should they: "*Charlotte Gray* is based on a best-selling novel

by Sebastian Faulks, unread by me, and on the basis of this movie, not on my reading list." His practical approach is also noted in his openness to movies fired by literary hacks. He gave *Love Story*, based on Erich Segal's bestseller, a sterling review, arguing that competent direction and the personalities of actors can invigorate prose that's "a cross between a parody of Hemingway and the instructions on a soup can." Clearly for Ebert, the commute from books to film is a heavily trafficked, two-way street, with no invariable rules of the road.

Above all, Ebert holds a literary adaptation accountable for capturing the spirit and themes of the novel that inspired it. The highly antici-pated Robert Redford-Mia Farrow remake of *The Great Gatsby* was a letdown, and Ebert's equitable evaluation is a paean to F. Scott Fitzgerald's novel. His chief concern is that the movie's faithfulness to production design overshadows the spirit and themes of the book. At its core, he feels Fitzgerald's story is about the cost of ill-starred idealism, anchored in Gatsby's doomed quest for the unattainable Daisy Buchanan. "In the novel, Gatsby never understands that he is too good for Daisy. In the movie, we never understand why he thought she was good enough for him. And that's what's missing," he writes. More is missing still, and he explains how the film's miscasting, unvigilant direction, and overproduced mise-en-scène continue to miss the novel's very point. The film clocks in at one-hundred and forty-six minutes, roughly the amount of time needed to finish the book, which Ebert recommends as the wiser investment. Another elephantine literary adaptation was Roland Joffe's *The Scarlet Letter*, a classic cinematic quagmire. If movies are considered the literature of our times, then Joffe's film is very bad literature indeed. Ebert wryly notes how the movie's anachronistic self-help values are incongruous with Nathaniel Hawthorne's themes of moral guilt and accountability, to say nothing of the film's ham-fisted performances, fascination with voyeuristic sexuality, and a finale that reduces Hawthorne's tale to a bodice-ripper: Hester Prynne actually rides away on horseback with Reverend Dimmesdale. Ebert quotes the director, who feels the book is "often looked at merely as a tale of nineteenth-century moralizing, a treatise against adultery." Ebert's riposte: "Actually, it is more often looked upon as a tale of seventeenth-century moralizing, and a treatise against hypocrisy. But nevermind." Early in the review he also quotes the movie's star, Demi Moore, who describes *The Scarlet Letter* as "a very dense, uncinematic book," providing Ebert with a red-letter closing: "Hollywood has taken that troublesome old novel and made it cinematic at last, although I'm afraid it's still pretty dense." His criticism rarely draws on outside material, but here he gives Joffe and Moore just enough rope. While the movie's fatuousness incites less ire than the care and talent poured into *Gatsby*, the subtext of the review is clear: Read the book.

Ebert lucidly takes apart new-fashioned classics as well, and his review of Brian De Palma's *The Bonfire of the Vanities* is a model of critical civility and circumspection. Tom Wolfe's satire of political hacks from all social strata in New York City is a burning indictment of 1980s avarice. In keeping with Wolfe's world of stockbrokers and socialites, De Palma's production was characterized by excess, and, even before a single frame was shown, the film's towering budget and gonzo casting decisions garnered malicious buzz among industry insiders and outsiders. Amid the intermural skirmishes, Ebert's calm assessment clarifies the film's worth. For him, the movie's two-dimensional characterizations are uneasy bedfellows with Wolfe's razor-sharp observations and pitiless study of human guile. Still, he never overreacts to De Palma's intentionally superficial approach, and, while his disappointment is palpable, he grants the film a fair hearing. Ebert gauges the mishaps,

Figure 18 There's mischief in her eyes: Stockbroker Sherman McCoy (Tom Hanks) and mistress Maria Ruskin (Melanie Griffith) keep up appearances in Brian De Palma's *The Bonfire of the Vanities*. Griffith's game, frisky charm livens up the proceedings. *Warner Bros.*

including Bruce Willis' listless performance as scrappy reporter Peter Fallow, against its quirky delights, like Melanie Griffith's "much more interesting" Maria Ruskin, the lubricious mistress of Sherman McCoy. He spots from the get-go that Griffith, alternately bedizened in plush furs, sparkly gowns, and the floppiest of hats, plays her role to a fare-thee-well. Saddled with silly double-entendres and malapropisms, she transcends the dumb-blonde archetype by pushing it as far as possible, and in a film generally burdened by miscasting, her game, frisky charm livens up the proceedings. She simultaneously adheres to De Palma's vision and makes the role her own. Ebert gets this, and in the final analysis suspects the movie will be enjoyed more by those who haven't read the novel. "The beauty of the Wolfe book was the way it saw through its time and place, dissecting motives and reading minds," he concludes. "The movie sees much, but it doesn't see through." With grace and perspicuity, Ebert weighs the accomplishments of Wolfe and De Palma. In doing so, he anticipates and distills four-hundred pages of *The Devil's Candy*, Julie Salamon's hand-wringing account of the film's checkered production.

Few tasks in translating pages into film are more crucial than preserving a novel's point of view, and Ebert is alert to this. In fact, his chief grievance with De Palma's *Bonfire* is the film's muddled perspective. Wolfe's third-person narrator not only reports but appraises the characters' shifting principles and imbroglios. Ebert believes Wolfe loathes all of the machers and schmoozers who inhabit the book, so it's a letdown that the film "doesn't seem to despise anyone all that much." Likewise, he was thoroughly frustrated by *Endless Love*, the film based on Scott Spencer's chronicle of adolescent angst and heartbreak. The book's narrator is David, half a pair of star-crossed lovers, with years of experience now separating him from his youthful indiscretions. For Ebert, the filmmakers' decision to abandon the book's narrative point of view and unfold the story chronologically is a calamity: "That means that the love affair between Jade and David, instead of being remembered as a painful loss, is seen in the 'now' as ... well, as a teen-age romance. Its additional level of meaning is lost." He pinpoints other boners, like the casting of Martin Hewitt as David, who "is too handsome, too heavily bearded, too old in appearance" to suggest a seventeen-year-old's bundle of nerves. So attuned to the novel's spirit is Ebert that even the stubble on an actor's face strikes a false chord.

Yet what most enrages him are the circumstances of David's impulsive behavior. In the novel, David concocts a scheme to set fire to Jade's home in order to "discover" the flames and gain esteem in her parents' eyes. In the movie, a friend suggests the idea to David, almost as an aside, and David acts on it. "Apparently the filmmakers thought the fire had to be 'explained,'" Ebert concludes. "The result is to take a reckless act and turn it into a stupid one, diminishing both David's intelligence and the power of his passion." Film historians describe Hollywood filmmaking as an "excessively obvious cinema," yet, here, Ebert objects to the conspicuous cause-and-effect chain, not in principle, but when such decisions reduce narrative complexity and depth of characterization. By the end of the film, the offense is two-fold: Lessening the intelligence of headstrong, vulnerable characters diminishes the intelligence of moviegoers as well. Still, despite the structural gliches, aspects of the movie work. For more than a few critics, the early 80s were open season on Brooke Shields, the star of *Endless Love* who remained popular with audiences. Here, Ebert argues she's "a great natural beauty" with "a strong, unaffected screen acting manner." After heedfully scrutinizing the film's narrative construction, his respect for Shields is both restrained and revealing. His commitment to analyzing all facets of a movie—regardless of critical vogue—is commendable, and his defense of her throws as much light on his aesthetics as his anger toward the film's form.

Endless Love is, finally, a movie that needs the urgency and regret of the novel's first-person perspective. Be that as it may, Ebert knows that a subjective point of view is no cure-all. On the other end of the spectrum are movies like *Heartburn*, Nora Ephron's thinly veiled account of her unhappy marriage to Carl Bernstein, or Arliss Howard's *Big Bad Love*, loosely based on the writings and life of Larry Brown. These films fall flat—so flat that even actors like Meryl Streep and Debra Winger cannot revive them. In each, Ebert theorizes that the point of view is the problem. Ephron penned the screenplay based on her book; Howard co-wrote, directed, and portrayed a version of Brown in his movie. In both cases, there simply isn't enough distance for the filmmakers to view their subjects with sufficient objectivity. In *Heartburn*, the result is especially unsatisfying: whitewashed characters dressed for revenge—sheep in wolves' clothing. With respect to Howard's film, which pleads sympathy for its middle-aged, divorced, alcoholic, unpublished, chain-smoking writer, Ebert observes, "We all have a tendency to go easy on ourselves, and *Big Bad Love* is unaware that its hero is a jerk." In these instances, Ebert understands that a subjective account can be blinding, either softening edges or limiting insight.

Though consistently incisive, Ebert doesn't always hit the mark. The adaptation of Jane Smiley's *A Thousand Acres* presents a troublesome case. Here, both the screenplay and Ebert's critique land somewhere between Scylla and Charybdis. Smiley's Pulitzer-Prize-winning novel is as dense and aromatic as the Iowa soil tilled by the Cook family. Paterfamilias Larry Cook (Jason Robards) lords over land and family, and turmoil ensues when he decides to divvy up his grounds among his three daughters: rebellious Rose (Michelle Pfeiffer), dutiful Jenny (Jessica Lange), and his youngest and favorite, Caroline (Jennifer Jason Leigh). The book is an ornate chalice, teeming with family folklore, buried secrets, and tense sibling rivalry. Smiley's epic scales the heights of melodrama, including adultery, child abuse, dementia, the reappearance of high-school sweethearts in middle age, infertility, and, yes, even allusions to *King Lear*. With nerve and beguiling elegance, Smiley barely navigates these theatrics: I nearly threw my hands up when, in the final passages of the book, Ginny attempts to poison one of her sisters with lethal homemade sausages. It's no surprise, then, that the book's sharply etched, audacious melodrama just about capsizes the film. The script mercifully excludes the tainted sausage, but not much else is sidelined. When the subplot of contaminated water wells and infertility is fleetingly mentioned, I winced. Threads that somehow sustain plausibility in Smiley's prose are challenging to translate to film without turning the entire fracas into a condensed season of *Dallas*.

In his review, Ebert admits to not reading the book, but he too believes the movie is overwhelmed by its content. True to form, he comments on the film's point of view:

> The movie is narrated by Ginny, the Lange character, apparently in an effort to impose a point of view where none exists. But why Ginny? Is she better than the others? At the end of the film she intones in a solemn voice-over: "I've often thought that the death of a parent is the one misfortune for which there is no compensation." Say what? She doesn't remember her mother and is more than reconciled to

Figure 19 In Jocelyn Moorhouse's *A Thousand Acres*, Michelle Pfeiffer and Jessica Lange are fully convincing as Midwestern sisters, and their chemistry elevates the film. In this scene, they maintain a standoff with their father at a church potluck. *Touchstone*

the death of a father who (thanks to recovered memory) she now knows molested her. What compensation could she hope for, short of stealing him from his deathbed to hang him on a gallows?

Let's tackle the first question: Why Ginny? No, she isn't better than her sisters, but, in a way, she undergoes the most meaningful psychological change. Throughout, Rose holds fast to her nervous indignation and Caroline maintains a strained independence, but Ginny transforms from a supportive wife and daughter to a woman who views her choices with greater complexity. In book and film, she becomes more self-aware, and, by doing so, generates the most sympathetic perspective. This is also what makes the film, in spite of narrative overload, so compelling. It's exciting to see Lange—whose characters often face adversity for being too smart for their own good—portray a more gullible woman than the sturdy Midwesterners she specializes in. And the usually sunny and winsome Pfeiffer is just as convincing as the bitter, unappeasable Rose. For two stars to convincingly portray sisters in the Corn Belt is a considerable feat. Both women creatively play against expectations and their chemistry elevates the screenplay and film beyond the level of unadorned CliffsNotes. Even Jennifer Jason Leigh seems right as the estranged Caroline, believing she has greater insight into family dynamics, and feeling superior for it. This time her aloofness and recalcitrance are welcome.

In terms of Ginny's voice-over, context is paramount. When she narrates the line to which Ebert objects, she isn't addressing her father's death; she's referring to Rose's passing, and the fact that she'll now be raising her nieces. Rose, for all of the petty and genuine grievances she nurses, is a loving mother, and this is the ultimate loss Ginny describes. No critic is expected to grasp every nuance in a film or book, but, in this instance, Ebert's critique of her voice-over is as spirited as it is imprecise. He also takes issue with the movie's pell-mell characterizations: "... I was unable to say who I was supposed to like and who I was supposed to hate—although I could name several characters for whom I had no feelings at all." Fair is fair, but, in this case, it would have helped to have read the novel. For the ambiguity is intentional—Smiley's very subject is the emotional apathy that takes root within families. In the book, Ginny eventually says of her sister Caroline, "Truly we were beyond like and dislike by now." But what Ebert discounts as ambivalence is Smiley's central theme: the obligations of timeworn family connections. In defense of a flawed movie, I share Ebert's hesitance about the overburdened plot; less so the negative assessment of the movie. Moreover, even when his arguments are flatfooted, the suitability of a film's narrative point of view remains an issue.

When it comes to translating characterization and motivation, Ebert privileges fidelity and complexity. Judith Rossner's *Looking for Mr. Goodbar* ends, famously, with its heroine strangled by another one-night stand. Richard Brooks' film also concludes with her violent death, but Ebert notes a critical difference: "In the book, Theresa might have picked up the guy *because* she knew he'd be trouble." So the film shies away from exploring her masochistic impulses, complexity is compromised, and the movie suffers. There isn't a more honest actor than Diane Keaton, and her performance as Theresa is so evocative that it's difficult to recall Rossner's book without thinking of her. Ebert praised her in *Goodbar*, but if her style isn't right for a part, he explains why. Consider her performance as Charlie, the actress-turned-spy in George Roy Hill's *The Little Drummer Girl*, which Ebert pinpoints as the film's weakness: "Keaton's Charlie is not young enough, passionate enough or, if I may say so, sluttish enough to recapture the wild, sloppy character in Le Carré's book." Again, he protects the actor, stressing that Keaton is gifted, just miscast. Regarding her work in Leonard Nimoy's *The Good Mother*, based on Sue Miller's novel, her unabashed qualities wear on him: "we get so many smiles, so much charming confusion ... that we begin to yearn for her to grow up." Keaton is better than this; she does what she can with Miller's maudlin book, Nimoy's uncertain direction, and—as Ebert stresses in his review—a script that's terrified of its subject matter. What's instructive, though, is his desire for complexity and fidelity. These are not instances of a critic drawing platitudinal comparisons between book and film. Ebert doesn't telegraph that he's well read; he simply is. And he holds a film responsible when its success rests on the novel's depth of characterization and on the director's subsequent casting.

Of all novelists past and present, Ebert's appreciation for life and art is most deeply influenced by Henry James. Discovering James in college challenged him to persist with the author's voluminous novels. Rewards would come, but not quickly or easily, and Ebert's perseverance as a reader complements his patience as a moviegoer. (Significantly, he treasures James as he does Ozu; both demand and reward time and attention.) It appears Ebert never sold his books after college graduation; he's journeyed with James well into adulthood, reading and re-reading him for the pleasures and insights. The intricacy and force of James' artistry are touchstones for many works of art, and his influence is seen in Ebert's off-the-cuff references to him, not merely in adaptations of his works. For instance, Ebert finds import in Woody Allen's *Match Point* by contrasting the attitudes and moral codes of its selfish protagonists with the scheming but far more self-aware characters in *The Wings of the Dove*. James' novels are standard bearers of a world where moral decisions matter. The social expectations that envelop his characters clash with relaxed modern values, and, though James' men and women often struggle and suffer, it's clear which world Ebert prefers.

His regard for James is all the more evident in his reviews of films inspired by his novels. At times Ebert moonlights as literary critic, paying sportive homage to James' style while reviewing *The Bostonians*:

> One of the qualities I like best in the novels of Henry James is the way his characters talk and talk about matters of passion and the heart, and never quite seem to act. One of his favorite words,

in many of his books, is "intercourse," by which, significantly, he seems to mean conversation, although you can never quite be sure. James's novels run long and deep, and because he was writing for a 19th century that was not always open to the kinds of passions felt by his characters, he beat a lot, if you will, around the bush, so to speak, with lots of commas and asides and subtle hints of unspeakable practices.

The last sentence is probably as much as a newspaperman can get away with. Ebert's full-length reviews are often shorter than James' sprawling paragraphs, yet the opportunity to reflect on James stirs something in Ebert, who rises to the occasion. *The Bostonians* takes place during the early suffragette struggles in Boston, focusing on the young, unformed Verena Tarrant (Madeleine Potter), a promising orator desired and pursued by two stronger personalities: her traditional suitor Basil Ransom (Christopher Reeve) and Olive Chancellor (Vanessa Redgrave), her sexually repressed political mentor. Ebert sizes up the film's pensive treatment of implied sexual and political battles with a cool, final assessment: the movie is "intelligent and subtle and open to the underlying tragedy of a woman who does not know what she wants, a man who does not care what he wants, and a girl who does not need what she wants." This aperçu echoes the film's achievements: an unusual contest of wills is dramatized, and James' sympathies toward his well-meaning, and at times unwitting, characters are preserved.

Figure 20 In Iain Softley's adaptation of *The Wings of the Dove*, when Kate (Helena Bonham Carter) and Merton (Linus Roache) consummate their connivery, they understand just how naked they are. *Miramax*

Ebert is every bit as enthusiastic about Iain Softley's adaptation of *The Wings of the Dove*, a striking film with flawless performances from Helena Bonham Carter, Linus Roache, and Alison Elliott. They comprise another tragic threesome, in a tale of British lovers preying on the emotional needs of a vulnerable American searching for romance. Kate (Bonham Carter) urges Merton (Roache) to wed terminally ill heiress Millie (Elliott) with the goal of inheriting her fortune. The fly in the ointment is that all three are alive to the perverse and desperate motives underlying their choices. Ebert admires how the film captures the book's tone, suggesting through prolonged silences, furtive glances, and clandestine embraces a visual equivalent of James' gift for indirect communication. In this respect, the film succeeds in finding a cinematic language that matches the emotional volatility simmering beneath the surface of James' novel. For Ebert, the movie pierces the novel's soul: "The buried message is that when it comes to money, sex, love, and death, most people are prepared to go a great deal further than they would admit. There is, if you know how to look for it, incredible emotional violence in the work of Henry James." And the movie suggests these emotional maneuvers in words and images of comparable potence. The characters are cognizant of the prices they pay for love and security, and, in the final scenes, when Kate and Merton consummate their connivery, they understand just how naked they are.

Jane Campion's version of James' *The Portrait of a Lady* is another classic of transatlantic deception. Isabel Archer (Nicole Kidman) is a naïve American orphan who travels to Europe in search of love, eventually yielding to the wheelings and dealings of Madame Merle (Barbara Hershey) and the painter Gilbert Osmond (John Malkovich), a man she will regret marrying. Ebert respects the integrity of the acting, with the exception of Malkovich's Osmond, too obviously rapacious to be persuasive as the dilettante. This shift in characterization, from imposter to snake-oil salesman, throws the film out of kilter. For Ebert, Isabel's love for Osmond transforms her from James' idealist to Campion's masochist. The masochism is not only unwarranted, it actually lessens her intelligence. Some viewed Campion's film as a feminist reading, but, to Ebert, any attempt to modernize James doesn't have a handle on the author's shrewd understanding of human nature and desire. Still, he's no hanging judge. He views Campion's film more as an interpretation than adaptation, and, with that caveat, cautiously recommends it. Furthermore, his critique provides another opportunity to hammer home the essence of Jamesian themes:

> The value of Henry James is that he teaches us to consider our motives. Today we rush heedless into life. We believe in "love at first sight." We get our values from TV and film, where the plot exists only to hurry the characters into sex. All modern emotions can be expressed in a sound bite. James's people think before they commit. When they choose wrong, they eventually learn how, and why. Today's Isabel Archer would dump Osmond, sue for her money back, and head for a spa to recuperate. I imagine James's Isabel forever in the loveless tomb of her own choosing.

Ebert holds dear James' severe and sympathetic understanding of human nature. His characters know that their decisions are instilled with ethical dimensions, that their choices impinge on others as well as on their own freedoms. Their words and actions show moral mettle, but in no way guarantee happiness. Comparatively, the modern world leaves much to be desired: "In *The Wings of the Dove* there is a fascination in the way smart people try to figure each other out. The film is acted with great tenderness. If the three central characters had been more forthright, more hedonistic, we wouldn't care nearly as much. But all three have a certain tact, a certain sympathy for the needs of the others."

If Ebert is drawn to their values, it is because he shares them. On one hand, he understands the human propensity for selfishness; on the other, he too is a writer with tact and concern for others. Decisions and values should be portrayed with moral weight, and this matters more to him than the triumph of virtue. Ebert's writing departs from the belief that there are values and causes higher than the self. As such, he cares deeply that stories of insight and verity—stories that examine the pain and promise of what it means to be human—be brought to the screen with perspective and integrity. This means that filmmakers, whether adapting Henry James or Tom Wolfe, must understand and convey the themes and points of view of the novels they bring to the screen. In the realm of words and deeds, Ebert thinks before he commits—and he urges filmmakers to follow suit. In so doing, he models a lifetime of incisive thinking, reading, and writing, which explains why he is so at home with James. By stressing the value of what James teaches, Ebert juggles the roles of critic, teacher, and literary scholar with aplomb, all the while savoring his own cup of tea.

Chapter 6

And I Still Can See *Blue Velvet*, Through My Tears

Of *Last Rites*, Ebert argues, "It is not only bad filmmaking, but it is offensive as well—offensive to my intelligence. Many films are bad. Only a few declare themselves the work of people deficient in taste, judgment, reason, tact, morality, and common sense. Was there no one connected with this project who read the screenplay, considered the story, evaluated the proposed film, and vomited?" Of another he writes, "*Very Bad Things* filled me with dismay. The material doesn't match the genre; it's an attempt to exploit black humor without the control of tone necessary to pull it off. I left the theater feeling sad and angry. On the movie's Web site, you can download a stripper. I'm surprised you can't kill her." Sweeping assessments like these are bookmarks of Ebert's gift for leveling a film with both hyperbole and wit. His responses also imply a tension: Great critics experience moral outrage at the movies, but nobody wants to be remembered as a moralist. In this respect, no critic is bolder than Roger Ebert in expressing how a film strikes his moral sensibilities. And no critic has expressed a deeper respect than Ebert for what James Agee called the aesthetic and moral discipline of the artist.

A defining moment in Ebert's career was his reaction to David Lynch's *Blue Velvet*. The film was not so much a movie as an event—a cinematic minefield that ignited genuine, passionate disagreement among moviegoers and critics. I was sixteen when it opened, and I vividly recall the sparks flying between Siskel and Ebert when they debated its worth on their show. Everyone was talking about the movie, and I desperately wanted to see it. After reading a *Newsweek* essay headlined "Black and Blue Is Beautiful?" my mom boycotted it. That left Dad, whose moviegoing tastes were more laissez-faire, and soon we were off to the Fox Eastgate Theater in Carbondale, Illinois, to see our first David Lynch film. We crammed into the theater's smallest auditorium, and I remember in horror looking down our short aisle and nodding to Mrs. Profilet, who awkwardly waved back. I watched *Blue Velvet* in a theater in which the farthest seat was sixteen feet from the screen, sitting next to my patient father, my high-school English teacher a few seats down the row.

But I'm getting ahead of myself. First consider Ebert's response, which quickly epitomized *the* negative reaction to the movie. In short, *Blue Velvet* explores the sordid underbelly lurking beneath the friendly veneer of American life. Young man Jeffrey Beaumont (Kyle McLaughlin) finds a severed ear in a field and his bizarre discovery leads him to Dorothy Vallens (Isabella Rosselini), a mysterious lounge singer whose husband and child are kidnapped by the psychotic Frank Booth (Dennis Hopper). As ransom, Frank degrades and rapes Dorothy, and, shockingly, she responds with pleasure to his violent, puerile sexual proclivities. Jeffrey becomes entangled in their perverse world, develops the wherewithal to survive, and eventually chooses between Dorothy and Sandy (Laura Dern), his high-school sweetheart. With its lush visual contrasts and the intimation that sexual hunger permeates every aspect of life, critics from Gene Siskel to Pauline Kael declared *Blue Velvet* a masterpiece. But Ebert challenged this critical consensus, and his review remains one of the most forthright, compelling instances of a writer's gut-level response to a movie's full-frontal emotional assault.

For Ebert, Lynch's film is an aesthetic mismatch of form and content, and his argument rests on the following foundations: 1) Any subject matter is fair game for a movie to explore, but the nature of a movie's content demands an appropriate form, and 2) Lynch's alternation of harrowing melodrama and small-town satire is a moral and emotional cop-out. "American movies have been using satire for years to take the edge off sex and violence," Ebert writes. "Occasionally, perhaps sex and violence should be treated with the seriousness they deserve. Given the power of the darker scenes in this movie, we're all the more

Figure 21 Dorothy Vallens (Isabella Rosselini) is a mysterious lounge singer whose husband and child are kidnapped in David Lynch's *Blue Velvet*. For Ebert, "Rossellini goes the whole distance" in an unworthy film. *M-G-M* and *De Laurentiis Entertainment*

frustrated that the director is unwilling to follow through to the consequences of his insights. *Blue Velvet* is like the guy who drives you nuts by hinting at horrifying news and then saying 'Never mind.'" He concludes with a racy, eye-opening analogy linking Isabella Rossellini's performance (which he admired) and her character's treatment at the hands of both Frank and director Lynch:

> In *Blue Velvet*, Rossellini goes the whole distance, but Lynch distances himself from her ordeal with his clever asides and witty little in-jokes. In a way, his behavior is more sadistic than the Hopper character.
>
> What's worse? Slapping somebody around, or standing back and finding the whole thing funny?

This mordant critique reflects three central themes that we have witnessed in Ebert's criticism: the critical relationship between a movie's style and content, a careful consideration of a film's moral implications, and, finally, a respect for and protective attitude toward actors.

A week after the movie's US release, Ebert interviewed Lynch, prompting further analysis and reflection. His second essay about *Blue Velvet* underscores its heightened level of controversy—this movie mattered. He critiques the film as well as colleagues such as Kael, Siskel, and David Kehr for praising the movie's style while ignoring

Rossellini's presumed humiliation at the hands of her director (and, at the time, lover, adding another layer of discomfort to the firestorm, although one generally untouched by critics).

In the interview, Ebert restates his hesitations about *Blue Velvet*, concentrating on the film's treatment of Dorothy and zeroing in on a disturbing scene: After a date, Jeffrey drives Sandy home, and Dorothy emerges from bushes in the front yard, naked and badly bruised. She runs toward Jeffrey, her arms stretched outward. At the same time, Sandy's ex-boyfriend and his cronies pull up to confront Jeffrey. Taking in the strange scenario, the boyfriend eyes Dorothy and jokes, "Is that your mom?" Ebert describes this scene as having great personal significance to Lynch, as it recalls a childhood memory of seeing a woman stumbling down the street, naked and in tears. (Ebert justly points out that the meaning has little import for audiences unfamiliar with Lynch's experience.) Lynch also paints, and he explained to Ebert that his paintings force audiences to "react," giving Ebert his closing lines:

> All right, and I have reacted to *Blue Velvet*, too. As an experienced and clever film critic, I even know how to write fashionable praise about the film—how to interpret the director's message, how to show I am bright enough to understand his subtleties. I can even rationalize his extremes, and explain how only philistines will dislike the work.
>
> I know how to write that kind of review, but damn it all, then I would be reviewing the movie's style but ignoring its lost soul. Maybe some critics have seen so many movies they have forgotten how ordinary people look at them. For most people movies aren't about style, they're about the characters in them, and what happens to those characters, and what it means. And in *Blue Velvet*, there are some scenes in which a woman is degraded and humiliated and made to suffer obscenely, and other scenes in which we're supposed to giggle because the call letters of the local radio station are WOOD, and they give the time "at the sound of the falling tree." Sorry, but I just couldn't get my lips to smile.

There is defensiveness here—the sound of a critic who wants more from his colleagues and feels pinned against the wall for it. A protective posture is not unwarranted; a common critical strategy involves suggesting that one's opponents are prudes. Peter Rainer's enthusiastic review of *Blue Velvet*, for instance, twice mentions the "people" who will not like or get it, as well as the "bluenoses" who protest sex and violence at the movies. Admirable in Ebert's stand is his refusal to dilute his point of view for fear of appearing the bumpkin. Without hesitation, he maintains his argument on the level of aesthetics and addresses the moral implications of the movie's style and content. Stating that the film has a soul—much less a lost one—is a daring move, itself an act of moral tenacity. His comments also engage one of the central functions of criticism: the art of expressing personal reactions to a much larger readership that encompasses cineastes—and my dad and Mrs. Profilet as well. Simply mentioning how "ordinary" moviegoers might respond to *Blue Velvet* is enough to be labeled a philistine, but, Ebert says, to hell with it. It is his vulnerability as a critic, his willingness to stand against the cognoscenti and test a film's—and an esteemed director's—moral pulse, his absolute seriousness in the face of moral and aesthetic dilemmas—all of this makes Ebert's response provocative and alive. In fact, his criticism is as raw, immediate, and unapologetic as *Blue Velvet* itself.

In the interview with Lynch, Ebert dismisses Pauline Kael's protracted *Blue Velvet* review as a "précis," and although there is more to it than that, he is not far off the mark. There is simply too much exposition in Kael's essay, and you have to wade through it. She comes closest to Ebert's concerns when she discusses Rossellini: "She has a special physical quality, too. There's nothing of the modern American woman about her. When she's naked, she's not protected, like the stars who are pummeled into shape and lighted to show their muscular perfection. She's defenselessly, tactilely naked, like the nudes the Expressionists painted." An elucidating comparison, but Kael ends the discussion too soon. In *Blue Velvet*, Rossellini *is* Manet's *Olympia*, but with a vicious twist: instead of an African maid and a black kitten, there are frat boys to the side, demanding she spread her legs. It is Ebert who raises the pricklier dimension of defenseless nakedness, both in the display of Rossellini's voluptuous body and in the film's violent treatment of that display. One need not share his distaste for the movie to recognize the moral legitimacy of these concerns.

At their most intense, the arguments between Siskel and Ebert were laced with moral outrage, and never more so than in the case of

Blue Velvet. I remember their wrangling on *The Tonight Show*, Ebert objecting to the film's mistreatment of Rossellini and Siskel defending the movie, adding, "She's a big girl, Roger." The supercilious tone bothered me, mostly because Ebert's stand was more complicated than the gibe implied. Their impassioned, widely reported dispute became the microcosm of *Blue Velvet*'s potential to provoke, and, within the context of Ebert's career, there were two addenda. At the 1987 Cannes Film Festival, Ebert asked Rossellini about her experience making the movie. She replied, "You were concerned for me? I heard you thought David took advantage of me. It is sort of touching. I could not read a single word written about the film, because it was so difficult. People had a right to be troubled... I don't believe one could do that role of Dorothy, take off her clothes and put herself in situations like that unless one sees something in the film that overcomes that embarrassment." Clearly, they differed in their assessments of the film's tone. Ten years later, following the publication of Rossellini's autobiography *Some of Me*, Ebert revisited the issue in "A Memory of *Blue Velvet*." In the book, she describes the ordeal of filming the scene in which Dorothy appears naked on the lawn, identifying the inspiration for her approach as Nick Ut's horrifying 1972 photograph of Kim Phuc, the Vietnamese child fleeing from a Napalm bombing in Trang Bang, her scorched arms stretched outward. Rossellini remembers:

> I wish I'd found some other approach for the scene in *Blue Velvet*; I did not like being totally exposed, I kept worrying about what my family would think when the film came out, and I searched and searched for other solutions until the last minute—also because people were gathering around the set to watch the making of the film.
>
> People came out with blankets and picnic baskets, with their grandmothers and small children. I begged the assistant director to warn them that it was going to be a tough scene, that I was going to be totally naked, but they stayed anyway. I went out and talked to them myself, but they were already in the mood of an audience and just stared at me without reacting to my plea and warning.

Ebert cites her words and adds:

Extraordinary. It is customary in movies to clear the set before nude scenes. Here we have the general public settling down with picnic baskets to watch Rossellini enact humiliation. But Rossellini was being humiliated not only in the film, but by the film. Where was Lynch? Why did he film the scene with total strangers watching? Did he feel it would enhance her sense of embarrassment?

Blue Velvet was in some ways a remarkable movie, and my one-star rating probably reflects personal aversion to that particular scene more than a balanced judgment of its artistry. But now that I've read Rossellini's book I feel more now than ever that a compact between actor and director was violated, and that what I was feeling was really there—painful, humiliating, and unwarranted.

In the hands of lesser writers, this final chapter might sound like sour grapes from a critic defending a longstanding position on a cult favorite. Yet Ebert does not treat her recollection as a final word in the matter. Her memory affirms his initial, painful response—no more, no less. Ebert's essay is another expression of his belief that "movies do not change, but their viewers do," and Rossellini's words prompt a fair question: "Where was Lynch?" As a critic, Ebert instinctively protects the actor. How much greater the offense when a director fails to display such compassion.

I've concentrated on Ebert's response to *Blue Velvet* because it's his most famous review, but his reaction to Lynch's film isn't an anomaly. A range of movies arouses his defensive posture toward actors. When Siskel and Ebert reviewed *Porky's II* (1983), both hated it, but Ebert argued that the film was cruel as well as bad, since Nancy Parsons imbued the role of Miss Balbricker, the draconian PE teacher and target of endless humiliation at the hands of teenagers, with a degree of empathy. Siskel was bemused by Ebert's defense, but, even in a rancid sequel, Ebert remains sensitive to the plight of actors. This, however, was an aside; at other times, his concern for actors colors his entire response. For instance, he believes *Fast Times at Ridgemont High* (1982) routinely debases its actresses: "Why does someone as pretty as [Jennifer Jason] Leigh have to have her nudity exploited in shots where the only point is to show her ill-at-ease?" At the bottom of the artistic food chain is *Fraternity Vacation* (1985), where at one point two women hook up with the male leads, then pretend to have venereal diseases. "How would you feel if you were an actress auditioning for a part, and the good news was you were the girlfriend of the star," Ebert posits, "and the bad news was that after you stripped and made a herpes joke, you disappeared from the movie?" In these cases, Ebert is at pains to establish his neutrality toward subject matter. "Let me make myself clear," he asserts. "I am not against vulgarity as a subject for a movie comedy." He enjoys, for example, the hearty bawdiness of *Animal House* or *There's Something About Mary*. Yet, for him, the creators of movies like *Fast Times* "have an absolute gift for taking potentially funny situations and turning them into embarrassment. They're tone-deaf."

Ebert is even more disturbed when a child appears to be manipulated. Beyond tone-deafness, he accuses those responsible for *The Good Son* (1993) of moral deafness as well. Here, Macaulay Culkin plays a nine-year-old who drowns his baby brother and attempts to kill his cousin, sister, and mother. "At times, hearing the things [Culkin's] made to say," Ebert writes, "you want to confront the filmmakers who made him do it, and ask them what they were thinking of." No need to include that final "of," but the concern is understood. By the end, Ebert notes the contradiction between the film's R-rating and inevitable appeal to Culkin's PG audience. "This is not a suitable film for young viewers. I don't care how many parents and adult guardians they surround themselves with. And somewhere along the line," he argues, "a parent or adult guardian should have kept Macaulay out of it, too." It's a devastating closing, using the language of the ratings system to shame calculating parents and directors. It recalls one of Pauline Kael's closing lines, expressing disbelief at the hundreds of parents who permitted their daughters to audition for the role of the demon-possessed girl in *The Exorcist*. When the parents watch this film, "are they envious?" Kael wondered. "Do they feel, 'That might have been my little Susie—famous forever'?" These moments are telling. When a new generation of critics came to the fore in the 60s, they looked at movies "in an amoral way," replacing those who believed an essential task of film was to be morally uplifting. According to Richard Schickel, "we were just movie people." And there's no question they approached films with greater openness and neutrality. Yet they also draw all sorts of moral boundaries in their criticism, and, in the case of Ebert, nothing leads him to confront filmmakers more than the sense that actors—adult or child, consenting or not—are exploited.

In the end, Ebert's reaction to *Blue Velvet* is meaningful for its gutsy passion, its influence in shaping the national debate, and how, with time, it continues to define his aesthetic. Admittedly, his vehement reaction got me to the theater. This points to another strength: Even when Ebert dislikes a movie, his reasoning awakens artistic and intellectual curiosity. Beyond his opinion, does Rossellini's long-run perspective confirm that he was right? It's difficult to say. She opens her book by playfully admitting she stretches and colors the truth. I am more certain of my own memory of watching *Blue Velvet* with my dad. As the lights went down, my heart was pounding for lots of reasons, not the least of which was that sinking feeling that I was not quite sure what I had gotten us into. I was drawn to the film and its simple, arresting images of good and evil, light and dark—by Rossellini's full, jungle-red lips whispering the title track into that circular 40s microphone, with Hopper in the audience, pining away and caressing his own swatch of blue velvet, clawed from her tattered robe; and then, by her lonely appearance on the lawn. The audience roared with laughter when the teenager cracked a joke at Dorothy's expense, and I felt ill. My understanding of audience psychology is more nuanced today; I know people can laugh for reasons other than amusement. But my feeling at that moment was a sense of isolation from a movie that cued its audience to laugh at a woman's pain. My overall response to *Blue Velvet* was muddy and complex. The film was disturbing, but I was sixteen and merely seeing it was a Rabelaisian transgression that got the blood flowing. I felt privileged by the opportunity to sit in that theater and think about it. Then and now, Ebert's essays help me to analyze my reactions, to more clearly survey the parts in relation to the whole.

Long before Rossellini's book, I sensed a violation of trust between actor and director. In March of 1987, my dad bought me a copy of *Vanity Fair* at a bookstore in the St. Louis Plaza Frontenac, one of my mother's favorite shopping haunts. The eye-catching cover asked a question all of us have wondered from time to time: "Will Diane Keaton Get to Heaven?" But, inside, there was also an interview with Lynch and Rossellini. Annie Leibovitz had photographed them, and they were a handsome, strapping pair. "'David is obsessed with obsession,' says Rossellini. 'He finds it irresistibly funny. He finds Frank comical in *Blue Velvet*, because Frank is so obsessed—even in the scene where Frank is raping me. When we were filming it, David couldn't stop laughing—he had to grab hold of himself not to disturb the scene.'" Reading this, I felt at the very least that Lynch did not have a handle on the force of his images and, by default, the tone of his film. I also remembered Ebert's initial review, which reads like prophesy: "What's worse? Slapping somebody around, or standing back and finding the whole thing funny?" Rossellini's remarks encouraged me to trust my instincts at the movies. Ebert's, too.

Chapter 7
Cross References

Ebert's sensitivity to the possibilities of life and art is heightened by his reverence for spiritual curiosity and old-school, muscular Christianity. His fascination with the moral and philosophical questions that spring from faith is firmly anchored in his Catholic roots. To write with appreciation for a religious upbringing and education is uncommon in a critic, and growing up in the church deepened his critical faculties, as well as his regard for communal experiences of grand images that movies and religion can satisfy. Of course, Pauline Kael argued, too, that seminal directors of the 70s like Brian De Palma, Martin Scorsese, and Robert Altman were informed by their pre-Vatican II upbringings. There is emotional urgency in their films, infused by an awareness of sin and guilt. As a writer, the same is true of Ebert. He shows enthusiasm for Scorsese's parables of guilt and redemption, Werner Herzog's determination to create startlingly fresh images, the visual flourish of Coppola's *Apocalypse Now*, and the Old Testament obsessiveness of characters in Andrei Konchalovsky's films. These movies—Ebert's greatest hits—are indicative of a critical sensibility steeped in an unsparing understanding of human foibles and the hope of the transcendent and eternal: the very idea that our lives and struggles are birth pangs for something greater.

These aesthetics were formed at an early age. As Ebert said in a 1994 interview, growing up Catholic profoundly influenced his spiritual and intellectual engagement. St. Mary's Grade School in Urbana was a modest one, with no athletic teams or science labs. The nuns did, however, have books and blackboards, and the first hour of each day was dedicated to exploring moral and ethical dilemmas. "I remember one discussion very clearly," he recalls:

> What would happen if you walked around a corner, and there was Kim Novak wearing an immodest dress? And you saw her before you could not see her? And then you had an impure thought? And then a car hit you and you died?
>
> First of all, the very subtext here is that women are an occasion of sin. Which I always thought would be terrifically thrilling for a woman. Imagine—if someone just looked at you and went to hell. Think of the power you would have!
>
> So you didn't mean to see Kim Novak, but you did see her. And you couldn't help but have an impure thought. Then you were dead, and you went to hell. Now, if you analyze that—not in terms of fifth- or sixth-graders, but in terms of the question itself—it becomes one of the deepest issues of Western theology, philosophy and morals. That is, are you guilty of committing a sin if you did not intend to commit it? Do sins have an abstract reality, or are they relative to your intentions?
>
> I think that spending one hour a day in grade school talking about questions like that was extremely good for my education—apart from whether what I was taught was right or wrong, or whether I would agree with it today. I think all of that has kind of sunk in and informs my writing.

It's becoming that the essence of his temptation was a movie star. These experiences, though not equaling the spiritual pungency of a Flannery or Frank O'Connor short story, contain the ingredients of spiritual dilemmas and epiphanies that sharpen critical faculties and inform great writing. It's no accident that Ebert was alienated by the early films of Pedro Almodóvar that assailed any form of religious tradition or authority. Likewise, Ebert warmed to Almodóvar when the director softened up and showed more sympathy toward a range of his characters. Ebert's Catholic upbringing is significant, not for the abuse Almodóvar endured, but for the formation of a morally engaged perspective that is open to the world. The clarity of his reminiscences suggests the long arm of an upbringing that encourages moral and ethical reasoning, and Ebert's religious training has been formative to his aesthetic in at least two ways: through his attraction to films that grapple with spiritual issues, and through his appreciation for the complexity that spiritual dimensions bring to movies.

Crucially, Ebert draws no distinction between art and religious art, and this is apparent in his analyses of films that portray religious subject matter. Ebert has little patience for Bruce Beresford's *King David*, a film with "absolutely no curiosity about what it was really like to be alive 3,000 years ago; no imagination about how people looked and behaved then; and, probably worst of all, no feeling for the powerful religious feelings they had." Noble religious intentions notwithstanding, great art inspires intellectual and spiritual curiosity. In sharp contrast is his appreciation for the two-fisted candor and unvarnished realism of Martin Scorsese's *The Last Temptation of Christ* and Mel Gibson's *The Passion of the Christ*. Blood flows liberally in both movies; these are not air-brushed portraits of a wispy, moony savior that populated the religious epics of Ebert's youth. As different as they are, Scorsese's and Gibson's visions stir and challenge viewers to contemplate the nature of Christ as God and man. For Ebert, they are not "religious" films per se, but great films, period—not because the filmmakers are devout, though they are, but because the movies' gritty depictions of first-century life stimulate and defy modern sensibilities. If religious epics of old did little to slake the religious thirsts of their characters, Ebert witnessed a transformation in these big-screen sensibilities over the course of his career—a transformation he heartily applauds.

Scorsese's and Gibson's films are two of the most controversial that Ebert encountered in his career, and, in his considerations of each, he reveals the fullness of his critical abilities. *The Last Temptation* arrived in a cloud of contention and prompted not one, not two, but three essays on the movie—the third, a kind of last-minute mea culpa that attempts to re-write the review that never quite got written. As a rebuttal to those who objected to the movie's portrayal of a struggling and embattled Christ, Ebert's first review is peerless. But, as criticism, it's weak tea. Of the filmmakers he observes, "They have paid Christ the compliment of taking him and his message seriously, and have made a film that does not turn him into a garish, emasculated image from a religious postcard." Or is it the author Nikos Kazantzakas who deserves the compliment? My point is that Ebert subtly builds a false dilemma. In one corner of the ring is the fey Jesus of "religious" films; in the other,

Kazantzakas, Scorsese, and screenwriter Paul Schrader's struggling, self-doubting Christ. At best, collapsing Kazantzakas' portrait with any of the biblical accounts is a sticky wicket. For Ebert's analysis to pass muster, these tensions need to be considered with greater care. Not addressing them leads to swift dismissals of the fundamentalists who objected to the film, but at the expense of more vigorous intellectual and spiritual debate.

Nonetheless, the movie is a sincere and fictional account of Christ's life, Ebert writes, made by a director and screenwriter with strong track records for films that explore the intersections of faith, guilt, and sin. Attention is paid to the movie's final dream sequence, where Christ is tempted by Satan to imagine a life where he marries, starts a family, and avoids going to the cross—a temptation that, Ebert notes, evokes its biblical precedent when Jesus is tempted and resists. But such measured reasoning is a letdown. By devoting most of his arguments to people who he admits are unlikely to see the movie and just as unlikely to read his review, it is a noble service in a lost cause. To his credit, he says as much in his final paragraph:

> I see that this entire review has been preoccupied with replying to the attacks of the film's critics, with discussing the issues, rather than with reviewing *The Last Temptation of Christ* as a motion picture. Perhaps that is an interesting proof of the film's worth. Here is a film that engaged me on the subject of Christ's dual nature, that caused me to think about the mystery of a being who could be both God and man. I cannot think of another film on a religious subject that has challenged me more fully. The film has offended those whose ideas about God and man it does not reflect. But then, so did Jesus.

A stinging analogy, but the acknowledgment fails to compensate for more astute criticism. Astonishingly, Ebert's follow-up essay sheds no more light on the film. In it, he argues that the values and presuppositions of an average horror movie are more offensive than anything in Scorsese's film. He contends that would-be censors are guilty of pride—pride in coveting their own image of Christ, pride in attempting to rob others the opportunity to think for themselves. This is all fine, but directing more arguments against those who favor censorship is like shooting fish in a barrel. After two essays and more than 2000 words, it is still possible to understand more about the plot of a standard horror film than Kazantzakas' creation. In the end, what are we left with? Enthusiasm that is not adequately illumined, and a fitfully persuasive refutation of critics who will not see the film. Increasingly, the reader must take it on faith that Scorsese's movie is worthwhile, and surely that's not what the director or Ebert had in mind.

Twenty years later, Ebert—acknowledging that his earlier reviews of *Last Temptation* were off-key—reconsidered the film in *Scorsese by Ebert*, a tribute to the director. Admitting the movie is "technically blasphemous," he mentions this "only to suggest that a film can be blasphemous, or anything else that the director desires, and we should only hope that it be as good as the filmmaker can make it, and convincing in its interior purpose." That's awkwardly put and not much of a rallying cry, but a definite reminder of Ebert's Law: A film is not about what it's about. It's about how it is what it's about. "In the title role, Willem Dafoe creates a man who is the embodiment of dutiful masochism. Whether he is right or wrong about his divinity, he is prepared to pay the price," Ebert writes, "and that kind of faith is more courageous than certainty would be." So Dafoe's uncertain, dutiful masochism is more courageous than ... *what*? Certain, undutiful masochism? Ebert never operates from strength when he reasons from false dilemmas.

More analysis of the acting itself would have helped this review. "Scorsese makes no attempt to suggest Christ's charisma," Ebert observes, "assuming it as a given." Yet, with Willem Dafoe in the role, this is precisely what cannot be assumed. Finally, Ebert states that the film "is as much about Scorsese as about Christ." "What makes [it] one of his great films is not that it is true about Jesus," he argues, "but that it is true about Scorsese." To me, this is a peculiar conclusion that suggests why Ebert isn't always Scorsese's most discerning critic. To read a director's life into a film—and treat that *as an intrinsically positive* critical value—is the type of auteurist nonsense that Pauline Kael rightfully rejected. Besides, Scorsese's quest for redemption is more richly expressed when it is implied, as in the struggles of Jake LaMotta in *Raging Bull* or even "Fast Eddie" Felson in *The Color of Money*. While transferring his spiritual doubts onto Christ, Scorsese refashions himself as a rehabilitated, can-do Judas. "Christ is the film,"

Ebert posits, "and Judas is the director." In the end, however, these metaphors suggest hubris, not greatness. Ebert shares Scorsese's Catholic background and obsessions, and, in a positive manner, his reconsideration shows that he, too, is self-critical. Recognizing the earlier effort was insufficient, two decades later, he's still willing to make amends. More importantly, however, the fact that he's never written a decent review of the film suggests the intensity of his identification with Scorsese. In the case of *Last Temptation*, both would benefit from the advice of Flannery O'Connor, another Catholic raised in the pre-Vatican II era. "Pay less attention to yourself than to what is outside you and if you must write about yourself," she urged, "get a good distance away and judge yourself with a stranger's eyes and a stranger's severity." And what's missing, finally, in Ebert's reviews of *Last Temptation* is just that: a stranger's—or even a friend's—severity.

Perhaps because the controversy was less polarizing or the focus of the film more concentrated, Ebert fares better in his analysis of Gibson's movie. As usual, he shoots straight. "This is the most violent film I have ever seen," he writes, situating the film within his religious experiences:

> Anyone raised as a Catholic will be familiar with the stops along the way; the screenplay is inspired not so much by the Gospels as by the fourteen Stations of the Cross. As an altar boy, serving during the Stations on Friday nights in Lent, I was encouraged to meditate on Christ's suffering, and I remember the chants as the priest led the way from one station to another:
> *At the Cross, her station keeping ...*
> *Stood the mournful Mother weeping ...*
> *Close to Jesus to the last.*
>
> For us altar boys, this was not necessarily a deep spiritual experience. Christ suffered, Christ died, Christ rose again, we were redeemed, and let's hope we can get home in time to watch the Illinois basketball game on TV. What Gibson has provided for me, for the first time in my life, is a visceral idea of what the Passion consisted of. That his film is superficial in terms of the surrounding message—that we get only a few passing references to the teachings of Jesus—is, I suppose, not the point. This is not a sermon or a homily, but a visualization of the central event in the Christian religion. Take it or leave it.

Ebert locates the film's content within the mundane, and, in doing so, humanizes himself and Gibson's shimmering, grisly images. I can certainly relate to drifting through the motions of a religious service as a teenager. For Ebert, Gibson's film brings a long-awaited visual gravity and spiritual urgency to the Stations. By zeroing in on Gibson's decision to portray only a fraction of Matthew's gospel, the film succeeds on its own terms. He reveres the movie, but that last sentence reminds the reader that all bets are off. This is a bruising work of art; all have been warned.

Ebert compares the movie favorably against the neutered religious epics of his youth. Some memories die hard, and he even takes a swipe at someone who complained to him that the characters in *Last Temptation* were unkempt. But the point is not worth the ink. More effective is his reasoned defense of the movie against concerns of anti-semitism. He emphasizes that the film's Jewish and Gentile characters possess an array of motives for their noble and ignoble choices, "each one representing himself, none representing his religion." Of the Jewish authorities in the movie who favor Christ's death, Ebert draws contemporary parallels among religious types who protect the status quo, like Catholic priests who ignore abuse, Protestant ministers who crave political power, and Muslim clerics who are silent on terrorism. Creatively taking hold of the film's many parts, he improves upon his earlier considerations of Scorsese's movie. "Is the film 'good' or 'great'?" he finally asks:

Figure 22 Mel Gibson's *The Passion of the Christ* is a shimmering, grisly work of art. His closing pietà makes direct contact with the viewer and features Mary Magdalen (Monica Bellucci), John (Christo Jivkov), Mary (Maia Morgenstern), Jesus (James Caviezel), and an actor playing a Roman soldier. *Icon Productions*

I imagine each person's reaction (visceral, theological, artistic) will differ. I was moved by the depth of feeling, by the skill of the actors and technicians, by their desire to see this project through, no matter what. To discuss individual performances, such as James Caviezel's heroic depiction of the ordeal, is almost beside the point. This isn't a movie about performances, although it has powerful ones; or about technique, although it is awesome; or about cinematography (although Caleb Deschanel paints with an artist's eye); or music (although John Debney supports the content without distracting from it). It is a film about an idea. An idea that it is necessary to fully comprehend the Passion if Christianity is to make any sense...

Critically speaking, this is having one's cake and eating it too. Recognizing the commitment and contributions of many is welcome. Concomitantly, all are subordinate to the grander goal of communicating the idea. He crafts a striking wrap-up, and the technique of understatedly praising the parts while never losing sight of the whole is spot-on. Over and against his lengthy reviews of *Last Temptation*, his *Passion* criticism is richer and more substantial. It is more intimate, more persuasive in its defense and understanding of the director's achievement, more illuminating of the whole, and, finally, more patient in its invitation to those who may disagree. The working title for Scorsese's film was originally *The Passion*, and, in relation to Ebert's engagement with both movies, this is appropriate. Ebert's criticism demonstrates his own passion for art that conveys deeply felt religious beliefs with unflinching realism and the single-minded devotion of true believers.

Another sign of Ebert's reverence for movies that provoke religious discussion is his enthusiasm for Michael Tolkin's *The Rapture*. Structurally, this is an odd, unnerving film—at first glance pornographic, then a born-again conversion narrative, eventually a toe-to-toe standoff with the Almighty. Sharon (Mimi Rogers) is a telephone operator by day, trapped in a sterile cubicle, repeating the same impersonal questions: "Operator 134. What city please? Is that a business or residence? Please hold for the number." By night, she cruises bars with a fellow swinger, seeking partners for group sex. Such extremes point to spiritual poverty, and, after a series of bizarre religious conversations with co-workers and door-to-door proselytizers, she experiences a born-again conversion. Flashforward six years. Sharon is convinced that Christ's second coming is imminent, drags her daughter to the desert to await his return, and when he fails to materialize, shoots the girl. In the final frames, the second coming indeed arrives, but a newly disillusioned Sharon despises God for allowing her to kill her daughter. Like Huck Finn, if that's how it is, she'll take hell instead.

Not a typical Hollywood ending, which is precisely what Ebert appreciates. In his review, he argues that he would feel cheated if the movie did not offer a vision, however simple and unsparing, of the final judgment. He praises Tolkin for holding fast to the integrity of his vision, for pushing the film and its protagonist to the edge. In a follow-up essay, he expands more on the film's theological implications. "Movies are often so timid," he argues. "They try so little and are content with small achievements. *The Rapture* is an imperfect and sometimes enraging film, but it challenges us with the biggest idea it can think of, the notion that our individual human lives do have actual meaning on the plane of the infinite."

There is no question it takes guts to end a film with the final judgment, but Tolkin's movie does not hold up under Ebert's approbation. Ebert defends *The Rapture*'s low production values, but its tattered vision of the apocalypse is the least of its troubles. A quick application of Ebert's Law reveals the movie for what it is. At the time of the movie's release, Tolkin argued that he wrote the script after watching hours of late-night religious television, and the film's scant insights into religious dedication suggest as much. *The Rapture*'s images of faith are a meretricious brew of religious cliché: part protestant evangelicalism, a touch of Mormonism, a heavy dose of Christian cults. In terms of Tolkin, this is not stupidity; it is arrogance born of ignorance. Regarding Ebert's Law, *The Rapture* depicts a painfully unintelligent woman's religious experiences and concludes with her defiance of an unyielding deity. And how about the "how"? Stylistically, the film is poorly researched and emotionally arid. It skirts the power of its subject by forcing its own stilted confrontation between creator and created. Or should I say "strawgod and strawwoman"? I am not so much appalled by Sharon's final choices as by a cynical script that requires all parties to perform in lockstep, not according to the logic of characterization, nor even according to a rudimentary grasp of Christian theology, but to the whims of a writer wielding a very dull axe. "The best work," Tolkin claims, "comes from an artist's limits to understand his material and ideas." I'm sure this aphorism helps him to sleep well, but the consequence is a film as benighted as *The Rapture*. Despite all this, I understand why Ebert sees the movie as original and alive, and his review helps me to appreciate, if not the film, then his own way of finding its courage. Ebert's review is a valuable offshoot of Tolkin's meager efforts, clearly tapping into his affection for intense religious debate and movies that go for broke.

Ebert observed that *The Rapture* is likely to offend fundamentalists and secularists alike, but, for him, this is laudable. Implicit in his criticism is a sense of fairness and respect for readers and audiences, religious or irreligious. His enthusiasm for *The Rapture* demonstrates this: If a movie is going to provoke, it should provoke in a manner that attempts a fair hearing for—or a fair skewering of—all. Ebert's writing is similarly judicious. As a point of contrast, consider John Simon's critique of *Marjoe*, the documentary of Marjoe Gortner, the child evangelist turned adult charlatan who exited the religious racket to pursue a career in, appropriately, show business. The film is ethically uncritical of Gortner's antics, and Simon defends the movie's implied cultural elitism: "One of the very few compensations for enlightenment (feeble though it be) in this essentially enlightenment-hating land is the privilege of sneering at the culturally inferior. It would be cruel to deny the poor sinner the pleasure of giggling at the poor redeemed, which is *his* form of hope. Give the great unwashed the blood of the Lamb to wash in; give those unwashed in it the right to their smug but pleasurable laughter" (italics his). Holding the "great unwashed" at arm's length is characteristic, and, as such, Simon's depreciation of churchgoers in the movie, as well as people of faith in general, is predictable. His point of view is more stimulating as a counterpoint to Ebert's, if only because it's impossible to imagine Ebert adopting this tone. In his essay on *The Rapture*, Ebert argues that Sharon is guilty of "the sin of pride" by presuming to know God's apocalyptic timetable. He, too, is sensitive to the sin of pride—in art and life—and, as a rule, he avoids the fleeting comforts of conde-scension. Ebert may be too quick to praise a film, but his criticism rarely leaves the scent of high-handedness.

Ebert loves to quote Godard, who argued that the way to criticize a movie is to make another. Enter Bill Paxton's *Frailty*, a terrifying thriller with theological undercurrents. It too deals with a disturbed religious parent, a widower who feels called by God to kill unrepentant sinners in his small Texas community. He even enlists the help of his boys, ages six and eight, inflicting incalculable psychological trauma on all. *Frailty* lays out a horrifying yet coherent set of values for its sincere and murderous father, and, in doing so, casts an unsettling spell. Ebert praises the movie's audacity, expressed in its daring narrative structure:

> The construction of the story circles around the angel's "instructions" in several ways. The sons and father are trapped in a household seemingly ruled by fanaticism. There is, however, the intriguing fact that when Dad touches his victims, he has graphic visions of their sins—he can see vividly why they need to be killed. Are these visions accurate? We see them, too, but it's unclear whether through Dad's eyes or the movie's narrator—if that makes a difference. Whether they are objectively true is something I, at least, believe no man can know for sure about another. Not just by touching him, anyway. But the movie contains one shot, sure to be debated, that suggests God's hand really is directing Dad's murders.
>
> Perhaps only a first-time director, an actor who does not depend on directing for his next job, would have had the nerve to make this movie. It is uncompromised. It follows its logic right down into hell. We love movies that play and toy with the supernatural, but are we prepared for one that is an unblinking look at where the logic of the true believer can lead?

Frailty's "how" thus deepens its spiritual mystery and underlying horror. Its narrative stimulates the mind and soul, and, for Ebert, what could be more appropriate for a movie that takes a long, clear-eyed view at the logic of a religious fanatic? That the film's editing, at times, leaves motivations ambiguous is all the more vexing. "Is Dad deluded into thinking an angel has ordered him to kill demons in human form, or did God really send him that message?" Ebert asks. "The movie offers us a choice: Dad is deluded, or God has changed His methods, abandoned the notion of free will, and become a psychological abuser. Under tradi-tional Christian theology, I believe Dad should have refused the angel's instructions, because Thou Shalt Not Kill."

Ebert holds up the straight-edge of orthodoxy to measure the film—a compelling resolution and more fruit from a tree that was watered each morning in grade school. Whether Ebert's praise is uncurbed, as in *The Rapture*, or as incisive and demanding as the film, like *Frailty*, this is a hallmark of great criticism: generous extolment that distills and illumines the writer's perspective and ethos.

Alongside passion plays and apocalyptic visions, Ebert prizes the texture and feeling that spirituality and faith can bring to film. He appreciates how religious belief muddies, deepens, and inspires human action and motivation. He respects Robert Duvall's *The Apostle* for creating from scratch a Christian evangelist who is winning, complex, and all too human. He holds Nancy Savoca's *Household Saints* in high regard for its understanding of the ways religious devotion is transformed among generations, not to mention its unpretentious portrayal of pre-Vatican II family life. He enjoys the likeable *Saved!* because its chief satirical weapon against the evangelical subculture is not cruelty, but "the values of a more tolerant brand of Christianity." When it comes to satire, Ebert generally favors a gentle rebuke to an aggressive broadside. But the presence of religious identity is not enough. It needs to have impact. In Gary Marshall's romantic comedy *Raising Helen*, the heroine falls in love with a handsome, available minister. Ebert questions the probability of a sexy Lutheran bachelor in Queens and then asks for more complexity: "To obtain comedy, you don't give Helen problems and then supply a man who solves them; you supply a man who brings in additional problems." Ebert knows that introducing an attractive, devout minister ought to supply a host of tensions, but not in this film's polished universe. For religious identity to matter, it needs to raise the stakes and permit characters to take risks that have costs as well as benefits. Just as importantly, Ebert resents the absence of religious belief when common sense and history demand its presence. For instance, he takes to task Ron Howard's *Far and Away* for ignoring the religious differences that would inevitably hinder its Irish Catholic-Protestant romance. Ebert's desire to understand the function of religious belief in the lives of characters is just one aspect of a larger hunger for intelligence and verisimilitude in film art. Religion is a reality of life. For filmmakers to shrink from it out of ignorance of history or fear of alienating audiences is intellectual, spiritual, and artistic slumming. For Ebert, great art enables audiences to think more complexly about the world and its systems of belief.

His sensitivity to the weight and import of religious images also appears in subtle ways, such as the distinctions in his and Pauline Kael's responses to Robert Benton's *Places in the Heart*. This tale of a small-town single mother in Depression-era Texas, struggling to harvest cotton and save the farm, shoulders a variety of spiritual motifs. Kael begins on a note of skepticism, questioning Benton's "smooth meticulousness" and confessing "an aversion to movies in which people say grace at the dinner table (not to the practice but to how movies use it to establish the moral strength of the household)." Resisting the movie's homespun charm and laundered view of America's past, persuasively questioning a narrative convention that lacks imagination, Kael is instinctively skeptical. Her criticism is also meticulous; the parenthetical aside displays sensitivity while sustaining the air of irreverence. When she asserts that the film is "about America, and about Christian love, and about forgiveness of those who fail to live up to it," it's not a compliment. Ebert admires the film more, but questions its stylized closing scene, where all characters, black and white, dead and living, partake in holy communion at the local church. While acknowledging the scene's visual power, he argues the movie "can't support such an ending, because it hasn't led up to it with a narrative that was straight and well-aimed as an arrow. The story was on the farm and not in the town, and although the last scene tries to draw them together, you can't summarize things that have nothing in common." The final scene of any movie is a privileged moment, and Ebert recognizes the ending's spiritual import and rejects it on structural grounds. For him, the scene itself is not Pollyannaish—it simply isn't earned by the weightlessness of the film's subplots. Significantly, then, while Kael is suspicious from the beginning, Ebert is not. Still, his birds-eye assessment rejects the closing as a violation of the movie's internal logic. Even their references to the film's title are telling. While Ebert cites the director, who states that "places in the heart" are treasured memories of his Texas childhood, Kael notes in another trademark parentheses: "(God knows it's got heart, but it doesn't need that slopes-of-Parnassus title. What places? A ventricle? An atrium? It turns out that the places are where we lived as children—where our roots are. But those places may not be in our hearts.)" Rooted in the soil of Central Illinois, Ebert accepts the title for what it is. Kael's critical ethos is more vividly displayed. The "God knows" and disingenuous questions are risible and they underscore her impertinence. Her references to "we" and "our" are also characteristic. She's now one with the audience, who isn't buying what the movie's selling either. Here, Ebert's and Kael's distinctive sensibilities are rooted in autobiography. Ebert, through silence, plays the believing game. He's not intrinsically suspicious of religious expression or sentiment, but it needs to function appropriately within a film. Kael is the confirmed agnostic and the subtext is clear: She's not about to fall for the film's conservative values. In the end, her irrepressible, ebullient prose assumes a pact between reader and writer that throws light on Ebert's more understated, dispassionate approach.

Finally, there's James Marsh's *The King*, a difficult, mesmerizing film about an evangelical minister (William Hurt) whose son—the consequence of a long-forgotten rendevous—comes home to roost. The young man, Elvis (Gael García Bernal), slowly insinuates himself into Pastor David's life and systematically destroys the preacher's family and ministry. The film is hard to shake, and Ebert responds deeply to its authenticity: "We have so many preconceived notions about the types in this movie (hellfire preacher, sexpot daughter, dutiful son, black sheep) that it's surprising to see them behaving as individuals; they make decisions based on what they know and when they know it, and that's always too little and too late." Ebert's analysis provokes spiritual exploration:

What the movie leaves us with are theological questions. Are the sins of the father visited on the son? Are we justified in protecting ourselves when fate threatens us? Are some people just plain bad? Should you think twice before doing the right thing? Are you sure

Figure 23 Pastor David (William Hurt) welcomes his long-lost son Elvis (Gael García Bernal) to his congregation in James Marsh's *The King*, a haunting film that left Ebert with a host of theological questions. *ThinkFilm* and *ContentFilm*

you know what it is? Underneath all these is a fundamental question: Why does God allow bad things to happen to good people? I was startled the other day when the pope visited Auschwitz and asked God the same question. The party line, in the pope's church and in Pastor David's, is that the Lord works in mysterious ways, his wonders to behold. Some wonders we can do without.

As a boy, Ebert began the day grappling with theological questions, and, as a man, he still wrestles with the problem of evil. He is always getting his hands dirty, holding art up to life and letting neither off the hook. In this spirit, he himself challenges the archetype of the cynical and irreligious critic. For sure, his reference to the "party line" is simple—a preconceived notion of its own that merits investigation. And the last sentiment is understandable, if glib; its tone and depth would give Dietrich Bonhoeffer pause. Ebert's meditation on *The King* suggests that when art inspires him to contemplate Christian theology, he would do well to return to his memories of the Stations, to Mary weeping over Christ partaking in the fullest measure of human suffering. Still, after all these years, Ebert remains the intellectual pugilist and novice theologian, hands wrapped and still sparring.

Chapter 8
Turned On

It's not that I'm not human. I too had the Farrah Fawcett swimsuit poster on my wall, head tilted, teeth glistening—and, in a favorite phrase of Ebert's—her nipples at attention. There was a distinctly American quality to her blonde athleticism, and the fact that her breasts were covered made her not less but more alluring. When she finally posed nude for *Playboy* at forty-eight, I felt sad, as if an era had ended and we'd let her down. All to say that Ebert's sense of sexuality veers, at times, to the *Playboy* archetype: late rather than early Farrah. At fifteen, I remember watching Ebert and Siskel review John Landis' *Spies Like Us* (1985), a dreary pairing of Chevy Chase and Dan Ackroyd as would-be CIA spies enmeshed in Cold War politics. Ebert recommended it—or recommended, rather, the curves of Vanessa Angel, a model playing a half-clothed Russian spy. On television, he was bewitched, and I was bewildered by and embarrassed for his enthusiasm.

Many, I think, struggle to assimilate Ebert, the Pulitzer-winning critic, and Ebert, screenwriter of *Beyond the Valley of the Dolls*. His participation in the project is part of Hollywood lore. It begins with "King of the Nudies" Russ Meyer, a World War II veteran who photographed the earliest *Playboy* playmates before directing movies. His first film, *The Immoral Mr. Teas*, was the tale of a middle-aged man with the indecorous ability to see women without their clothing. *Teas* was profitable, and Meyer continued making movies in the 60s, including *Faster, Pussycat! Kill! Kill!* and *Vixen!*, which cost $72,000 and grossed $6 million. *Vixen!*'s success led to a front-page article on Meyer in the *Wall Street Journal*, which prompted Ebert to write a letter to the editor, praising Meyer's career. Meyer wrote to thank Ebert, had lunch with him in Chicago, and a friendship was born. That Ebert defended Meyer's talent in print is an early instance of Ebert's chutzpah, his willingness to take risks. So when Meyer was invited to direct his next project at Twentieth Century Fox, he asked Ebert to pen the screenplay. Ebert took a six-week leave from the *Chicago Sun-Times*, flew to California, cranked out the script, earned $15,000 ("Pretty good in 1969"), and, for a brief season, indulged in the lush life.

And that script was a humdinger. In short, *BVD*—the perfect acronym—is the story of the Carrie Nations, a three-girl band that lands in LA and is soon discovered by Ronnie "Z-Man" Barzell, a young record producer. Kelly, the lead singer, hopes to collect an inheritance from Aunt Susan, the head of a modeling agency. The trio is rounded out with Casey, the lesbian daughter of a senator, and Petronella, torn between her love for a straight-laced law student and a heavyweight prizefighter. Critic John Simon invested hundreds of words in his plot synopsis, proving that *BVD* is beyond précis. Let it be said that the women's involvement in the music industry leads them through a maze of drugs, romance, sexual escapades, and violence. And for the history books, in one of the film's many climaxes, Z-Man rips open his shirt, revealing two breasts. When gigolo Lance laughs at the gender-bending disclosure, Z-Man decapitates his would-be lover to the tune of Twentieth Century Fox's theme song. Beyond this, the film peaks with an orgy and bloodbath at Z-Man's estate, leading to a joint wedding ceremony for the lucky survivors.

The late 60s was a rare moment when a handful of independent filmmakers like Meyer gained access to the big studios that were frantically trying to figure out what audiences wanted. Many families were choosing television, and Twentieth Century, struggling to differentiate its product and appeal to youth, wasn't above releasing a Russ Meyer film. Ebert was an eyewitness, and his involvement stands as a critical, visible juncture in his quest for the sweet life. Ten years earlier, Janet Leigh had spent three weeks filming *Psycho*—and the next four-and-a-half decades talking about it. In a similar vein, Ebert is endlessly asked, "Why did you write *Beyond the Valley of the Dolls*?" It's tough to live down an arrested adolescence when the corpus delicti becomes a cult classic. Rather than putting the movie behind him, however, Ebert puts it in perspective—for him, it's the "best rock camp horror exploitation musical ever made."

Notorious for its X-rating in 1970, the film betrays the conservative Midwestern roots of its writer. The screenplay's kitchen-sink assortment of clichés reveals a screenwriter in love with movies, as well as shapely women. Ebert stresses that none of the film's cultural iconography—including characters and events inspired by Phil Specter, Cassius Clay, the Manson murders—was based on firsthand knowledge or research. *BVD* is a twenty-something Midwesterner's daydream of the swinging Hollywood night life, a vision of the drug culture from a writer raised in downstate Illinois. Ebert's raucous naïveté—combined with Meyer's kinetic pacing—makes the film a uniquely soft-core comic strip.

The movie was savaged by critics. Gene Siskel awarded it one star. John Simon was fascinated and mortified. There's "something for everyone—campy intellectual, long-faced moralizer, or swinging voyeur. Clever," he observed, "but not so clever as it is swinish." Rex Reed declared it one of the worst films of the year, second only to Twentieth-Century Fox's *Myra Breckinridge* (which he starred in). Only *Time*'s Richard Corliss argued that it was one of the ten best films of the decade. Although *BVD* made money for Twentieth Century, the studio downplayed its association with Meyer, and, after one more film with him, severed the relationship. Through the years, however, the movie has developed a dedicated following. It still "plays like gangbusters," Ebert says in its defense. "I feel vindicated today," he argues, pointing out the movie's prominence in retrospectives of Meyer's work at Yale, the Museum of Modern Art, and the Cinémathèque Française. Still, these votes of confidence are iffy. The last time I visited the Cinémathèque, a retrospective of Richard Fleischer's films was playing. Anyone for a double bill of *Mandingo* and *Amityville 3-D*? Or shall we head back to the café?

To *BVD*'s credit—and this applies to many of Meyer's films—the women have surprising agency; they take hold of their futures while men spin their wheels. At the same time, rapid-fire editing cannot hide the fact that these women landed the jobs not so much for the size of their talents as their bras. "I've never been that interested in what goes on below the waist," Meyer has said, acknowledging the limits of his imagination. By collaborating with him, Ebert shared his adolescent enthusiasm. "Since women's breasts are the most aesthetically pleasing part of the human anatomy," Ebert concludes, "it is only a blessing if your culture celebrates them," a manifestation of 1950s America, where women were occasions for sin and fell into one of two categories: *June Bride* or *Wicked Woman*. Meyer's and Ebert's fascination with bosoms was very much in step with the post-war, "bigger is better" mentality—the jutting tail fins, sleek musclecars, and bombshells—both blonde and hydrogen. Not to mention *Playboy*'s so-called philosophy, which sought to untether sexual expression from cultural and religious mores, while upholding the centerfold as a female ideal. Pauline Kael once observed that "in the pre-bunny period," smart, snappy actresses like Jean Arthur and Myrna Loy "made American women distinctive and marvelous" in the movies. But there's nothing distinctive or marvelous about the doe-eyed, cookie-cutter bunnies hopping about and on each other in *BVD*. The film can be praised for its eye-popping cinematography, playful montages, and willingness to satirize every known movie cliché. Yet, apart from the visual and satiric punch, by defining beauty and sexuality so narrowly, it diminishes the range of human experience and desire. So many D-cups, so little substance.

The film's quality aside, Ebert's memories reveal a man at peace with himself, and his friendship with Meyer underscores his personal and professional development. From a practical standpoint, he gained technical experience not only in screenwriting, but in witnessing the creation of a film from pre- to post-production. And the trip to LA provided other initiations. Meyer biographer Jimmy McDonough writes:

> Meyer reveled in revealing Ebert's sexual proclivities to the press, cheerfully recounting one night early into the writing of *Dolls* when there was a small get-together at his home including Uschi [Digard], Ebert, and some wanna-be starlet who had stripped before Meyer earlier that day at Fox in hopes of getting a part. "Roger got head right on the edge of the pool," boasted RM. "Flapping like a seal. A great scene!" (After which Meyer declared there would be no more exchanges of wondrous body fluids until *Dolls* was completed.)

> Ebert had some clarifications in regards to this tale. "I will leave it to Russ to tell his version of this story, since it is more action-packed than mine. The auditioning actress and the girl in the pool were two different women, nor did both events happen on the same day. Actually it's surprising Russ would tell this story the way he does, since he was adamant about not connecting the 'casting couch' with his sex life."

Here, Ebert—who never hesitated to publicly exaggerate Gene Siskel's foibles—shows he can get as good as he gives. Apocryphal or not, Meyer casts himself as a professional and sexual mentor—Ebert's bawdy, loving uncle. And Ebert's the novice—the corn-fed critic discovering pool-side delights. All accounts suggest they bonded over their passions for movies, food, and hour-glass figures. So be it, but their lifelong friendship—evinced here in Meyer's tattling and Ebert's forbearance—testifies to their mutual loyalties.

More beguiling is the critic and man Ebert became. Even if *BVD* weren't a distinguished prelude, he surprised his critics by writing forthrightly and at times insightfully about sex in the movies. Pauline Kael applied sexual metaphors to moviegoing, most memorably in her book titles: *I Lost It at the Movies*, *Kiss Kiss Bang Bang*, *Reeling*, *Taking It All In*, and so on. Of course, her titles carried multiple meanings, but the sexual thread weaved them together. She also used sex as a metaphor for artistry: In *Hardcore*, a film she disliked, director Paul Schrader "doesn't know how to turn a trick." Equating movies and sex isn't Ebert's game, but he was influenced by Kael's candor—and frankly, because he's a man, his sexual disclosures could be more direct. "*I Am Curious (Yellow)* is not merely not erotic," he declares, "it is antierotic. Two hours of this movie will drive sex out of your mind for weeks. See the picture and buy twin beds." He ends on an equally pragmatic note: "The one interesting aspect is that the hero succeeds in doing something no other man has ever been able to do. He makes love detumescently. The hell with the movie; let's have his secret." Ebert's wrap-up is revealing, on several fronts. He's practical—at the very least, an erotic film should be erotic. He has a welcome sense of humor about sex and movies. He apparently isn't multi-orgasmic, but he is, above all, honest. There's a lightness in his straightforwardness that smooths the edges of his confession—another contrast to Kael. She wanted movies to unloosen our shackles, but the repetition of sexual metaphors grew tiresome. It was a relief when she named her final collection *For Keeps*. What was next? *Going Down On the Movies*? Ebert is blunt, but he's not aiming to redefine the moviegoing experience. And because his confessions leave him vulnerable, he's all the more likeable.

For that matter, Ebert's point-blank responses to sexuality in movies can be a bracing, oddly touching tonic. A nascent feminist, he coined the term "Horny Teenager Movies," a genre that irritated him, where male adolescents looking to get laid have personalities that females are denied. Take *Spring Break* (1983), for example: Ebert's final word is served straight-up, no chaser: "What a letdown for horny movie critics." James Agee surely felt that from time to time, but he couldn't reveal it to readers of *The Nation* in the 40s. Ebert's reference to "critics" provides a bit of distance, but when I read that sentence at thirteen, it was like ice water to the face. I thought, he's one of us—just more honest. In his one-and-a-half star review of *Perfect* (1985), he acknowledges an old saw: "They say you never enjoy a movie about a subject you know something about." "I know something about journalism and nothing about health clubs," he concludes, "and I hated the movie's journalism scenes, but I thought Jamie Lee Curtis was really hot as the aerobics instructor." Here, he's a man's man, appreciating the curves of a leading lady. Unlike his response to *Spies Like Us*, though, he keeps his libido in check. Curtis is stunning, but *Perfect* lacks the spirit and snap of her pelvic thrusts.

So what else turns Ebert on? "Graphic detail is not erotic," he says. "What's erotic is character, situation and suggestion, along with attractive nudity." With this in mind, Taylor Hackford's *An Officer and a Gentleman* (1982) has it all. Richard Gere is a struggling naval cadet; Debra Winger, the daughter of an officer candidate who falls for him; and Louis Gossett, Jr., the drill sergeant who whips him into shape. "There's romance in this movie, all right, and some unusually erotic sex," he writes, "but what makes the film so special is that the sex, and everything else, is presented within the context of its characters finding out who they are, what they stand for—and what they will *not* stand for" (italics his). Dennis Quaid and Ellen Barkin generate serious chemistry in Jim McBride's *The Big Easy* (1987), a tale of police corruption in New Orleans. Their love scene is "all the more erotic because the two lovers do not perform like champions in the sexual Olympics," he argues, "but come to bed with all the insecurity of people who are almost afraid to believe it could, this time, be for real." There's nothing insecure about Kathleen Turner in Lawrence Kasdan's *Body Heat* (1981), a modern film noir with "a power that transcends its sources." For Ebert, the driving force is not the sex scenes, but the tension between Turner and William Hurt. From the moment that it's clear that Hurt will do anything for Turner—including killing her husband, "the movie stops being an exercise and starts working." And in a parenthetical aside that deserves a megaphone, he argues: "(I think the moment occurs in the scene where she leads Hurt by her hand in that manner a man is least inclined to argue with.)" Gross and unerotic is Paul Verhoeven's *Basic Instinct* (1992), with Michael Douglas and Sharon Stone slamming one another against walls and headboards. "This is not a movie where the outcome depends upon the personality or behavior of the characters," he writes. "It's just a wind-up machine to jerk us around."

In his review of *Wild Orchid* (1990), Ebert pushed further, addressing the relationship between the critic and the erotic film. "We engage in a conspiracy of silence about erotic movies. We discuss their plots, their characters, the truthfulness of their worlds. We never discuss whether or not they arouse us—whether we're turned on." And he doesn't stop there: "Critics are the worst offenders, occupying some Olympian peak above the field of battle, pretending that the film in question failed to engage their intelligence when what we really want to know is whether it engaged their libido." In response to *Wild Orchid*, the answer is "no," and Ebert's rationale is compelling. The film is a love triangle involving psychological and sexual betrayals in Rio de Janeiro. An international lawyer (Carré Otis) is used by a wealthy negotiator (Jacqueline Bisset) as romantic bait for a real-estate playboy (Mickey Rourke). Ebert discusses the implausible script and the absence of chemistry among the leads, concluding: "Apparently the lesson to be learned here is that sexuality itself is not enough, nor is nudity or passion. What is required is at least some notion that the personalities of the characters are really connecting. Unless they find each other sexy, why should we?"

Along with characterization and chemistry, Ebert also judges eroticism by weighing the relations between form and content—yet another application of Ebert's Law: A film is not only what it's about, it's about how it is what it's about. Consider the case of Stanley Donen, the director of glorious entertainment like *On the Town*, *Singin' in the Rain*, and *Funny Face*. In 1984, *Time*'s Richard Schickel lamented the existence of Donen's dark doppelgänger, who also directed *Blame It on Rio*, a tawdry fantasy of a middle-aged man having a fling with his best friend's troubled teenage daughter. "There are not two Stanley Donens," Donen countered. "There's only one, and I stand up for *Blame It on Rio*. I think it's a good picture. I thought I told it like it is ... It is about how men are, some men, not all men. A beautiful girl wants to screw. You have to be pretty powerful to turn her down." Likewise, there are not two Roger Eberts, and all of his sensibilities, for better or worse, are at play in his review of Donen's film. He isn't necessarily against a story that explores an older man chasing a younger woman amid topless beaches. "But in *10*," he posits, "Bo Derek was old enough to take care of herself, God knows, and her affair with Dudley Moore was handled with at least some wit and sophistication." *Blame It on Rio* "has the mind of a 1940s bongo comedy and the heart of a porno," and, for Ebert, hearts and minds are won through unity of form and content.

But what if a film had the heart *and* mind of a porno? The same standards for eroticism apply. Although "not a member of the raincoat brigade," Ebert reviewed a handful of infamous X-rated films of the 70s. For the record, he preferred soft-core. "Carefully deployed clothing can, indeed, be more erotic than plain nudity," he argues, favoring the airbrushed *Emmanuelle*, possibly "the first movie influenced by magazine centerfolds." All the same, explicit detail bores him, and he dismissed the heavy breathing and sexual gymnastics in *Deep Throat* and *Debbie Does Dallas*. An exception, though, was *The Devil in Miss Jones*, which "actually seems to be about its leading character—instead of merely using her as the object of sexual variations." In fact, his defense of *The Devil* may have been written as much for his mother as his readers. "None of this will make sense, I suppose, to the majority of movie-goers who have never been to a hardcore film, and never intend to," he concedes. "But for those of us who do attend occasionally (even if only out of professional duty, ahem), the most depressing thing about them is their cheerlessness, their grim preoccupation with the mechanics of a situation, and their total exploitation of actors." It's telling, too, that "cheerlessness" is one of his chief complaints against hard-core.

In the end, Ebert wants films to be consistent, and the range of his reactions to three of Ken Russell's sexually charged movies further demonstrates as much. In *The Devils* (1971), the director "has really done it this time":

He has stripped the lid of respectability off the Ursuline convent in Loudon, France. He has exposed Cardinal Richelieu as a political schemer. He has destroyed our illusions about Louis XIII. We are filled with righteous indignation as we bear witness to the violation of the helpless nuns; it is all the more terrible because, as Russell fearlessly reveals, all the nuns, without exception, were young and stacked.

The Devils is an exploitive hothouse of a movie—deserving of Ebert's sardonic turn. Russell's tone is as hysterical as those lonely nuns, deflating the film's social and religious criticism. Ebert cuts through Russell's hypocrisy, smoking out a sham historian.

Ebert is more forgiving of Russell's *Crimes of Passion* (1984), where he acknowledges the inherent difficulties in making an erotic film. "Sex is an activity of great and serious importance to its participants, but as a spectator sport," he argues, "it has a strange way of turning into comedy." *Crimes* is the story of Joanna (Kathleen Turner), a fashion designer who moonlights as China Blue, an exotic hooker. Enlivening her evenings are Grady (John Laughlin), a client trapped in a loveless marriage, and the Reverend Shayne (Anthony Perkins), a crazed street preacher. Because Russell is more captivated by Joanna's lurid nightlife than Grady's family troubles, the film's two halves—violent erotic thriller and domestic drama—don't cohere. Ebert blames several culprits for the failure: Russell, who should have found a way to balance the uneven material; a ratings board that demanded several sex scenes be excised; New World Pictures, for permitting the cuts; and, finally, sex itself, "because there is nothing quite so ridiculous as someone else's sexual fantasies, and nothing as fascinating as our own."

Surprisingly, the corrective to Russell's *Crimes* is Russell's *Whore* (1991), a sober study of an LA prostitute (Theresa Russell) who, at times, narrates her story directly to the camera. The film's unpretentious approach fits the material, and Ebert's critique gains force through comparisons to *Crimes* and a recent box-office winner, *Pretty Woman*. *Whore*'s grittier texture throws into relief *Crimes*' bipolar structure. "*Whore* is not about a world where the heroine can do anything with her days," he observes, "except try to pull herself together after the night before." Upon release, the director accused the ratings board of being capricious for granting *Whore* an NC-17 rating, while previously giving *Pretty Woman*—a glossy, Cinderella romance between hooker and john—a more marketable R. "He may have a point, but then again," Ebert notes, "*Pretty Woman* was about a character who lived in an

R-rated world, and *Whore* is about a woman who lives in the real one."
Again, consistency is key. Note that Ebert recommended both films.
Pretty Woman's effectiveness rests squarely on its fairy-tale vision,
whereas *Whore* finds a compelling match between its documentary
approach and depiction of street-life indignities.

Even so, there's more to Ebert's take on sexuality than directness,
humor, and proportion. There's insight. Enter Bernardo Bertolucci's *Last
Tango in Paris*, a cinematic turning point that prompted a critical clash of
pens—and the first to star a major American actor in a role that was an
explicitly sexual jaw dropper. The film cemented Bertolucci's reputation
as a leading director, continued Marlon Brando's career revival, and
prompted Pauline Kael's most famous review, in which she likened
the film's October 14, 1972, debut to Stravinski's notorious *Rites of
Spring*—a review so ecstatic that United Artists reprinted it in a two-page
New York Times advertisement. Kael's praise was effusive; she argued
that Bertolucci and Brando—in using sexuality not as exploitation, but
as an extension of character—redefined film art. *Last Tango* depicts the
relationship between Paul (Brando), a forty-five-year-old American expat,
grieving over his French wife's suicide, and Jeanne (Maria Schneider), a
twenty-year-old Parisian, engaged to a young, inchoate filmmaker. They
run into each other while apartment hunting, immediately have sex, and
continue to meet in the flat—anonymously, on Paul's terms—for three
days of sadomasochistic couplings. Through their liaisons, Paul confronts
his grief and Jeanne discovers a danger that's absent in her life. Reacting
to this, Kael's review is intensely personal. "[Jeanne] lends herself to an
orgiastic madness, shares it, and then tries to shake it off—" she notes,
"as many another woman has, after a night or a twenty years' night."
More than describing Jeanne, Kael evokes her own experience of the
movie. Since it is Paul suffering the confusion of sex roles—in the film,
Paul penetrates and is penetrated by Jeanne—Kael is enthralled. "If
Brando knows this hell," she asks, "why should we pretend we don't?"
Here, she conflates Brando and Paul, identifying with the tragedy of the
seemingly passé notion of the sexually aggressive male and enraptured
female. "For adults, it's like seeing pieces of your life," she writes, "and
so, of course, you can't resolve your feelings about it—our feelings about
life are never resolved." Characteristically, the "we," "you," and "our"
stand in for "I" and "my," and Kael writes like a critic deeply ambivalent
about having been bruised and buggered.

To her, *Last Tango* was "the most powerfully erotic" and possibly "the most liberating" film ever made. It's no surprise, then, that Paul's rejection of social mores is appealing to her. Paul—who is introduced with hands pressed against ears, raging against a roaring train, crying out "Fucking God!" and ends by sticking his gum under the railing of a balcony—Paul exemplifies the subversive gesture that Kael treasured at the movies. "Bertolucci has a remarkably unbiased intelligence. Part of the convulsive effect of *Last Tango in Paris* is that we are drawn to Paul's view of society," she argues, "and yet we can't help seeing him as a self-dramatizing, self-pitying clown." Kael, however, isn't unbiased in her appreciation of Brando. The length she spends praising him tips her hand: Paul's/Brando's violent, vulnerable allure far outweighs the character's bufoonery.

While Kael accepts the film's tango as a "speeded-up history" of age-old sexual battles, critic John Simon finds only implausibility. He wants realism in the details. "The couple's Paris flat," he wryly observes, "would be guarded with machine guns against casual copulators off the street." And he demands realism in the big picture, too. "There are no real characters here," he argues, "only movable pegs on which to hang a makeshift plot and shiftless actors' motivations." He then posits a theory (one shared by Ingmar Bergman) that *Last Tango* is a closeted

Figure 24 A cinematic turning point that divided critics: In Bernardo Bertolucci's *Last Tango in Paris*, Paul (Marlon Brando) confronts his grief over his wife's death and Jeanne (Maria Schneider) discovers a danger that's missing in her life. *M-G-M*

gay fantasy, with Paul a latent homosexual and Jeanne adopting the young man's role. For Simon, it's hypocrisy, for the film postures "as the revelation of ultimate heterosexual truths." Furthermore, he argues the portrayal of the couple is misogynistic, and he attributes Kael's (and other female critics') enthusiasm to Brando worship. He "is still the supreme heartthrob of many professional and lay female filmgoers, and this movie," he argues, "into which he has admittedly poured autobiographical utterances and in which he lays his body and sexuality two-thirds bare, makes him more present, available, vulnerable than ever before." All in all, nobody cuts through Brando adulation as incisively as Simon; *Last Tango*'s lead, in every sense, has no clothes.

Ebert, on the other hand, declared the film "one of the great emotional experiences of our time." "For the movie is about need," he writes, "about the terrible hunger that its hero, Paul, feels for the touch of another human heart." His analysis is less audacious than Kael's or Simon's—that "touch of another human heart" sounds like a greeting card. Still, Ebert revealingly places the movie's sex within the context of relationship and desire. For instance, he grasps the "tragic imbalance between Paul's need and Jeanne's almost unthinking participation in it." Instead of seeing their differences as merely disturbing or misogynistic, the unevenness generates "tremendous dramatic tension; more, indeed, than if both characters were filled with passion." Consequently, the film isn't liberating for him in the same way that it is for Kael, as a release from convention and an omen of greater realism. Instead, its power is the portrayal of sexual aggression as "just a physical function of the soul's desperation." Paul "has no difficulty in achieving an erection," he observes, "but the gravest difficulty in achieving a life-affirming reason for one." And this encapsulates Ebert's appreciation of movie sexuality: Sex needs to express character and situation, and, through positive or negative example, it should be life-affirming.

For Kael, the film's open treatment of emotionally charged, physically violent sex is startling. Throw in Brando as the sexual aggressor, and it's "the most powerfully erotic film ever made." Powerful, yes—but, for Ebert, the film isn't enjoyably erotic because nobody's having a good time. Again, he stresses characterization: "the sex isn't the point; it's only the medium of exchange." Kael opens with this insight (*Last Tango*'s sex "expresses the characters' drives"), but it gets lost in the shuffle. Throughout her review, she acts as sociologist (the sex model of past generations is collapsing), apostle ("the movie breakthrough has finally come"), historian ("movies are a past we share"), telepathist ("Bertolucci wasn't surprised by what Brando did; he was ready to use what Brando brought to the role"), confessor ("If Brando knows this hell, why should we pretend we don't?"), psychologist (some will prefer to feel embarrassed for Brando, "so they won't have to recognize how deep down he goes and what he dredges up"), and bobbysoxer ("We are watching *Brando* throughout this movie"). Of course, if Kael didn't overreach—if she, too, didn't bring everything within her to bear on the film—the review wouldn't be remembered, either as personal criticism or historical record.

Comparatively, Ebert's prose mirrors the film's concentration on Paul's emotional crisis, and, in the end, he assays the film's larger vision. The movie's point, he writes, "is that there is a land in the human soul that's beyond the rational—beyond, even words to describe it":

> Faced with a passage across that land, men make various kinds of accommodations. Some ignore it; some try to avoid it through temporary distractions; some are lucky enough to have the inner resources for a successful journey. But of those who do not, some turn to the most highly charged resources of the body; lacking the mental strength to face crisis and death, they turn on the sexual mechanism, which can at least be depended upon to function, usually.

Ebert can be a psychologist, too. Paul's sexual proclivities are expressions of intellectual and spiritual decay—and that's why the film is more emotional than erotic. By framing Paul's sexuality as a plausible portrait of middle-aged, masculine crisis, Ebert holistically engages the film's themes. He acknowledges *Last Tango*'s infamy ("A lot has been said about the sex ..."), but where Kael sees bold eroticism and Simon sees bad behavior, Ebert sees lost souls.

Elsewhere, it must be noted, his consideration of the film's sexual politics is less persuasive. "It is said in some quarters that the sex in this movie is debasing to the girl," Ebert argues, "but I don't think it is. She's almost a bystander, a witness at the scene of the accident." I suspect anyone who's been raped, sodomized, or repeatedly called a "pig," might disagree. Regardless, the argument doesn't work—at times, Jeane's body *is* the crime scene, although she invites much of the abuse. Ebert even employs ad hominem: "Only an idiot would criticize this movie because the girl is so often naked but Paul never is. That's their relationship." True, but there are many ways to film a sadomasochistic union, and the movie's ambiguous stance toward Paul and Jean's liaisons is puzzling. In this respect, John Simon more effectively raises prickly, necessary questions about form and content. The movie "seems to be muttering something about the need to grow up and abandon childish notions of sexual paradises," he observes, "yet those are the only thing it droolingly revels in." By defending the movie's content, Ebert ignores its style.

Still, in contrast to Simon's disgust and Kael's rapture, Ebert's enthusiastic yet even tone is better fitted, and it stands up over time. Case in point: Attempting to rehabilitate Maria Schneider's vacuous performance, Kael compares her to "a bouquet of Renoir's screen heroines and his father's models," her voice to Leslie Caron's in *An American in Paris*, her face to Jane Fonda's in *Barbarella*. Conversely, Simon describes her as a "buxom guttersnipe, with the face of a perverted cow and the acting ability of a petulant ox." In both instances the associations backfire: Schneider belongs in neither Kael's pantheon nor Simon's barn. In one line, Ebert is more sensible: "Schneider doesn't seem to act her role so much as exude it." "On the basis of this movie, indeed," he argues, "it's impossible to really say whether she can act or not. That's not her fault; Bertolucci directs her that way. He wants a character who ultimately does not quite understand the situation she finds herself in." Here, he finds a tenable middle ground that reflects Schneider's uncertainty and skirts exaggeration.

Ironically, Kael's breathless praise increased the probability that, for some, the movie could only disappoint. Her critique is deeply felt, but it's first and foremost about her—how the film challenged *her* expectations of movie eroticism, how *she* identified with Brando's sexual confusion and insanity, how the movie drew on *her* knowledge of film history. Alternately, Simon's approach is both knottier and naughtier. Beginning his analysis by quoting Kael, he needlessly writes within her shadow. Despite this, he deftly punctures the film's pretensions. But though his arguments for a gay subtext are not without interest, he's too reactionary to pull it off. When he describes a stilted conversation between Paul and his deceased wife's lover as "just the sort of thing aging inverts would prattle about," he affirms his own unchecked stereotypes. My point is, with varied goals and temperaments, Kael and Simon stand *between* the film and their readers. Ebert admires *Last Tango*, but isn't overprotective or self-indulgent. He evenhandedly showcases the film and its meanings, all the while conveying his respect for sexuality that unveils characterization. In doing so, he provides a direct, lasting encounter with *Last Tango*.

He might also have said, "Let's meet back here in twenty-three years." In 1995, Ebert revisited *Last Tango* following its revival at Facets Multimedia in Chicago. In the essay, he reminds his readers of Kael's provocative review, and gently allows that the revolution never happened. "It was not the beginning of something new," he argues, "but the triumph of something old—the 'art film,' which was soon to be replaced by the complete victory of mass-marketed 'event' films." He connects the second viewing to a college memory:

> I once had a professor who knew just about everything there was to know about *Romeo and Juliet*, and told us he would trade it all for the opportunity to read the play for the first time. I felt the same way during the screening: I was so familiar with the film that I was making contact with the art instead of the emotion.

But, once more, the focus is on emotion—this time, its absence—and the impossibility of recapturing it. He still sees things anew. Schneider appears younger than ever—"her open-faced lack of experience contradicting her incongruously full breasts"—and he gracefully acknowledges that she's in over her head. "Both characters are enigmas, but Brando knows Paul," he writes, "while Schneider is only walking in Jeanne's shoes." When Paul finally lets down his guard and admits that he likes her, "the moment is wonderful because it releases the tension, it shows what was happening in that apartment, and we can feel the difference when it stops." Seeing the movie "is like revisiting the house where you used to live," he says, "and where you did wild things you don't do anymore." Ebert conveys just enough; *Last Tango* still haunts, but its flat is no longer home. In a third and final reflection, following Brando's death in 2004, Ebert demonstrates that, over time, he's grown protective of the film. He retracts his claim that Schneider merely walks in Jeanne's shoes; he now feels that she "meets [Brando] in the middle." In 1995 he argued that Brando "is in scenes as an actor, she is in scenes as a thing." "Wrong again," he writes in 2004. "They are both in scenes as actors, but I was seeing her as a thing, fascinated by the disconnect between her adolescent immaturity and voluptuous body. I objectified her, but Paul does not, and neither does the movie." Well, wrong again, at least on behalf of Paul and Bertolucci. As Ebert fends for the movie, Brando, and himself, his insights shrink. "[I]sn't it remarkable," he asks, "that no film since 1972 has been more sexually intimate, revealing, honest, and transgressive than *Last Tango*?"

Come again? Taking nothing away from *Last Tango*'s legacy, any movie by Catherine Breillat (*Perfect Love*, *Fat Girl*, *Romance*) humbles the film. No less because she insists on exploring sex from a woman's vantage point—precisely what's lacking in *Tango* and nearly all movies. In praise of Breillat, Kathleen Murphy argues: "Her vision is clearly not for those turned on by balloon boobs and dumbsticks on automatic; shagging as sexy as planes refueling in mid-air; man on top/full breast but no penile exposure/crescendo of moans and cut! sex scenarios— all the components of the cartoon school of filmmaking that infantilizes (and masculinizes) the American sexual imagination." Ebert goes back and forth with Breillat's films, but he much admired another deserving movie: Frederic Fonteyne's *An Affair of Love* (2000). It's startling to witness two adults having extended, intelligent conversations about the realities of sex, and I wouldn't trade ten minutes of it for all of *Last Tango*'s huffing and puffing.

A trip to France isn't necessary, either. As a corrective to *Last Tango*, I submit Lance Young's *Bliss* (1997), a curious, unsettling movie that explores the sexual struggles between newlyweds Joseph (Craig Sheffer) and Maria (Sheryl Lee). It begins with two creative cross-cuttings. "There's some things I've never told you about Maria," Joseph anxiously confesses to his best man, en route to his wedding. "She has some problems." Cut to Maria in her wedding gown, riding to the chapel with her distant parents, looking every bit as skittish. It's a playful glance at last-minute jitters, but the seeds are planted: They've only scratched the surface of their issues. Now, jumping forward six months, another cross-cutting: Joseph and Maria are in couple's therapy, sharing mutual frustrations. This is juxtaposed with pleasurable moments of them in bed, suggesting that at least one area of their union is going swimmingly. Then, back to the counseling session.

When their psychiatrist, Dr. Alfred Colson (Spaulding Gray), inquires about their sex life, Maria admits that she never achieves orgasm. Joseph is stunned. Underlining his pain are the snapshots of their sex, which isn't exactly Jane Fonda in *Klute*, feigning orgasm while keeping an eye on the time. We're as surprised as he, and the movie has set its tone: aiming to frankly explore sex, it keeps both characters and audience on their toes.

Things heat up when Joseph learns that Maria is seeing another therapist, Dr. Baltazar Vincenza (Terence Stamp), known for his unorthodox treatment of sexual and psychological pain. Outraged after realizing that Maria has slept with Vincenza, Joseph confronts him. Baltazar patiently defends his methods and their debate ends in a standoff. Meanwhile, Maria compulsively cleans their home, and when it's clear she isn't getting better, the men strike a deal: Baltazar steps away from her, agreeing to mentor Joseph in Eastern views of sexual arts. A tutelage commences, including instruction in yoga breathing and tantric sex—all aimed at bringing together mind and body, as Joseph works diligently to separate orgasm and ejaculation. According to Baltazar, "conscious sex that achieves bliss" can heal the unconscious, but while Joseph becomes a more patient lover, Maria remains a slave to her compulsions. Interestingly, she continues her psychotherapy, and the movie is novel in this respect, too. "The film avoids the temptation to pit the two therapists against one another... Truth is the objective," Ebert notes, "not proving who's right or wrong." Maria eventually has an emotional collapse, whether from a nervous breakdown (the psychoanalytic perspective) or a body memory (Dr. Baltazar's point of view), and soon recalls childhood sexual abuse. As she takes steps to deal with her past, her relationship with Joseph grows stronger.

The movie is risky but it hangs together with Lance Young's straightforward writing and directing, as well as the remarkable acting. "*Bliss* is a daring movie not because of the sexuality it contains," Ebert writes, "but because it is so intent about it." The movie's sexual conversations are unusually explicit, but the actors' resolve—their honesty and earnestness—provides an emotional ballast. Talented and underrated, Craig Sheffer is amazing. His Joseph undergoes the most change, and, while he's often wounded, his blithe willingness to think differently about life and sex is equally persuasive. And the movie puts him to the test. On a high from working with Baltazar, Joseph walks home one night, freely announcing to passersby, "I love myself.... I feel the love." This scene could be cringe-worthy, but Sheffer's winsomeness and the relaxed spring in his step recall Gene Kelly's unaffectedness on city streets. At the height of their discord, Maria banishes Joseph from their home; he checks into a thin-walled hotel and hears the inevitable couple having sex. Later, he runs into the guy. "Y'know, it's not good for you to have so many orgasms," he sensitively warns. "You need to learn to preserve your yang and prolong your sexual activity. Good for you, good for your wife." The student is now an amiable evangelist, and the fellow, nervously appreciative. Sheryl Lee is effective, too, as Maria. The couple's therapy sessions feel genuine, and Lee's mysterious allure—she looks like she's full of secrets—matches up with Maria's many moods and surprises. And Ebert justly declares Terence Stamp as "the key to the film's success." He plays Baltazar "with a great and solemn conviction, and very sparingly—there are no unnecessary notes." With his white mane, slippers, and Nino Cerruti threads, he's a sexy Yoda. And his measured, calm voice brings clarity and a hint of the sacred. Nothing can rattle him. After Joseph rebukes him for sleeping with Maria—in counterpoint to Brando's "Fucking God!"—Baltazar raises a finger and gently asks: "Cup of tea?" In Stamp's salad days, he was the randy demigod in Pasolini's *Teorema*, bringing chaos to a bourgeois Italian family. In winter, he's a patient guru, bringing sexual resourcefulness to a tense American marriage. It's hard to imagine a richer, more satisfying arc for this one-of-a-kind actor.

Other aspects of mise-en-scène shine, including Baltazar's apartment, a triumph of production design. With buffed hardwoods, Persian rugs, a roaring fireplace, walls lined with cobblestones and book shelves, fresh flowers exploding from crystal vases, enormous windows with light streaming through—it's a fantasy unto itself. No wonder Baltazar has an impromptu dance session with Maria one night; he's got the space for it. And what a contrast—this gorgeous, warm, inviting abode—compared to *Last Tango*'s infamous, barren apartment. Am I seriously choosing *Bliss* over *Tango*? It's "not an 'adult film'" Ebert argues, "but a film for and about adults: It's provocative, and it has a heart." It's got a mind, too, and the antidote to Brando's bleating and braying is Stamp's soothing and spooning. Indeed, the movie's final image of Baltazar dissolves into a bird's-eye view of

Figure 25 In *Bliss*, Dr. Baltazar (Terence Stamp) mentors Joseph (Craig Sheffer), a struggling husband, in the sexual arts. This risky movie hangs together with Lance Young's straightforward directing, and Stamp's and Sheffer's remarkable performances. *Triumph Films*

Joseph and Maria, resting naked in each other's arms. Then, fade to black: "For Pauline"—who, though otherwise unidentified, I'm sure is a very happy woman. In the final analysis, *Tango* is punishing; *Bliss* simply is.

Ebert is complicated. In a 1984 *Playboy* interview, Gene Siskel named Nastassja Kinski as the actress he would most like to see unclothed. "That's *extremely* bad behavior," Ebert barked, in a follow-up conversation with Lawrence Grobel. "There was a time when nobody would have understood a remark like that and it would have been grounds for a duel." Later in the Grobel interview, after Siskel turned the tables, Ebert could not deny that, when the lights go down, he's been known to yell, "The movie gets four stars: three stars for her being in it, four stars if she removes clothing." He then confessed that, like Jimmy Carter in an earlier *Playboy* interview, he has lust in his heart. Years later, Ebert was perplexed when Robert Zemeckis' *Beowulf* (2007), containing computerized nudity, escaped with a PG-13 rating. "If I were 13," he said, "Angelina Jolie would be plenty nude enough for me in this movie, animated or not." To be sure, Ebert, *is* 13 at times, like when he encourages Neve Campbell "to never wear any garment that comes within a foot of her neck," or when he's relieved to see a topless Halle Berry in *Swordfish* (2001) because he feared Hollywood "had forgotten about breasts." The same critic, though, who applauds that scene argues that the only flaw in *Monster's Ball* (2002) "is the way [director] Marc Forster allows his camera to linger on Berry's halfclothed beauty." "This story is not about sex appeal," Ebert posits, "and if the camera sees her that way, we are pretty sure that Hank [her lover] doesn't. What he sees, what she sees, is defined not by desire but by need." Here, he sensitively takes into account a character's body and soul. Make what you will of his enthusiasm for shapely women, which shows no signs of retiring; but don't forget, either, that "what's erotic is character, situation and suggestion." "You know, sex in movies is either hell or heaven," the woman says, in the French romance *An Affair of Love*, "but never between the two." "In life," she adds—and, I would include, in Ebert's criticism—"it's often between the two."

"All you need to make a movie," Jean-Luc Godard asserted, "is a girl and a gun." Working with half that equation, Ebert has fancied many actresses over the years, including Ingrid Bergman, Jane Fonda, Debra Winger, Rosanna Arquette, Kim Basinger, Angelina Jolie, Daphne Zuniga, Jennifer Lopez, and Neve Campbell.

But Lillian Gish? In his review of *The Whales of August* (1987), he celebrates its stars, Lillian Gish and Bette Davis—Gish, 91; Davis, 79—whose careers incarnated the history of American film. "Many of the

Figure 26 Lillian Gish is Sarah Webber, celebrating the memory of her husband on what would have been their 46th wedding anniversary in Lindsay Anderson's *The Whales of August. Alive Films* and *M-G-M*

crucial moments in the movie play mostly in closeup," Ebert observes, "and I could not help meditating on these famous faces as I watched them." He goes on:

> At her great age, Gish still sometimes looks girlish, capable of teasing and practical jokes, but the moment when she lets her hair down in front of the portrait of her dead husband is a revelation, because it contains a genuine erotic content, a sense of memory of her character's romance with this man. Davis contains surprises, too. In so many of the roles in the third act of her career, her face was a painted mask of makeup—not out of vanity, but because she was often cast as a painted madwoman or harpy. Here, devoid of much makeup, her features emerge with strength and a kind of peace that is no longer denying age. Both women, in other words, are beautiful.

John Simon once described Russ Meyer as "a brothelkeeper with delusions of intellectual grandeur," and it was writer G. K. Chesterton who observed, "Every man who knocks on the door of a brothel is searching for God." As a young man, Ebert went knocking—and, from Chesterton's vantage point, his quest for the sweet life was a search for transcendent intimacy—intimacy that couldn't be discovered in ephemeral jolts of pleasure, whether at the movies or by the pool. Ebert's collaboration with Meyer was a lively chapter in his biography, but his definition of eroticism and beauty has come to encompass more than hour-glass figures. The writer who jump-started his career chasing playmates is also the critic who found eroticism and beauty in Lillian Gish's and Bette Davis' unruffled resplendence.

Chapter 9
Misfires

After fifteen years, I still haven't recovered from teaching *Apocalypse Now* or reading Ebert's unbridled enthusiasm for it. "It's one of the central events of my life as a filmgoer," he writes. For him, it embodies all that's extraordinary at the movies: a grand theme, spellbinding images, innovative use of sound, performances that go for broke, an overwhelming sensory experience. I respect the special place Francis Ford Coppola's film has in Ebert's oeuvre, but his sustained fervor is unconvincing. Yes, it's got Robert Duvall's "I love the smell of napalm in the morning," as well as that striking shot of a camouflaged Martin Sheen emerging from the river, shrouded in smoke.

But the film makes me ill. I've seen it at least ten times. First, on videocassette in high school, and then in English 104: Intro to Film, as a freshman at the University of Illinois. In graduate school, I taught it several years at gunpoint, as part of the Intro to Film curriculum. In 2001, at a friend's insistence, I endured *Redux* in 70 mm. at the Cinerama in Seattle, and, again, when Ebert selected it for his 2010 festival. I am tired of hearing bright moviegoers give this film a moral, historical, and intellectual free pass. I have served my time. I am apocalypsed out.

At times—despite his intelligence, his critical acumen, his generosity of spirit—Ebert blows it. More specifically, he can refuse to let a movie work on its own terms. Beyond that, his criticism is hampered now and again by glibness, pragmatism, sentimentality, affection for content at the expense of style, and a boyish enthusiasm that posits easy solutions and misses what's really happening on the screen. My purpose here, then, is to haggle with him over movies—some beloved, some dismissed—where his assessment is less than persuasive, and to offer a counterpoint that considers a performance, a scene, or a film from a slightly different angle.

Ebert knows how to get a laugh, but his humor can skim over a film's modest appeal. Consider Paul Aaron's *Maxie* (1985), the story of a deceased Roaring 20s flapper and would-be movie star whose spirit temporarily takes residence in the body of Jan (Glenn Close), a staid San Franciscan and secretary of a Catholic bishop. Critics dismissed the movie and American audiences ignored it, opting instead for Glenn Close in *Jagged Edge*, a snappy whodunit that opened just a week later. Ebert was unimpressed, giving *Maxie* ½ a star—and this from a critic whose three-star reviews, at times, are the equivalent of a gentleman's C. Because the movie "does as little with its original inspiration as is humanly possible," he offered the screenwriter a laundry list of possible improvements:

> (1) Jan becoming Maxie during sex, to [husband] Nick's consternation; (2) The bishop turning out to be Maxie's old beau, before he went into the seminary; (3) Maxie in a San Francisco leather bar; (4) Nick preferring Maxie to boring old Jan; (5) Nick being possessed by Maxie's old boyfriend, who goes after her, only to find the boring Yuppie, Jan, in his arms; (6) Maxie enlisting her friends from the Other Side to possess everyone else at the office party, so that W.C. Fields is talking with Calvin Coolidge, etc.

These suggestions would be a shot in the arm, with the exceptions of (1) and (4), which more or less happen on screen. (Was Ebert distracted in preparing his list?) But the French adored *Maxie*, a simple, endearing, supernatural homage to screwball comedy. And Glenn Close gives it all she has, particularly when Maxie instills Jan with a newfound, mischievous verve. Ebert's right, of course. The script doesn't take risks—but Close does. As Maxie, demanding some hooch and belting out "Black Bird" at an office party, she finds a vividness that holds the movie together. She's lit beautifully, and the ethereal halo that envelops her earth mother in *The Natural* is again used to striking effect. Here, she's a carnal pixie, sprinkling fairy dust on decorous surroundings. If more people had noticed her performance, they wouldn't have been floored by her sensuality in *Fatal Attraction*. Her seductiveness was there all along, simmering, but not yet brought to a rolling boil. And as Nick, Jan's dazed husband, Mandy Patinkin gets his own laughs. He doesn't want to cheat on Jan, but he desires Maxie's spontaneity. "Wanna ravish me?" he sweetly asks, clad in his pj's and standing in their bedroom doorway, uncertain if he'll encounter Jan or Maxie. He's asking—and begging. Straitlaced but hungry for more, his expression here—that gentle smile and arched eyebrows—is alone worth at least another star. What's missing from Ebert's list is the film's earnest, oddball charm.

Regarding Robert M. Young's *Extremities*, where Farrah Fawcett plays a rape victim who turns the tables on her attacker, Ebert shows that when he's unimpressed with a performance, he can be glib. The plot is based on William Mastrosimone's play: Marjorie (Fawcett) is attacked by a would-be rapist (James Russo) and barely escapes. He makes off with her purse and identification, later turning up at her home to finish what he started. After he torments and attempts to rape her, she gains the upper hand by spraying bug repellent in his eyes and caging him in the fireplace. Convinced there still isn't enough evidence to convict him in court, she begins digging his grave in her backyard, and the film's second half involves her roommates (Diana Scarwid and Alfre Woodard) returning from work and trying to talk her out of it. "*Extremities* is a film in which a male psychopath tortures a female psychopath for an hour," Ebert writes, "and then they trade places. I know that isn't what the filmmakers believe the film is about, but I can only go by what's on the screen." This isn't a promising opening—it's a bit early for humor, but let's see how he analyzes the gap between the filmmakers' aim and movie. His first criticism is that "the only scenes with any dramatic force are the ones that exploit sex and violence." "Only" is too strong, but he pinpoints a serious weakness: the film lingers too long on Russo's sadistic treatment of Fawcett. Half the attention devoted to her humiliation would suffice, and this isn't a minor criticism—it means excising about fifteen minutes of ugliness.

But does it really belong "on the same shelf with trash like *I Spit on Your Grave*"? Actually, the film opposes exploitation. The opening itself, crosscutting between Fawcett and Russo, is a visual stunner. And it examines how a woman like Fawcett is targeted. As she leaves work, plays racquetball, and stops by an ice-cream parlor, he rides a motorcycle wearing a black helmet—a shiny insect cruising damp city streets for prey. On the soundtrack, Bonnie Raitt's gravelly voice belts out "Stand Up to the Night," setting an eerie tone. Fawcett and Russo cross paths outside a strip mall, but not before a point-of-view shot reveals his selection process. In the parking lot, he darts from woman to woman—one is with a man, another less physically attractive. Then Fawcett appears.

Ebert's second concern is the lack of characterization. "Fawcett is a woman who does not seem to have a job or a past; she shares a house with two other women, and plays racquetball, and fools around with her roommate's boyfriend," he observes. "Those are the only details we learn about her that do not directly apply to her violent experiences." True, the film concentrates on Fawcett's violent encounters, but the details are more apparent than he allows. The opening montage shows that she works at a natural history museum and is taking a few days off. In fact, as she leaves work and says goodbye to a security guard, she walks past a wooly mammoth and glides beneath the looming teeth of a mastodon—a potent image for primal battles that await. It's strange that Ebert asserts he can only go by what's on the screen, only to miss what's on screen. Yes, she plays racquetball, but even this sets up the violent turnaround: Fawcett's in good enough shape to take on her attacker. Ebert certainly has a point: the film is light on character development. But his analysis fails to acknowledge Fawcett's cultural evocativeness, which provides its own backstory, and fails to consider the film's position among other movies of its era that dealt with rape.

Fawcett skyrocketed to fame in 1976 during her yearlong stint as one of television's crime-fighting beauties in *Charlie's Angels*. She left the show, floundered in middling movies, and starred in "Extremities" off-Broadway. This led to her stalwart performance as a battered wife who exacts revenge against her husband in *The Burning Bed*—the most widely watched movie in television history—and Fawcett soon landed the film version of "Extremities." When she lets down that famous mane in the opening sequence, her iconic stardom flows with it: a woman who first appeared as a sex symbol, then fought mightily to offer more than a pearly smile and blonde curls. Ebert isn't a television watcher, and that's fine, but this subtext is critical for understanding the film's effectiveness.

Figure 27 Marjorie (Farrah Fawcett) enlists her roommate (Diana Scarwid) for help in Robert M. Young's *Extremities*. Ebert may have wanted more details about Marjorie's life, but many moviegoers already knew her. *Atlantic* and *M-G-M*

Then, too, *Extremities*—alongside *The Burning Bed* (1984)—is very much of a piece with other films of the period that dealt with women, sex, and violence. On the international scene, Marleen Gorris' *A Question of Silence* (1982) concerns three women who endure daily humiliation at the hands of men, and finally attack and kill a condescending male boutique owner. After a female psychiatrist is assigned their case, she refuses to argue for their insanity. This film, as well as Chantal Akerman's *Jeanne Dielman, 23 Quai du Commerce, 1080 Bruxelles* (1975)—which quietly depicts the title character peeling potatoes, washing dishes, raising a son, and occasionally working and defending herself as a prostitute—was also criticized for not providing enough background to explain the woman's behavior. Questioning male perspectives that establish social and courtroom justice, these films called for a redefinition of abuse. In the case of *Extremities*, Ebert may have wanted more details about Marjorie's life, but many moviegoers already knew her.

"Fawcett's performance is hard to follow," he writes. "She doesn't seem frightened enough when Russo first appears at her home, and after he begins to mistreat her she uses lots of sobs and sniffles instead of letting us see her character's mind at work." His disappointment hinges on Fawcett's reaction to Russo's reappearance, and if she isn't frightened enough, it's because she's approaching the confrontation with a degree of choice. She hasn't returned to work, she knows Russo has her address, she's considering buying a gun, she changes the locks but allows her roommates to leave for work—even letting one borrow her car. And she reads a book on prehistoric life with her back to an unlocked front door. At the very least, the film implies that Fawcett, following a week of sleepless nights, is testing her mettle and anticipating his return. And upon his reentry, if there isn't "any true electricity, any feeling that her character is truly consumed by violence," as Ebert posits, then why initially describe her as a female psychopath? To Ebert, she "seems more inspired by petulance than revenge," but what Fawcett portrays, I believe, is revenge tempered by a thirst for control. She was consumed by the first attack, reverses roles, and responds—at times, waspishly—to his caged threats. Yet, for Ebert, nothing will do. "By the film's last shot, a long close-up of Fawcett's face," he concludes, "we are so confused that we don't know what she's supposed to be thinking, or what she may have learned, or even, for that matter, if there's anyone at home." Of course it isn't clear what she's learned. She endured two attempted rapes, overpowered her predator and dug his grave, battled roommates over a course of action, and elicited a confession from her attacker at knifepoint. The final close-up of Fawcett's enigmatic smile rightly captures her cautious sense of relief and victory, as well as the film's stance on the unlikely possibility for justice. Criticizing Fawcett's close-up is like saying that Garbo isn't expressive enough in the final shot of *Queen Christina*.

Focusing on Fawcett, Ebert misses two forces that give the film a lift: Fawcett's roommates Alfre Woodard and Diana Scarwid, the former a social worker and the film's voice of reason; the latter a jittery beautician, easily panicked by Russo. Bustling about in the morning, Woodard dons a business suit and squeezes fresh orange juice; Scarwid juggles a cigarette, doughnut, licorice stick, Pop-Tart, and coffee; and Fawcett combs the yellow pages looking for a gun. These women have an easy chemistry: on their way out, Woodard blows Fawcett a kiss, and Scarwid pecks her cheek. At times like this, I wish Ebert had watched the film next to Pauline Kael. She never reviewed it, and I can't imagine her liking it, but she always appreciated the jolt of good character actors. She would have gotten a kick out of Woodard's sprightly authority and Scarwid's tawdry working-class heroine. When Woodard returns home and announces, "Look guys, cherry cheescake," only to spot a beast in her living room, her horrified expression is exactly what's needed. When Scarwid cries, "Jesus Christ, we can't just keep him here, like a pet!" the laughter isn't unintentional, as Ebert claims—it's a much-needed release from the film's stifling tone. These actresses are like open windows on a muggy afternoon, bringing an air of reality to a macabre stalemate.

"Fawcett is admirable; evoking the pathos of beauty that turns from a blessing into a target," writes *Newsweek*'s Jack Kroll. "Her own beauty is deepening into courage and talent." But *Halliwell's* calls the movie "anything but entertaining," and both have a point. *Extremities* is a raw, unyielding film, although Fawcett demonstrates here—and in other movies like *The Apostle* or *Dr. T. & the Women*—that, in the right role, her stardom had magical, incandescent qualities. Ebert's punchy sense of humor rides roughshod over this, as it does over many details, and his final remark—wondering "if there's anyone at home"—is too cute by half.

Ebert's Midwestern pragmatism, when applied narrowly or to the wrong material, can also disappoint. His frustration with Neil Jordan's *In Dreams* (1999), for instance, is understandable—and a letdown. Admittedly, this silky nightmare is challenging to interpret and describe. Claire (Annette Bening), a clairvoyant who illustrates children's books, begins experiencing frightening dreams of children in need. Soon enough, her own daughter disappears, and she is convinced a serial killer is both responsible and telepathically communicating with her. Ebert's major concerns are two-fold: The plot is overburdened and unrealistic. Again, the lists: he questions the heroine's ability to survive multiple falls and a monstrous traffic pileup, her escape from a psychiatric ward, her ever-present dog. "With that much plot," Ebert asks, "does this movie really need the drowned ghost town, the husband's affair with an Australian woman, the flashbacks to the dominatrix mom, and the garbage disposal that spews apple juice?"

As a matter of fact, yes. *In Dreams* operates within the logic of a nightmare, so it's unhelpful to hold it to the expectations of a more conventional thriller. And the movie actually needs the drowned ghost town, not only for a stunning opening sequence, but for its connection to the killer's past and its symbolic import for buried secrets. As for the husband's affair, it establishes marital mistrust, which explains Claire's latent jealousy of her daughter, whom the husband favors. Mentioning the Australian woman is a red herring—making the character sound arbitrary. She has to live *somewhere*, and, since the husband's a pilot, it's plausible he would take a lover abroad. And the flashbacks to the dominatrix mom? Well, a stiletto heel is more visually arresting than, say, a fist or a gun. Finally, the garbage disposal plugged with apple juice is another variation of an apple motif that saturates the film.

But I'm not as disappointed in Ebert's one-and-a-half-stars as his prosaic approach, where an easy laugh trumps the tougher task of addressing an unruly film. And it's his flippant tone that sets off Kathleen Murphy in *Film Comment*. For her, the movie is a free play of associations, a "cinematic hallucination, wilderness territory where imagining is unfettered by civilization's police (or genre conventions)." Her affection for the movie barely tops her anger at those who dismissed it. "Jordan's flawed, gorgeous film has been virtually buried by pans so literal-minded and snide," she claims, "they look like panic attacks." Although she doesn't name Ebert, she quotes him several times, and he's the most influential of those she takes to task. "Imperfect as it is," she adds, "*In Dreams* should make a movie-lover's eyes dance for sheer delight in visual poetry." Her defense fittingly reflects those glittering imperfections. The analogy to the panic attack, for example, is wide of the mark; in fact, it is Ebert's insouciance that irritates. Simply put— and richly contrasted with Murphy's passionate urgency—Ebert isn't worked up at all over the movie; there's no adrenaline racing through his pen.

In an ad hominem aside, Murphy again squares off with Ebert: "One of the most willfully stupid reviews of *In Dreams* began, '[It's] the silliest thriller in many a moon, and the only one in which the heroine is endangered by apples.' (Checked out Genesis recently?)" Okay, that *is* quite a few moons ago. If I may, Murphy is responding in kind to Ebert's glibness, which sets the tone for his review. At the same time, there aren't enough toeholds within the film to easily guide the viewer toward a generous or Genesis interpretation of all those apples. I realize that's precisely what Murphy admires—there are no easy interpretive destinations, yet her imaginative reading of the motif isn't as evident as she implies. To put it another way, as fodder for exegesis, *In Dreams* is a stubborn work of art. As eisegesis—by letting us into the nightmare from many vantage points—it's, well, a dream.

Figure 28 Claire (Annette Bening), a clairvoyant who illustrates children's books, enters her own silky nightmare in Neil Jordan's *In Dreams*, a film that "should make a movie-lover's eyes dance for sheer delight in visual poetry" (Kathleen Murphy). *DreamWorks*

Again, there is middle ground. Murphy assiduously captures the movie's opulent surfaces, and her rapturous respect for the film's collapsing of dreams and reality is contagious. Her words bring to life the extraordinary opening of a submerged city, the haunting sequence where winged children perform Snow White in the woods, the lovely work by Annette Bening (soon to be showered with awards for less daring movies), and the continuity between *In Dreams* and Jordan's other toothsome nightmares, like *The Company of Wolves*. Yet she writes protectively, and, at times, gilds the lily: "Scanning Jordan's slant-rhymes demands suspension of the contemporary taste for ironic distanciation in favor of a kind of tranced hyperawareness, open to the flow of interwoven word and image." Ebert's approach, conversely, is pedantic, and he ends with more questions. "Whole subplots could have been dumped; why even bother with the other woman in Australia?" Already asked. "Although the drowned village supplies some vivid images, wasn't it a huge expense just for some atmosphere?" Who cares? It's a critical setting and unforgettable image. Entire films would be lucky to have one as breathtaking. And this is what Murphy understands: the film's splendiferous cinematography is more than atmosphere—it's content as well as style. "And how many viewers," Ebert wonders, "will be able to follow the time-shifted parallels as Claire's escape from a hospital is intercut with the killer's?" Probably no fewer than those who try to make sense of a dream. Or a movie titled *In Dreams*. "Over the top? Out of control, as many pursed-lipped reviewers sneered?" Murphy asks, and answers: "You betcha!" A lot like *In Dreams*, Murphy's defense is just as gloriously over the top—she's positively drunk on Jordan's images. But we don't know her fellow critics are purse-lipped; we just know that Ebert's tone is less illuminating and inviting—and, in this instance, he makes it tough for a defendant to understate her case. Is his pragmatism a wet blanket and her intoxication a plush duvet? You betcha.

Over and against Ebert's glib pragmatism, he's generally a senti-mental guy—but even his sentimentality gets in the way of incisive criticism. Consider his review of James L. Brooks' *Terms of Endearment*, a film that deeply affected him. Aurora Greenway (Shirley MacLaine) is a cobra-like mother who withholds and demands love from daughter Emma (Debra Winger), a free-spirit as relaxed as Aurora is high-strung. Against her mother's wishes, Emma marries Flap (Jeff Daniels), an aspiring English professor. The movie charts the turbulent mother-daughter relationship over many years, as Emma raises three children in a chaotic home with a philandering husband. The women stay connected by telephone, and Aurora, a widow, slowly builds a romance with Garrett Breedlove (Jack Nicholson), a lecherous former astronaut and next-door neighbor. Still a young mother, Emma suddenly develops cancer.

Ebert's response is forthright and genuine: "This is a wonderful film." And he finds a metaphor for the movie's shifting tones in the stories that families share. "You'll mention someone who has passed away, and there'll be a moment of silence," he writes, "and then somebody will grin and be reminded of some goofy story." In fact, for Ebert, the film's finest accomplishment is its juggling of disparate tones. "This is a movie with bold emotional scenes and big laughs, and at the same time," he argues, "it's so firmly in control of its tone that we believe we are seeing real people." Pauline Kael and John Simon, however, were incredulous. "It's exactly the kind of bogus picture that will have people saying, 'I saw myself in those characters.' Of course they'll see themselves," Kael observes. The director "guides the actors with both eyes on the audience." Simon is even more colorful. For him, the film "rattles on through farce, comedy, drama, and tragedy as Brooks understands them, always with great concentration on the audience's anatomy: ribs to be tickled, sides to be split, eyes to be drenched, hearts to be broken—and carefully mended." "A more calculating and manipulative movie would be hard to imagine, and yet," he notes, "there is a kind of innocence, too. Brooks seems to be the sort of con-man who cons himself into believing he is creating true art."

Each of these reviews misfires—or, to put it differently, *Terms* is best understood by pooling their insights and letting the dross fall away. Ebert responds to the movie on an emotional level, as I think most did who flocked to see it during the 1983 holidays. He affirms the film at face value; its shifting tones are acceptable because "life's like that." Revealingly, he never mentions Brooks' background in sitcoms—an insight that's central to Kael and Simon's arguments that the movie is fueled by the rhythms of television comedy. Again, for Ebert, the movie is like family conversation, moving from laughter to pain. But a work of art is different than a conversation at a funeral or around a dinner table, and *Terms*' willingness to punch every button—from slapstick to melodrama to tragedy—is regrettable. Brooks could strike myriad tones in *The Mary Tyler Moore Show*, when, in one famous episode, Mary remains indignant as her newsroom colleagues delight in the ironic death of "Chuckles the Clown," a television entertainer attacked by an elephant. Yet, after burying her emotions for a few days, they surface when she nearly keels over in laughter at his eulogy. This emotional roller coaster is plausible in a sustained, thirty minute sitcom with seasoned comediennes; but stretched to feature-length over a lifespan of thirty years, the approach is manipulative. In this respect, Kael and Simon offer more astute criticisms of the movie's structure.

But Ebert is also off-key regarding some of the movie's performances, though not with Debra Winger. Everyone admires her, if "admires" isn't too soft a word. Ebert: "She outdoes herself. It's a great performance. And yet it's not a 'performance.' There are scenes that have such a casual gaity that acting seems to have nothing to do with them." Kael: "All this retro-forties virtue piled on the cartoon underpinnings of TV comedy shows might seem utterly nuts if it weren't for Debra Winger." The actress is "incredibly vivid," she adds, "and she has fresh details in her scenes." Even Simon acknowledges that moments are effective—"especially with actors as good as Debra Winger."

Yet that's the shared ground. *Terms* is "so firmly in control of its tone," Ebert argues, "that we believe we are seeing real people." Winger's Emma? Absolutely. But MacLaine's Aurora? No. It makes sense that Ebert has the least to say about MacLaine. She plays the role like an embattled vaudevillian, hell-bent to entertain. When Aurora explodes at the dinner table, waving her silverware and screaming, "Why should I be happy about being a grandmother?!" it's a showy star turn. I have no doubts Aurora is fretting about her age, but, if realism were intended, she could have humiliated herself in a hundred more subtle ways. In fact, it would be more poignant and entertaining had her insecurities leaked out rather than exploded. Kael and Simon are attuned to this. "Aurora's surely not meant to be believable?" Kael asks. "She's a TV-museum piece, like the characters in 'Mary Hartman, Mary Hartman' or 'Soap.'" "MacLaine plays a mostly ludicrous character mostly ludicrously, which may be right," Simon observes, "but I find her a bit too obvious and coarse at times." At times? In spirit, only a few feet separate MacLaine's Aurora and her later work as a veiled Debbie Reynolds in *Postcards from the Edge*. The actress and her characters are hungry for attention, demanding obeisance from co-stars and moviegoers. It's only Winger's sense of reality that centers the film, suggested as much by the failure of the movie's sequel, *The Evening Star*, that posed the question that few cared to ask: "What happens to Aurora on her own?"

Winger "doesn't reach for effects," Ebert argues, "and neither does the film, because it's all right there." But Winger's effortlessness, I think, actually throws into relief the film's—and Ebert's—eagerness to please. "There isn't a thing that I would change," he states. Really? Not even the underwritten roles of Patsy, Emma's life-long friend, or Aurora's gullible suitors? Not even Emma's shoehorned and unmotivated trip to New York City? Or MacLaine's overreaching? Then, too, the movie looks like television; the cinematography is forgettable. Between them, Kael and Simon cover this ground, while Ebert's perspective suggests a bias: The downside of sentimentalism. He's too quick to drop his popcorn and embrace a movie after he's fallen in love with its characters. Kael and Simon's strength is that they can extol performances and still hold a director accountable for a film's infractions. And one need not adopt their jaded tone to see this. In her closing remarks, Kael argues that *Terms* is "pious"—that it "uses cancer like a seal of approval." "At the

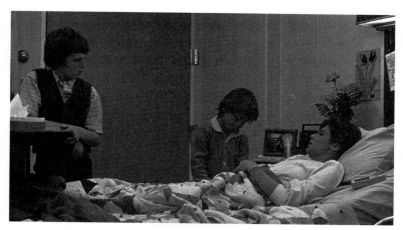

Figure 29 Debra Winger prepares her sons, played by Troy Bishop and Huckleberry Fox, for her death in James L. Brooks' *Terms of Endearment*. Even without words, their body language suggests everything, and this farewell is one of the most moving scenes in American film. *Paramount*

end, the picture says, 'You can go home now—you've laughed, you've cried.' What's infuriating about it," she concludes, "is its calculated humanity." Simon concurs. A deathbed scene between a young mother and her two sons "is bound to elicit conspicuous Kleenex consumption among the gullible." It's difficult to know how to respond to this. Cancer is a fact of life, and some mothers must say goodbye to their children too soon. I understand Kael's frustration—that the *function* of cancer, in bringing everyone together, is cynical. At the same time, the subject of death, particularly coming at the end of a film, shouldn't be off-limits. I think it comes down to how it's played, and Winger—and Troy Bishop and Huckleberry Fox, who play her sons—are more than equal to the task. Their farewell is one of the most moving scenes in American film. The boys have suffered from and resent their parents' feuding, and yes, on her deathbed, Emma does what she can to prevent Tommy (Bishop), her oldest, about ten, from feeling guilt in years to come for not having liked his mother of late. The younger, Teddy (Fox), about six, is more emotional and already sympathetic to Mom. Simon writes that here the movie enters "Erich Segal" territory, but the earthy way it's written is anything but. At scene's end, Teddy stands at the door, tears streaming down his face, and Emma says, "I was so scared, but I think it went really well, don't you?" He nods his head, fighting tears. She's framing the memory for them, however awkwardly, and while Kael and Simon may experience unwanted flashbacks to *Penny Serenade* and *Love Story*, there's never been a parting so lovingly anchored in a messier reality or a more genuine emotional pull.

Ebert's always agued that if a thriller is intended to excite, and a comedy to provide laughs, then why shouldn't a tearjerker elicit tears? "Don't trust any critic who writes about *My Dog Skip*," he warns, "without remembering his childhood dog." But the reverse also holds: Don't trust any critic of *My Dog Skip* who's primarily thinking of his childhood dog. In the end, Ebert's affection paired with Kael's and Simon's reservations yields the greatest insight. His frankness, his willingness to wear his heart on his sleeve—all of this is refreshing. But more telling, instructive criticism is thwarted by his boundless enthusiasm and sentimentality.

At times, Ebert is so drawn to the message even he fails to adhere to Ebert's Law. Such is the case with Rod Lurie's *The Contender*, a political drama that explores what Senator Laine Hanson (Joan Allen) endures after accepting President Jackson Evans' (Jeff Bridges) invitation to serve as second in command, following the untimely death of his Vice President. Laine is no stranger to politics: Her father was a Republican governor; the President is a Democrat, and she has been both—a former Republican who crossed party lines when moving from the House to the Senate. Her critics cite this as evidence that she's a turncoat, but, to Laine, the transition embodies her allegiance to her country over partisanship. The confirmation process promises to go smoothly until Senator Sheldon Runyon (Gary Oldman), a political rival of Evans and head of the Judiciary Committee that must approve the nominee, discovers a sordid sexual episode in her past. Photos surface and witnesses step forward, all suggesting that Laine participated in group sex as a college freshman during a sorority hazing ritual. Instead of refuting the rumors or expressing regret, Laine surprises her colleagues by simply refusing to engage the controversy. Since men are never questioned about their college sexual histories, she reasons, women should be held to the same standard. Eventually, it's also revealed that Laine began her affair with her husband while he was married to one of her close friends. These controversies derail the confirmation hearings, but the President sticks close, determined that a female Vice President will be his "swan song."

"Most American movies pretend there are no [political] parties," Ebert writes. "Even in political movies, characters rarely reveal their affiliations." Which is why Ebert loves *The Contender*. It "takes sides," he writes, "and is bold about it." "Its sentiments are liberal and Democratic," he observes, "its villains conservative and Republican." Yet what Ebert considers "frankly partisan" is actually shamedly, sheepishly partisan. Returning to Ebert's Law, the problem isn't so much the content as it is the *way* in which the film makes its case. "There is a remarkable scene between Hanson and Runyon, who have lunch together in a private club," he writes, "the Republican shoveling down his meal and talking with his mouth full as if he would like to chew on her too." Worse than Runyon's table manners, the movie reduces political beliefs to penne versus steak. Laine is an elegant, refined vegetarian—and, having served her country without regard for personal income—she's selfless. Against her, Runyon—with his receding hairline, bad perm, and oily skin—doesn't stand a chance. He's offended by group sex, is against abortion, and eats charred meat. The scene *is* remarkable—for its two-dimensional stereotypes of Republicans *and* Democrats.

And just how bold is *The Contender*, really? Ebert's accurate in describing its political prejudices; Runyon is Snidely Whiplash—but not once does the film call him a Republican. God forbid, that a movie with so many Democratic heroes, would actually call its pro-life, pro-God, anti-affirmative action rabble rouser a member of the GOP. This isn't verisimilitude; it's spinelessness—and the artistic equivalent of "don't ask, don't tell." Later, when a reader mentioned the movie's political imbalance, Ebert defended the film, pointing to its "positive Republican portrayals—the Allen character's father, played by Philip Baker Hall, and Democratic sleazeballs—the characters played by Christian Slater and William Peterson." This is amusing. Hall, the only character identified as Republican, is pissed off because his grandson has heard the name of Jesus in a private (!) school. Definitely your garden-variety Republican. Slater performs admirably as a fledgling Democrat who initially agrees to carry Runyon's water in order to serve on the committee. After upbraidings from the President and Laine ("You're young," she admonishes), he falls into line. In short, he's impressionable, but hardly a sleazeball. Ebert's right, though, about Petersen's Democrat, who's a charlatan. But, unlike Runyon, he still manages to earn a passive-aggressive pat on the back from the President: "You didn't mean harm."

Why is Ebert so out to lunch here? It's hard to say, but his reaction is a reminder of the value of Kael's perspective. Her political sensibilities, which, like Ebert's, were liberal and Democratic, never permitted her to swallow political claptrap. Of the Vietnam drama *Coming Home*, after observing that the suicidal, hawkish husband was not only wrong on the war, but lousy in bed, she asked, "When did liberals become such great lovers?" Regarding the black-and-white characterizations in *American Beauty*, she asked: "Can't educated liberals see that [the movie] sucks up to them at every plot turn?" For Ebert, *The Contender* is bold, but a bolder film would call a Republican a Republican—and it wouldn't score all of its points by knocking down a straw one. More self-righteous than anything, the movie certainly takes sides. Laine and her President hate everything about their opponents, excepting their self-satisfaction, flag-waving, and finger-pointing—which they adopt without irony. When Laine lectures the confirmation committee on why she's an atheist, stirring music buttresses her homily. "My church is this very chapel of democracy," she reproves. "I do not need God to tell me what are my moral absolutes. I need my heart and my brain and this church." On this count, Lurie is a true believer.

As a moralizer, however, and as a director, he's awfully cagey. Wherever Laine turns, she's exonerated. Being asked to account for the alleged orgy is a moral affront; who, after all, can say what is wrong or right? When asked to account for sleeping with a married man, she mutters, "Love is an involuntary reflex and I fell victim to it." If the movie approves of a value (men and women deserve equal treatment; nobody can say that college orgies are wrong, even when the women are drunk), Laine is applauded—it's the individual's choice. If the movie disapproves (don't sleep with your best friend's husband), Laine is chastened—but it was, after all, out of her control. Having sex with a married campaign manager was apparently involuntary. "They've caught you being a human being," President Evans assures her. "That's all."

But that's not all. After spending three-quarters of its length arguing that youthful sexual indiscretions are nobody's business, final revelations make it crystal clear that Laine never partook in the sexual escapade. So one is invited to feel moral superiority over the fuddy-duds who argue that group sex is deviant, as well as moral relief, knowing that Laine would never do that. I guess Lurie thought it too disturbing that thinking liberals would live by the values he force-feeds. But why, then, do we need the earlier flashbacks of a young naked blonde on all fours, in a three-way, with frat boys cheering? To assure us that it happened? Yet Laine, through her ambiguous responses, makes it clear that it may very well *have* occurred. In his review, Ebert describes the villain Runyon as a man with "unwholesome curiosity about other people's sex lives." Amazing, that a movie obsessed with hypocrisy embodies it.

Still, there are consolations. Jeff Bridges' folksy, but not too folksy, turn as President Evans is a delight. He exudes savvy authenticity, and the movie provides him with a playful motif: he likes to eat. Not only that, but the White House chefs are at his beck and call, so he orders whatever he wants, for whomever he wants, made to perfection. He understands that hearts and minds are as likely to be persuaded in the kitchen as the Oval Office. It's endearing, until the fifth time he discusses food, when—like everything else in this movie—Lurie hits one note, too often. The other grace note is Sam Elliott as Kermit Newman, Evans' "I've-seen-everything" advisor. With his chiseled features, matchless baritone, and thick brush of salt-and-pepper hair, he embodies moral authority, and his ability to cut through horseshit humbles the movie. "Listen, Laine, I don't care who you fucked, and how many times, in how many positions," he says, "as long as it doesn't threaten the

Figure 30 With his chiseled features and matchless baritone, Sam Elliott embodies moral authority as Kermit Newman, advisor to the President, in Rod Lurie's *The Contender*. DreamWorks

administration." By the time he gets around to this, late in the game, I was as exasperated as he. And I'd agree with the first two-thirds, with one revision: "as long as it doesn't threaten the intelligence of the movie."

And then there was the apocalypse. Ebert has written more about *Apocalypse Now* than any film in his career. (Four essays, total: the original 1979 review, a portion of *Two Weeks in the Midday Sun* covers the film's premiere at Cannes, a reflection in *The Great Movies*, and a 2001 review of the extended version *Apocalypse Now Redux*.) The story is on a mission. Captain Willard (Martin Sheen), a trained assassin for the US Army, is ordered to exterminate "with extreme prejudice" Colonel Kurtz (Marlon Brando), a decorated Special Forces officer and Green Beret. Once assigned the task of defending the Cambodians, Kurtz—now apparently worshipped by a tribe—has gone insane. Willard soon joins a Navy Patrol Boat and travels upstream to terminate Kurtz's command. Ebert's initial review celebrates the movie and obliquely defends director Francis Ford Coppola, who confessed at the 1979 Cannes Film Festival that he was still undecided how his film should end, inviting criticism and controversy. Coppola was accused of being indecisive, bombastic ("This isn't a film about Vietnam," Coppola declared. "This film is Vietnam"), and wasteful. (The movie cost $31 million and nearly drove the director to financial ruin.) But Ebert rightly argues that the film's merits are ultimately what's on the screen. Addressing critics who felt the use of Joseph Conrad's *Heart of Darkness* and the casting of Brando as Col. Kurtz were diversionary efforts to compensate for a weak script, Ebert writes:

> Such criticisms are made by people who indeed are plumbing *Apocalypse Now* for its ideas, and who are as misguided as the veteran Vietnam correspondents who breathlessly reported, some months ago, that *The Deer Hunter* was not "accurate." What idea or philosophy could we expect to find in *Apocalypse Now*—and what good would it really do, at this point after the Vietnam tragedy, if Brando's closing speeches did have the "answers"?

This line of reasoning isn't reassuring. Who needs content or historical accuracy, he seems to be saying, when the subject is as complex as America in Vietnam? And with a sleight of hand, an "idea"—by which,

I take him to mean a coherent value or message—is dismissed as an inarguable, and thus unrealistic, "answer." For Ebert, the film's message is clear: "war is hell." "We do not go to see Coppola's movie for that insight—something Coppola," he claims, "but not some of his critics, knows well." Coppola understands, he argues, that movies are better at presenting moods and feelings than abstract ideas. *"Apocalypse Now* achieves greatness not by analyzing our 'experience in Vietnam,'" he writes, "but by re-creating, in characters and images, something of that experience."

This is fine, if slippery. Regarding the use of Conrad's story, he feels "the narrative device of the journey upriver is as convenient for [Coppola] as it was for Conrad." "That's really why he uses it," he asserts, "not because of literary cross-references for graduate students to catalogue." Yet, if Coppola is simply looking for a narrative device to justify a chain of events, why invoke Conrad at all? Kael, for instance, argues that Conrad's novel made no sense for Coppola's purpose. "[W]e no longer think of blackness and going native in the same terms," she says. "We don't think of being in the jungle with no clothes on in the same way English readers of that period thought of it." This is not a superfluous observation; it's a fair criticism when a director and co-screenwriter inject the structure and memory of a seminal novel into a modern context. And Ebert unfairly caricatures his opponents— people who are concerned about the implications of Conrad's story. He is too quick to let Coppola off the hook, and too quick to send-up his critics as myopic graduate students.

There's also a question of history, and those who expect historical accuracy and analysis in a film that depicts history. Again, Ebert argues that engaging the Vietnam conflict by recreating "in characters and images, something of that experience" is an achievement. Movies are less than ideal forums for analysis of abstract ideas, he writes, but surely we don't have to choose between analysis and feelings. Think of Renoir's *The Grand Illusion*, Marcel Ophül's *The Sorrow and the Pity*, Costa-Gavras' *Z*, or Tim Robbins' *Dead Man Walking*. Each has a point of view and communicates it by analyzing a range of attitudes and perspectives. Certainly none falls short of conveying mood and emotion with grand, potent visuals. And the subject doesn't have to be war, occupation, or the death penalty. Movies like Jean Cocteau's *Beauty and the Beast*, Sydney Pollack's *Tootsie*, or Paul Thomas

Anderson's *Boogie Nights* analyze social and romantic relations at specific points in time—and they're no slouches as entertainment or visual poetry. So it's possible for any film to communicate powerfully through visuals and analysis, which is where *Apocalypse Now* falters—as well as Ebert's defense. "It doesn't look at the facts of war, of what we were doing there," Kael asserts. "Instead we are carriers of metaphysical evil, we are demons." What she's calling for—a sense of history and perspective—is different than the "answers" Ebert dismisses as unrealistic. Facts, analysis and a coherent point of view are not enemies of film style.

That said, a movie still has a right to pursue historical truths without analyzing detailed historical events. So what, then, can we make of Coppola's re-creation of America in Vietnam, born of emotion and mood, rather than analysis? Ebert cites two scenes that point to Coppola's accomplishment: One where Captain Kilgore (Robert Duvall) initiates a helicopter attack on a small village, and a later one where Captain Willard and his men kill a Vietnamese family in a fishing boat. Ebert first saw *Apocalypse Now*—and that striking helicopter raid—in the Palais at the Cannes Film Festival, and it's difficult to imagine a more extraordinary venue. He recalls himself and others actually ducking during the helicopter attack. To him, it's the greatest of all movie battle scenes—it's "simultaneously numbing, depressing, and exhilarating." "As the rockets jar from the helicopters and spring through the air, we're elated, like kids for a half-second," he reports, "until the reality of the sequence sinks in." It's a memorable scene, for sure, but what prevails, ultimately, is that sense of exhilaration. The silhouette of the helicopters lined for battle against a tangerine sky, the outrageous blasting of Wagner's "Ride of the Valkyries" that accompanies the attack, Duvall's flamboyant, cockeyed performance (which is largely played for laughs). Such pyrotechnics overshadow the tragedy of schoolchildren under attack and the Vietcong's retaliation. (Furthermore, any film where actors have to stand atop each other's shoulders to see who screams the loudest, simply to make an impression amidst the cacophony, is a failure on the director's behalf. Duvall is a showstopper here, but it's because he will not be outdone by his director.) The sequence's visual point of view is also anchored in the helicopters, muting the intensity of what happens below. In fact, the overpowering force of this scene throws the entire film off-kilter, leading Kael to ask, "How can you go further than the craziness that the Robert Duvall character plays?" You can't, which makes the middle portion drag, and all but sinks the film's endless third act. "The movie's feeling for bombs bursting," she argues, "is like what Mussolini's son-in-law talked about, about how he loves the bombs bursting over Ethiopia." And Ebert is onto something when he admits briefly responding to the helicopter attack like a child. The scene—the entire film, in fact—cues that response, and for much longer than a half-second. For Ebert, this sequence produces mixed emotions but Kael, I think, is more precise: "It sure doesn't make you hate war."

For Ebert, a scene that depicts the slaughter of Vietnamese civilians at the hands of American soldiers is equally effective. The men board a family's boat and insist they show their papers. A woman reaches for something and a soldier shoots her—only to reveal that she was trying to protect a puppy. Before the soldiers can send for help, Willard—determined that nothing will interrupt their mission to destroy Kurtz—shoots the woman again. To Ebert, the events transpire "with such sudden, fierce, senseless violence that it forces us to understand for the first time how such things could happen." This interpretation is reasonable, but it doesn't account for the scene's manipulative nature or the way it destroys suspense. First, the manipulation. The events are too stilted to promote an understanding of wartime atrocity. I share Kael's reservations when she sighs, "[Y]ou want to say, 'Oh Francis, the old puppy number.'" Second, since the murder confirms Sheen's psychosis, his eventual assassination of Kurtz is a matter of waiting for the other shoe to drop. "The film has no structure," Kael points out. "There's no possible confrontation between Sheen and Brando," she concludes. "Sheen is already a coldblooded killer who murders an injured girl, so what has he got to change into?"

This miscalculation regarding Captain Willard—this lack of trajectory, of character development—occurs much earlier, in fact, during the famous, overheated montage that introduces him. Willard is stranded in Saigon, drunk, naked, battling cabin fever in a hotel room, flailing around like a pathetic, wounded boar. He's at war with himself—literally smashing his mirror image, and the scene revels in his unhinged, masturbatory self-confrontation. He finally collapses into a puddle of blood and self-loathing—and this is where his characterization *begins*. Willard is introduced "in such a moral, physical, and spiritual funk that it's impossible to conceive how he could be further undone by a journey into a heart of darkness," Richard T. Jameson writes, "nor have we reason to impute to him any capacity for illumination." A mission to the heart of darkness requires discovery—and though Willard drifts inexorably up river and Sheen struggles valiantly with the role—Willard truly has nowhere to go.

If *Apocalypse Now* is uncritical of its boyish enthusiasm for exploding bombs, it's also retrograde. The only women who appear include a Vietcong who places a bomb in an American helicopter and is instantly gunned down, the peasant girl who protects her dog, and the *Playboy* bunnies who arrive to entertain the troops. Their CSO show provides a splashy set-piece: a bright floating stage, surrounded by water, oversized phallic missiles, and lascivious American troops. The playmates descend from a helicopter—one dressed as a cowgirl, another in stereotypical Native American garb—and briefly shimmy, strut, and fondle weapons for the catcalling soldiers. When the men grow restless and storm the stage, the women are forced to evacuate. It's true, of course, that soldiers can develop a mob mentality, that *Playboy* centerfolds entertain troops, that this entire sequence can be seen as critical of the men's behavior. This is war, some will argue; this is how men act. Depicting sexist attitudes isn't sexist. But why, then, does the film adopt the point of view of the soldiers? Why the back shots of the women's rear ends? It's one thing for a character to be a *Playboy* centerfold, another for a director to reduce her to that.

If there were any doubts about these sensibilities, the *Redux* version puts them to rest. Coppola's extended cut includes two more scenes with women: a visit to a ghostly French plantation and a scene where the men rediscover the bunnies, whose helicopter ran out of gas. At the plantation, there's a tense dinner debate between Willard and lingering French colonists. Afterward, Willard retires, and a French widow disrobes and joins him in bed. The follow-up with the centerfolds, however, is the real howler. When the soldiers cross paths with them, their manager pimps them out for two barrels of fuel. Another soldier encircles their stranded helicopter to watch. One shot is especially illustrative: As the Playmate of the Year (Colleen Camp) explains her loneliness—how she longs to be seen as more than a shapely body—Lance (Sam Bottoms) opens her blouse and ogles her breasts. In the shot's composition, Camp's head is sliced in half. The camera—placed at Lance's eye level—takes in everything from her lips to her chest. When Lance lays her down, the camera moves above her head, peering downward, again upstaging her face with her chest. The entire scene is played for laughs, and in the two times I've watched it with packed audiences, it gets them. The joke, however, isn't on Camp, who dutifully enacts her bunny routine, or on Bottoms, who is believably more interested in sex than war. The joke is on Coppola, whose point of view is as sophisticated and nuanced as a horny soldier's. Actually less so, since Lance attempts to console her after she stumbles on a corpse during foreplay.

And about the message. If Ebert sees it as "war is hell" and Kael reads it as "White man—he-devil," John Simon detects a cop-out. "Battles may seduce the desperate or crazed combatant," he posits, "but what is an allegedly antiwar filmmaker doing mucking around in this tainted ecstasy?" To this end, Ebert often quotes Truffaut, who argued that it's impossible to make an antiwar film because war is inherently thrilling. Here, Simon and Truffaut anticipate film scholar Frank Tomasulo's penetrating analysis of the film, where he claims that its conflicting attitudes toward war and America's presence in Vietnam allow it to be embraced by dove and hawk alike. But the film's "fence-sitting stance" doesn't help audiences understand much about Vietnam. "A text without a context is a pretext," he states, "a pretext for real historical analysis and a pre-text for wars and war movies to come."

For the centennial of cinema in 1996, Ebert composed "one hundred great moments from the movies." They included Fred Astaire and Ginger Rogers dancing; Gene Kelly singing in the rain, sporting his mile-wide grin; James Stewart, crying "Please God, let me live again" in *It's a Wonderful Life*; Robert Mitchum's reply—"Smoking"—after Kirk Douglas offers him a cigarette in *Out of the Past*; Burt Lancaster and Deborah Kerr rolling on the beach in *From Here to Eternity*; and Cary Grant and Eva Marie Saint hanging from Mount Rushmore in *North by Northwest*. Farrah Fawcett saying "Choose. Him or us. *Choose. Him* or *us*" to one of her roommates in *Extremities* was nowhere to be found, but Debra Winger saying goodbye to her children in *Terms of Endearment* and Robert Duvall's "I love the smell of napalm in the morning" in *Apocalypse Now* made the cut, as well they should. Yet, not only Duvall, but Coppola and finally Ebert himself are hooked on that smell of napalm. Simply put, there's a difference between a great scene and a great film, and Ebert can lose sight of that. At times, he imposes his expectations onto movies, and can be glib, pragmatic, and sentimental to a fault. He also privileges content over style, displays an uncritical, boyish enthusiasm, and settles for a laugh.

And come to think of it, my first viewing of *Apocalypse Now* wasn't on videocassette. It was the *ABC Movie of the Week* in a three-hour version that was genuinely exciting to stay up and watch. I was twelve.

Chapter 10

I Ain't a Pretty Boy No More

More than any critic, Roger Ebert champions the underdog. And his enthusiasm for the overlooked is another offshoot of his critical empathy. He loves a resurgence—Ingmar Bergman directing Ingrid Bergman in her final film, *Autumn Sonata*; Sidney Lumet following his Lifetime Achievement Oscar with the stunning *Before the Devil Knows You're Dead*. He also trumpets resurrections. After appearing in a string of second-rate films, Jon Voight portrayed an escaped convict in *Runaway Train*. His harrowing account of the limits of human freedom was, for Ebert, arguably the "best single scene" of his career—a perfect match between a character and an actor at the end of their ropes. Ebert prescribes comebacks, as well. "Mickey Rourke's role [in *Once Upon a Time in Mexico*] is to carry a little dog in his arms, look sinister, and seem capable of more colorful dialogue," he observes. "It's time for him to be rehabilitated in a lead." And he celebrates artists reasserting their stature or seizing higher rungs. "*Working Girl* is Mike Nichols returning to the top of his form," he points out, "and Melanie Griffith finding hers." Again, his strength is not in describing a performance, but conveying its import within the context of a career. About *Working Girl* (1988), he writes, "This is Melanie Griffith's movie in the same way that *The Graduate* belonged to Dustin Hoffman":

> She is not an obvious casting choice, but she is the right one, and in an odd way her two most famous previous roles, in *Body Double* and *Something Wild*, work for her. Because we may remember her

from those sex-drenched roles, there is a way in which both Griffith and her character are both trying to get respectable—to assimilate everything that goes with "serious hair."

His parallels amplify Griffith's accomplishment. If Pauline Kael lionized the filmmakers and actors she adored, Ebert foregrounds those who are taken for granted. So much so that his review of *Another Day in Paradise* (1999)—a middle-aged, drug-running version of *Bonnie and Clyde*—becomes an encomium to Griffith and James Woods: "A movie like this reminds me of what movie stars are for," he writes.

> We see them many times and in many movies over a period of years, and grow used to their cadences and their range. We invest in them. Those that we like, we follow. James Woods is almost always interesting and often much more than that. Melanie Griffith has qualities that are right for the role she plays here. The kids, [Vincent] Kartheiser and [Natasha Gregson] Wagner, are talented but new. It's a sign that you're a movie lover and not just a fan when you start preferring the fine older vintages to the flavors of the month.

Illuminating an actor's worth, Ebert's praise heightens our moviegoing pleasures. And the fact that it's Woods and Griffith he's praising is meaningful. Woods tirelessly brings intelligence and verve to every role. His characters' fast-talking bravado and hard-as-nails façade often mask desperate vulnerabilities and cravings for respect. Effective though he is, he still seems underappreciated—especially in contrast to more celebrated colleagues like Robert De Niro or William Hurt. In Ebert's own way, by turning a review into a hymn, he redresses the imbalance.

Other actresses, too, would have been suitable in *Another Day*— Sharon Stone would also have chemistry with Woods, and Sigourney Weaver could handle the sawed-off shotguns—but Griffith's fragile strength, her steely sensitivity, set her apart. Regarding Griffith, Pauline Kael once inquired, "Has anybody ever looked better in smeared lipstick?" and *Another Day* pushes the envelope further: Has anybody ever looked better in smeared lipstick, while wielding a .22 and protecting her clan? Like Tess Harper, her signature role in *Working Girl*, Griffith is easily underestimated. But not in Ebert's eyes. In *Another Day*, she's "the last rose of summer: still fragrant, but you can see her energy

Figure 31 In Larry Clark's *Another Day in Paradise*, James Woods and Melanie Griffith portray a pair of middle-aged drug runners. Griffith's fragile strength and steely sensitivity set her apart. Her soulfulness binds together family and film. *Trimark* and *Chinese Bookie Pictures*

Figure 32 And Woods' sly, fast-talking bravado masks desperate vulnerabilities.

running out." He's drawn to her delicate beauty, and, by the end, her soulfulness binds together family and film.

Ebert's respect for outsiders also has international currency. The Cannes Film Festival is the ultimate event for cinephiles, and its American ambassador is Roger Ebert. After a long night of debate, table pounding, and generous doses of French 75s, I would declare *Two Weeks in the Midday Sun: A Cannes Notebook* (1988) as Ebert's finest moment. The sum of his portraits in this volume reveals critical artistry and insight—replete with his own sketches—that achieve the sublime. Capturing the hurly burly of Cannes, Ebert's account of the 1987 festival succeeds in all respects: as a critical tour de force, a charming memoir, a concentrated study of the politics of film distribution and exhibition, and a movie lover's dream. Yet, even in the midst of star-studded premieres and parties, it's the outsiders who catch his eye.

Eschewing interviews with international sensations like Elizabeth Taylor or Gérard Depardieu, Ebert zeros in on actors and filmmakers who, though not on the A-list, provide more complex copy than most stars. "If I were going to compile some sort of a Cannes journal," Ebert reasons, "I needed a central figure, a hero, and Menahem [Golan] might supply it. He had the advantage of not being part of the Cannes establishment; the festival seemed to need him but not to like him, to resent the fact that the most adventurous buccaneer at the festival was a self-made Israeli." As heads of Cannon Films, Menaham Golan and Yorum Globus—also known as the "Go-Go Boys"—were the most prolific and infuriating movie magnates of the 1980s. Their output was an assortment of cheapjack action films (*Missing in Action*, *Invasion U.S.A.*), threadbare sequels (*Death Wish 4*, *Superman 4*), and bold, imaginative epics (*Runaway Train*, *Shy People*). In my youth, the appearance of "Cannon Films" in a darkened theater was tantalizing—the movie was bound to be either extraordinary or extraordinarily appalling. Unapologetic promoters, they were still smarting in 1987 from earlier rejections at Cannes. As Ebert reports, a Cannon film had never walked away with a Palme d'Or or a major acting award, and although Golan was once asked to serve as an official judge at the festival, the invitation was rescinded by the French when his artistic credentials were disputed.

But Golan has the qualities that Ebert admires: a willingness to hold court, to charm enemies as well as friends, to color outside the lines, and to go for broke, both personally and professionally. At the same time, and paradoxically, he has a palpable need for acceptance and appreciation. If Golan is the hero, he's surrounded by a supporting cast that confirms Ebert's respect for the outsider. Fresh from her role in the controversial *Blue Velvet* (1986), Isabella Rossellini honored the memory of her father, director Roberto Rossellini, with the presentation of the first Rossellini Award. To Ebert, the accolade is reserved for "those who persist, despite everything, in believing that the cinema need not be held hostage to greed." Though Ebert hated *Blue Velvet*, he praised her acting as being consistent with her parents' daring personal and professional choices: "There seemed to be a family inclination to follow where the heart led, regardless of public opinion."

Or take director John Sayles, the gold standard of independent American filmmaking—the quintessential Hollywood outsider. At the 1987 Cannes premiere of *Matewan*, a film that depicts violent coal-mining strikes in turn-of-the-century America, a reel was accidentally repeated, and Ebert asked the director about the snafu. "'[The projectionist] was doing the best he could,' Sayles said. 'A lot of projectionists wouldn't even have noticed that they'd skipped a reel.'" Sayles is a patient individual, I'm sure, but it's Ebert who stresses his integrity and humility, as artist and man.

And few would consider Faye Dunaway as a Hollywood outsider; in 1987 she was just that. After five years living and working in London, she was a virtual expat. On the heels of some forgettable movies and a failed marriage, she returned to the States, and her performance in *Barfly* as a no-nonsense alcoholic was luminous. Ebert visited the LA film set, understanding the movie was a risk for all: Dunaway, who needed a role to fit her talent; director Barbet Schroeder and star Mickey Rourke, whose track records had been hit and miss; and Charles Bukowski, the underground poet peering from the shadows, permitting his life to be immortalized on film. At its Cannes premiere, Ebert championed *Barfly*, poised as formidable competition for the Palme d'Or and Best Actress honors.

For Ebert, Cannes is more than premieres, cocktails, and hobnobbing. He even descended to the basement of the Palais, where videos are hawked in bulk; where, and from his point of view, a man who sells movies, sight unseen, shares equal billing with international celebrities. "It was in an obscure backwater of this circus, a few years ago, that I met Ken Hartford," Ebert recalls, "the man who sells movies by the pound. He struck me then as the most honest man at Cannes, and I have had no reason to revise that opinion." Smart and free of pretense, Hartford is at peace with the conflict between art and commerce. He essentially purchases bargain-basement feature films by the pound, gives them exotic titles, commissions artists to create movie posters (who he admits rarely see the films), and sells the movies to foreign markets. "'Basically, I sell crap,' he said cheerfully," revealing Ebert's equally cheerful affection.

In the hands of other critics, the focus would be different. Andrew Sarris might concentrate on the premiere of Francis Coppola's latest. Pauline Kael would be enraptured by her favorites: Cher receiving the Best Actress honors or Brian De Palma filming his latest production on the red carpet of the Palais. Rex Reed would be chasing after screen gods and goddesses, past and present. Ebert, however, attends the world's glitziest film festival and returns with snapshots of Menahem Golan craving acceptance, Isabella Rossellini honoring her father, John Sayles maintaining his independence, Faye Dunaway renovating her career, and Ken Hartford merrily selling movies by the pound.

In the mirrors of their faces, I believe, Ebert sees himself. He enjoys a comeback because he knows what it's like to be an outsider. His review of John Waters' *Hairspray* (1988), a celebration of early 60s teenage dance competitions, takes us back to his adolescence. "Nobody I knew dressed as cool or danced as well as the kids on 'The Hop,'" he recalls, "and there was a sinking feeling, on those long ago afternoons in front of the TV, that the parade had passed me by." His teenage memories invariably emphasize insecurity and self-consciousness. "God, 13 can be horrible," he laments, in an aside that's more vivid than the film under discussion, *Cheaper by the Dozen 2*. "I remember as a high school freshman, standing around at the Tigers' Den teenage hangout in Urbana, cupping my hand to my mouth and checking to see if I had bad breath. At any given moment there would be half a dozen other kids also sniffing in dread and suspicion, all of us chewing Doublemint like crazy."

Well into bachelorhood, Ebert was the eternal lonely guy. He disliked the romantic comedy *Splash*, where regular guy Tom Hanks falls for mermaid Daryl Hannah. Ebert felt the movie was too conventional, and wanted Hanks and John Candy—who plays Hanks' brother—to switch roles. "Then we'd be on the side of this big lunk who suddenly has a mermaid drop into his life and has to explain her to his creepy, swinging-singles brother," Ebert observed. "Plus, there's the sweet touch that this transcendently sexy mermaid has fallen for the tubby loser with the heart of lust, and not for his slick brother. See what I mean?"

I see more. Just as revealing is his review of *The Butcher's Wife*, a romance where Demi Moore loves burly George Dzundra, but eventually lands in the arms of Jeff Daniels. "I was disappointed that *The Butcher's Wife* lost faith in its original romantic inspiration." "Is it not possible," he asks, whimsically, "for a portly butcher to have a ripe young wife?" No leading man himself, Ebert's experiences shape his style: he's drawn to those who, for whatever reasons, are "over in the corner." They're usually the most engaging people in the room.

"Do you think Roger will ever get married?" Ebert's mother, Annabel, repeatedly asked his friends. Well, the sweet touch that Ebert longed for in *Splash* finally arrived when he met attorney Charlie "Chaz" Hammel-Smith in 1988. They married in July 1992, when Ebert was fifty. At the wedding he declared, "I'll never be lonely again." And he hasn't. Their partnership is an enduring one, with Chaz standing beside him, nursing him back to health during his battles with cancer. "I think that I am better in marriage," she says. "I like taking care of people and having someone there in my corner and being in someone's corner."

As well as being a stalwart companion, she's also vice president of The Ebert Company and executive producer of *Ebert Presents*. And she's a patient, elegant match for Roger. "His wait for the perfect mate," according to family friend Betsy Hendrick, "was well worthwhile."

Figure 33 A perfect match: Chaz and Roger Ebert at the 61st Annual Directors Guild of America Awards, where Roger received the DGA Honorary Life Membership Award, Hyatt Regency Century Plaza, Century City, CA, January 30, 2009. *Sara De Boer/Retna Ltd./Corbis*

Watching movies binds them together, too, and they enjoy honoring gifted, underappreciated filmmakers. Perhaps inevitably, then, they designed his own festival, christening it "Roger Ebert's Overlooked Film Festival." They would eventually drop the "overlooked," but, for a decade, they defined the adjective with flexibility and ingenuity. The festival has continued to specialize in small, independent films like Rolf de Heer's *Dance Me to My Song*, Hilary Birmingham's *Tully*, or Kevin DiNovis' *Surrender Dorothy*. It has also spotlighted movies that garnered critical attention, but never found the audiences they deserved—say, Errol Morris' *Gates of Heaven*, Paul Schrader's *Mishima*, Alex Proyas' *Dark City*, Kenneth Branagh's *Hamlet*. Although Ebert's guest list honors filmmakers, it's not only the names above the titles. Anne V. Coates edited *Lawrence of Arabia*. Eiko Ishioka designed *The Cell*'s arresting costumes. Scott Wilson acted with distinction in *Shilo*, *Junebug*, and *Come Early Morning*. Theirs aren't household names, but they're why we love the movies. Ebert's festival also encompasses genres and formats. Of the twelve-to-fourteen films screened over five days, he'll include a silent film and a musical, and the choices can be surprising. George Cukor's *My Fair Lady*, for instance, is hardly overlooked. But when Ebert secured a restored 70 mm. print and invited Marni Nixon—Audrey Hepburn's voice in the musical numbers, and one of film's most undervalued artists—to the post-screening interview, you can appreciate his creativity. Perhaps most of all, his festival departs from others in its celebration of movies and friendship rather than movies and distribution deals. And when Nixon joined Ebert on stage and he declared, "You *are* the Debbie Reynolds character in *Singin' in the Rain*," like a well-watered flower, she glowed. Anticipating the screening of Paul Cox's *A Woman's Tale*, Ebert writes, "I have had good times with Cox in Cannes, Montreal, Toronto, Honolulu, Chicago, and Calcutta, and now at last in Urbana-Champaign."

The reference to Urbana-Champaign is yet another defense of second-hand roses: He sticks up for his hometown and alma mater. "Looks like it's the University of Illinois!" cracks Tom Cruise's suburban Chicago teenager in *Risky Business*, when it appears he's shut out from attending an Ivy League university. Off-screen, Ebert bristled when Gene Siskel, a Yale man, ribbed him for attending a state school. Again, it's difficult to think of the University of Illinois as an institutional underdog, but stereotypes endure. At a ceremony commencing

Ebert's 2006 festival, University of Illinois President B. Joseph White confessed that, after accepting his position, friends privately asked why he wanted a job in the "cultural backwaters" of Central Illinois. When Ebert reached the podium, he responded with incredulity: "Cultural *backwaters*? Try 'cultural *forefront*'!" Then he fiercely listed a history of the university's achievements, not the least of which includes the development of the supercomputer and innovations in talking pictures. Ebert's defense of his university is self-defense. His life silences the naysayers who associate success with metropolitan living or the Ivy League, and nobody makes a more persuasive case for including Urbana-Champaign among the film-loving cities of the world than he.

A rousing moment that united Ebert's respect for the underdog and his alma mater was the screening at his 2005 festival of *Murderball*, a documentary that explores with unsparing directness the lives of men who compete in full-contact wheelchair rugby. On the morning of April 21, the film was screened in Huff Gym, on the U of I's campus. In attendance were the filmmakers and several hundred men and women who live in wheelchairs. The setting was appropriate, as the University of Illinois pioneered the development of university-wide wheelchair accessibility and athletic programs. Later that day, Ebert shared the movie with a full audience at his festival. The post-screening interview was something to behold: Directors Dana Adam Shapiro and Henry Alex Rubin joined Ebert on stage. Flanking them as if in a Western stand-off were Mark Zupan, the surly, determined star of the American team, and his former coach and arch rival, Joe Soares. Adding more tension to the conversation, Soares—recently fired from the Canadian team—had reapplied to be the USA's head coach, a move that would reunite him with the very players who label him a traitor in the movie. Though hostile toward one another on screen, Zupan and Soares were gentlemen that day, each speaking to Ebert and the filmmakers, never to one another. When an audience member asked Zupan how he felt about the possibility of working with Soares again, he smiled, indicating that time would tell. (The job would not go to Soares.) This is Ebert at his most discerning and industrious: honoring a worthy film that sees its participants with complexity and compassion, giving directors an opportunity to explain their process, letting the stars discuss their lives and challenges, and, just as importantly, serving as mediator among forceful personalities. Furthermore, it was clear that Ebert himself walked away changed. When Zupan explained that losing the use of his legs at eighteen was the "greatest thing that's ever happened to me," Ebert—obviously taken aback—paused and said, "That is very hard for me to hear." Zupan later elaborated for all: "This *is* hard. You're not going to adjust overnight. My first two years after getting hurt were like being an infant again. But be grateful for what you have, instead of focusing on what you don't have."

Another pleasure of Ebert's Overlooked Festival is seeing how the films speak to one another. A grander, encompassing theme was evident in 2007. The festival was launched with *Gattaca*, an austere portrait of a future where technologies can pinpoint when a human life ends. Want to know your expiration date? *The Weather Man* followed, examining a middle-aged television newsman's struggles to find meaning in life, despite his professional accomplishments. *La Dolce Vita*—the film that serves as a yardstick for Ebert's life—elegantly explored similar terrain. Then, a documentary on Freddie Mercury, the lead singer of Queen, whose extravagant talent and life ended with his death from AIDS. The final screening was of *Beyond the Valley of the Dolls*, reuniting Ebert with cast members and musicians. When The Strawberry Alarm Clock—a band that appears in the film as themselves and broke up in 1971—played a set after the screening, the affair turned into a homecoming.

It was impossible to watch these films and not consider issues looming large in Ebert's own life. As we've seen, movies for him are conduits for introspection. The characters in these films ponder the prospects of aging and death, resulting in soul-searching, fear, and dread. Through them, Ebert invites us to examine our lives as he examines his own. That there is more to life than the pursuit of pleasure is an issue that he can no longer ignore. It's an issue that gnaws at us, as it does him.

As mentioned at the outset, Ebert knew that Mickey Rourke—after squandering much of his talent in the 90s—was ripe for a comeback. The rehabilitation arrived in the form of *The Wrestler*, the tale of Randy "The Ram" Robinson, a washed-up professional wrestler struggling to pay the rent, relate to others, and simply hang on. It was a plum role, where an actor's personal difficulties deepen the characterization. "It is routinely said that *The Wrestler* is Rourke's 'comeback performance,'" Ebert observed:

Figure 34 "I don't hear as good as I used to and I forget stuff and I ain't as pretty as I used to be": Mickey Rourke delivers the performance of his life in Darren Aronofsky's *The Wrestler*. *Fox Searchlight*

It is not only that. It is his comeback on his own terms, as a full-force, heedless, passionate physical actor with strong undercurrents of tenderness, loneliness, and need. He did a lot of his own wrestling in the film, including a scene where he deliberately cuts himself, and he was painfully honest in the scenes with women. What you see is a man with what he knows is the role of his lifetime, and willing (I am convinced) to die for it.

"Now I don't hear as good as I used to and I forget stuff and I ain't as pretty as I used to be," Randy cries out—his body ravaged from years of wrestling and steroids. "But goddamnit, I'm still standing here and I'm The Ram... You know what? The only one that's going to tell me when I'm through doing my thing is you people here."

Ebert understands. In 2002, he was successfully operated on for thyroid cancer. In 2003, he underwent surgery to remove a cancerous growth on his salivary gland, and, later that year, was treated at the neutron radiation facility at the University of Washington in Seattle. In June 2006, he underwent another surgery for salivary cancer, but a carotid artery burst near the site of operation. "It was sheer good chance that this happened at the hospital and not at home, where I would certainly have died. It was touch-and-go," he writes. "The bleeding seemed impossible to stop. The affected tissue had been weakened by radiation. Only within the last year has my wife informed me that at one point it appeared I had died. She sensed I was still alive, and asked the doctors to keep working. I am happy that they did." A portion of his jaw was removed, and a tracheotomy maintained his breathing. Under heavy sedation, Ebert has little memory of July and August. The bleeding stabilized in September, and his first public appearance was at 2007's Ebertfest. His neck wrapped with gauze, his lower lip drawn, his back in pain, he enjoyed most of the films from a La-Z-Boy in the back of the theater. Unable to speak, he communicated through a computer-assisted voice generator, confessing that some had advised him not to appear in public. His responses borrowed iconic movie lines, like *Gone With the Wind*'s "Frankly, my dear, I don't give a damn" and a paraphrase from *Raging Bull*: "I ain't a pretty boy no more." But, instead of drawing the blinds, Ebert engaged his public, sending a message that illness is nothing to be ashamed of. He recognizes the continuity: "The original appeal of *Siskel & Ebert* was that we didn't look like we belonged on TV." And it's as if the threat of death itself, like *Murderball*'s instructive brutality, has been one of the greatest things to happen to him. Through it all, Ebert's mind is strong, and his productivity, staggering. He writes voraciously for rogerebert.com and speaks through the voice generator. Not even cancer has prevented him from thinking and writing about movies. Like Rourke's, Ebert's comeback is on his own terms. As America's ambassador of film, his has been the role of a lifetime, and it is for this, too, that he's willing to die.

Epilogue: Heroes

The first week of July 1997 was a lonely one for movie lovers. Robert Mitchum, one of the great, laconic tough guys—our sleepy-eyed icon of film noir—died on Tuesday, July 1. With a trench coat and fedora, a cigarette dangling from his lower lip, Mitchum was often enveloped in shadows and smoke. At RKO, he recalled, his films were "lit by matches." The following day, James Stewart, arguably the most beloved American movie star, passed away. Stewart's image was too varied to summarize a genre, but archetypal moments include his passionate filibustering in *Mr. Smith Goes to Washington*; fussing with and falling for Margaret Sullavan in *The Shop Around the Corner*; returning home, with gratitude, in *It's a Wonderful Life*; and obsessing over Kim Novak in *Vertigo*. Both men worked with the greatest directors of their time, Mitchum starring in 125 films and Stewart collaborating with Frank Capra, Anthony Mann, John Ford, and Alfred Hitchcock. Their voices were as recognizable as their faces: Mitchum's throaty, full-bodied, too-hell-with-it growl, and Stewart's higher-pitched, adamant-yet-tremulous drawl. They were two sides of the American coin: Mitchum, the cynical outsider who walked home alone; Stewart, the passionate idealist who believed in the system.

Arriving on deadline, Ebert's tributes to each were characteristic. He praised Mitchum, always his favorite actor and interview, whose worldweariness was the lost soul of noir. And he applauded Stewart, who—contrary to popular sentiment—took risks with his career, hitting a range of emotionally complex notes. The timing of their exits inevitably led to comparisons, and there was a general sense that Stewart's passing overshadowed Mitchum's in the press. For a moment, Mitchum seemed destined to play the outsider in death as in life. But, on July 9, Ebert addressed this in a third essay, "Mitch and Jimmy: Some

Thoughts." His defense was simple: Both were exceptional, and Mitchum's talent—always darker, and therefore more challenging to embrace—was worth revaluation. "So, Mitchum or Stewart?" he asks. "I cannot choose. I cannot do without either of them."

Ebert has always appreciated heroes with dents in their armor. He liked Daniel Craig's James Bond in *Casino Royale* because, "if you prick him, he bleeds." In *Defiance* (2008), Craig brought the same humanity to Tuvia Bielski, the leader of the Bielski settlement, the group of Jews who survived in the wilderness during World War II. Tuvia insisted that all Jews, regardless of age or strength, be a part of their group. His brother, Zus (Liev Schreiber), was skeptical, believing the way to fight the Nazis—and ultimately protect more Jews—was by accepting only the fittest. Yet Tuvia's philosophy triumphed, and the movie explores the tensions that erupted in their small band of survivors. In his review, Ebert wants the film's scope to move beyond the guerilla fighters; he longs for the wider vision of a *Schindler's List*. On that count, however, I think Pauline Kael got it right; films like *Schindler's List*, in attempting to define history on many planes, often become didactic. The fact is, *Defiance* is better than Ebert allows. Its compact scope presents a world that is less known, and, because of that, all the more captivating.

"Early in the film," Ebert observed, "there's a scene where a feckless middleaged man named Shimon Haretz (Allan Corduner) hopes to join the group and is asked what he does."

> He thinks maybe he's ... an intellectual. This is no use to the partisans, although he is allowed to stay. At the time of the story, the region was largely agrarian and peasant, and many were skilled craftsmen, artisans and laborers. I thought, I'm also an ... intellectual. Of what use would I be in the forest? The film works in a way as a cautionary tale. Most of us live in a precarious balance above the bedrock of physical labor. Someday we may all be Shimon Haretz.

As one who isn't getting around so easily anymore, his words are humbling, even disconcerting. "Of what use would I be in the forest?" Very little, in terms of heavy lifting. Nonetheless, Ebert's contribution has always been life-giving. The leaders are at each other's throats? He'll step in and mediate. The partisans are exhausted after days of moving with little to eat? He'll tell a joke with style, easing the load. Tevia is losing confidence? Ebert will recall his past achievements. A young man and woman want to marry? He'll plan the ceremony, eying the challenges ahead. At the end of the day, people are still at each other's throats? He'll continue to negotiate, always sensitive to the outsiders.

Like such heroes, Ebert's mentors amplify his legacy as well. Pauline Kael's "later reviews are fully formed aesthetic objects," writes essayist Craig Seligman, "and the movies that occasioned them tend to drop away, like excrescences." And Kael, who once called *An Officer and a Gentleman* "crap, but crap on a motorcycle," might have liked that analogy. "In truth, they drop away from all her reviews," he continues. "When I read Kael now, the pictures she wrote about seem like footnotes to *her* work" (italics his). But the movies will never be footnotes to Ebert's work. He shares the stage. And, by initiating intelligent critical debates—at times in our own living rooms—he made the movies *ours*. This requires a different type of confidence, and Ebert's sensibility—as indefatigable reporter and judicious, trustworthy guide—has made him an original. His prose isn't as theatrical as Kael's or as fastidious as John Simon's—that's the cost and consequence of writing for a daily, pulling a punch now and then, reviewing every film that opens every Friday—a punishment never inflicted on Kael or Simon. What we've gained in Ebert, though, is a body of work that's not only characterized by rigor and insight, but also by humility. In "The Love Song of J. Alfred Prufrock," T. S. Eliot writes, "I have heard the mermaids singing, each to each. / I do not think that they will sing to me." "Don't we all know that feeling?" Ebert responds.

> That feeling that other people in other places are singing in the sunshine, but here in the shadows of our own miserable existence, the parade has passed us by. It is a key discovery of adult life that almost everyone else feels the same way, too, and that anyone who believes he's leading the parade is either stupid, mistaken or a saint.

It should come as no surprise that one of his favorite films is Charlie Kauffman's *Synecdoche, NY* (2008), a house of mirrors that reflects the competing identities, relationships, and homesteads of a human life. In it, theater director Caden Cotard (Philip Seymour Hoffman) and his loved ones are played by actors of various genders, ages, and races. The unusual casting dramatizes the manifold roles we inhabit and project upon others, exploring the intellectual and spiritual crises that Ebert has wrestled with—and put into words—for years. Oddly, Hoffman and Dianne Wiest (who also plays Cotard in later years), with their sweater vests, eyeglasses, and round figures, even resemble Ebert. The film begins with Cotard at forty, travels with him for four decades, and culminates—literally—in his final breath. "This is the ultimate law—the seed dies to live, the bread must be cast upon the waters, he that loses his soul will save it," C. S. Lewis writes, adding, "But the life of the seed, the finding of the bread, the recovery of the soul, are as real as the preliminary sacrifice." Ebert's career demonstrates these truths: He has chased after dreams, experienced great professional success and not a little personal dissatisfaction, relinquished his ideals of perfect love and the good life—there's quite a distance from Farrah Fawcett to Lillian Gish—and, in doing so, found greater wisdom. Ebert isn't a critic who's simply waiting to see if a film measures up, or to compare this one to that. There's a sense of discovery and hard-won development in his work that mirrors the way life is lived, and it is his willingness to discuss that growth—to use it as a centerpiece of his criticism—that sets him apart.

Were Pauline Kael on trial for her life, a jury of Meryl Streep, Oliver Stone, Clint Eastwood, Natalie Wood, and Kevin Costner—all victims at her whipping post—wouldn't need much time to deliberate. "Geniuses, almost necessarily, *are* monsters," writes Craig Seligman, in Kael's defense. "There's something monstrous in the titanic will it takes to produce a world-class oeuvre," he argues, "not to mention the coldness it takes to pronounce somebody else's work wanting." But Ebert has suggested another way. Of course, critical genius involves artfully and truthfully bending words to one's will, all the while illuminating art. Certainly a titanic drive is essential, but coldness isn't intrinsic to critical greatness, whether panning or not. To the point, Ebert shattered the stereotype of *All About Eve*'s Addison DeWitt—the biting, mercurial theater critic who loathed all, including himself. With humility and pluck, Ebert has shown you can champion Brian De Palma, sternly advise Burt Reynolds and Goldie Hawn, gush over Debra Winger, go head-to-head with David Lynch, admire *both* Pauline Kael and Andrew Sarris, *both* Angelina Jolie and Lillian Gish, *both* James Stewart and Robert Mitchum.

Figure 35 Heart and soul: James Stewart and Robert Mitchum, circa 1978. *Michael Ochs Archives/Getty Images*

For decades, Americans have invited Ebert into their homes—first through newspapers, then television, books, and the internet. It was easy to open the door, because he viewed movies—and the characters that decorate them—as friends. "Forget it's a thriller," he writes of *The Big Easy*. "See it because you want to meet these people." Or at least as potential friends. "By the end of [*Everybody's All-American*], we not only feel we know these people, we feel we know them too well," he argues, "and would like to make some new friends." His artful casualness is everything we appreciate in a friend: one who's truthful, literate, large-hearted, witty, argumentative, and empathetic. He's taken his passions for movies and life, transformed them with words, and given us a carefully etched portrait of intellect and spirit, not to mention a clear set of critical values. "The typical newsroom is open space filled with desks, and journalists are actors on this stage; to see a good writer on a deadline with a big story is to watch not simply work," Ebert writes, "but performance." He has enlarged his stage and audience, from the newsroom to the world. But, for a moment, forget that his is one of the longest, most rewarding performances in film criticism and American letters. Read him because you want to meet this guy. "So, Mitchum or Stewart?" he asks. "I cannot choose. I cannot do without either of them." Of course he can't: Ebert needs both because he *is* both. Like Stewart, he's earnest, with a boyish, all-American spirit that's independent of age. As the symbol of his profession, Ebert, too, has become a national treasure. Yet, like Mitchum, he's no stranger to a barstool or a broken heart. He tasted life's pleasures, wised up, and befriended ennui. "Stewart was the heart," he argued, of American movies, "and Mitchum was the soul." By personifying so much that was worthy in each and by sharing that love with us, Ebert is surely both.

Notes

Introduction

xvi   "sprout mushrooms": Pauline Kael, "Not for the Ages" (review of *Angel Heart*), in *Hooked* (New York: E.P. Dutton, 1989), 287.

xvii   "that a movie could suggest": Roger Ebert, "Introduction," in *Roger Ebert's Book of Film*, ed. Roger Ebert (New York: W. W. Norton, 1997), 14.

xviii   "'This is a great night,'" and "I loved Rick's": Charles Bukowski, *Hollywood* (Santa Rosa: Black Sparrow Press, 1989), 183.

"'Pardon me'" and "'And neither do you'": Ibid., 188.

xix   "Either/Or when we yearn": Jennifer Maier, "Happiness Is Being Danish," *Dark Alphabet* (Carbondale: Southern Illinois University Press, 2006), 3.

Chapter 1: Godchild

1   "Her American-good-girl innocence": Pauline Kael, "A Fresh Start" (review of *Barbarella*), in *Going Steady* (Boston: Atlantic Monthly Press/ Little, Brown, 1970), 172.

2   "Nothing succeeds better than": John Simon, "From Sensibility Toward Sense: Susan Sontag, *Under the Sign of Saturn*," *The Sheep From the Goats: Selected Literary Essays* (New York: Weidenfeld & Nicolson, 1989), 24.

4   "How do you make a good movie": Pauline Kael, review of *Bonnie and Clyde*, in *Kiss Kiss Bang Bang* (Boston: Atlantic Monthly Press/Little, Brown, 1968), 47.

"all men of goodwill": Richard Schickel, review of *Bonnie and Clyde*, *Life*, October 13, 1967, 16.

5   "*The Wild Bunch* is the first masterpiece": Richard Schickel, "Mastery of the 'Dirty Western'" (review of *The Wild Bunch*), *Life*, July 25, 1969, 8.

"Claude Chabrol's *La Femme Infidèle*": Andrew Sarris, "*La Femme Infidèle*," in *Film 69/70*, Joseph Morgenstern and Stefan Kanfer (eds) (New York: Simon and Schuster, 1970), 121. (Originally published in *The Village Voice*, November 13, 1969.)

"Remember when the movie ads": Pauline Kael, "Exiles" (review of *Z*), in *Deeper Into Movies* (Boston: Atlantic Monthly Press/Little, Brown, 1973), 63.

"the Academy Awards of Journalism": J. Douglas Bates, *The Pulitzer Prize: The Inside Story of America's Most Prestigious Award* (New York: Birch Lane Press, 1991), 4.

7   "the national dream beat": Roger Ebert, "In Memoriam: Gene Siskel," *Roger Ebert's Movie Yearbook 2000* (Kansas City: Andrews McMeel Publishing, 1999), 754.

"Is this the night Rog" and "when will Gene": Richard T. Jameson, "Jameson on Film, Down the Tube: T.V. vs. the Movies," *Pacific Northwest*, July–August 1986, 55.

8   "Is this film more interesting": Ebert, review of *Monster-in-Law*, in *Roger Ebert's Movie Yearbook 2006* (Kansas City: Andrews McMeel Publishing, 2006), 114.

9   "I feel like Roger Ebert": Joel H. Cohen, "Home Away from Homer," *The Simpsons*, season 16, episode 20, directed by Bob Anderson, aired May 15, 2005.

10   "If Kael and Sarris were": David Bordwell, "Foreword," in *Roger Ebert, Awake in the Dark: The Best of Roger Ebert* (Chicago: University of Chicago, 2006), xvi.

"*Sun-Times* writers always felt": Ebert, email message to author, March 15, 2009.

11   "This is the kind of film": Roger Ebert, review of *Innocence*, in *Roger Ebert's Movie Yearbook 2003* (Kansas City: Andrews McMeel Publishing, 2002), 285.

"*The Last Picture Show* has been described": Ebert, review of *The Last Picture Show*, in *Roger Ebert's Movie Home Companion 1987 Edition* (Kansas City: Andrews, McMeel & Parker, 1986), 297.

12   "Movie art is not the opposite": Pauline Kael, "Trash, Art, and the Movies," *Going Steady* (Boston: Atlantic Monthly Press/Little, Brown, 1970), 106.

"The wide movie audience appears to resent": Pauline Kael, "Virgins, Vamps, and Floozies" (review of *Outrageous Fortune*), in *Hooked* (New York: E.P. Dutton, 1989), 274.

13   "the apostle of common feelings": Charles T. Samuels, "Going Steady" (review of *Going Steady*), *New York Times Book Review*, February 22, 1970, 36.

"exonerates her readers": Ibid.

"flatters people sharing": Ibid.

14   "Nobody's publishing film books": Richard Corliss, "All Thumbs: Or, Is There a Future for Film Criticism?," *Film Comment*, March–April 1990, 16.

"David Bordwell on Ozu": Roger Ebert, "All Stars: Or, Is There a Cure for Criticism of Film Criticism?," *Film Comment*, May–June 1990, 46.

"The hazel eyes that laser out": Richard Corliss, "Tom Terrific," *Time*, December 25, 1989, 74.

"vivid prose": Richard Corliss, "Then Again," *Film Comment*, May–June 1990, 52.

"I simply don't want people to think": Corliss, "All Thumbs," 18.

15   "Not many people shine": Richard Corliss, "A Screen Gem Turns Director," *Time*, October 14, 1991, 72.

"Serious discussion of good movies": Ebert, "All Stars," 46.

"Go further": Corliss, "Then Again," 51.

16   "Even if my movie's never released": Jeff Nichols, at Ebertfest, following the screening of *Shotgun Stories*, April 25, 2008.

"steadily eroded by too calculating": Andrew Sarris, "Auteurism Is Alive and Well and Living in Argentina," *Film Comment*, July–August 1990, 22.

17   "My nature is to be antagonistic": Roger Ebert, "Playboy Interview: Siskel & Ebert," interviewed by Lawrence Grobel, *Playboy*, February 1991, 52.

"Siskel and Ebert picked up": Andrew Sarris, "Foreword: Allen Smithee Redux," *Directed by Allen Smithee*, Jeremy Braddock and Stephen Hock (eds) (Minneapolis: University of Minnesota, 2006), vii.

18   "My web site and blog": Roger Ebert, "See You at the Movies," *Roger Ebert's Journal* (blog), *Chicago Sun-Times*, March 25, 2010. http://blogs.suntimes.com/ebert/2010/03/see_you_at_the_movies.html.

Chapter 2: Rule of Thumb

21   "the raised thumb represented": For a complete discussion of the meanings of the thumb in Roman culture and beyond, see Anthony Corbeill, "The Power of Thumbs," *Nature Embodied: Gesture in Ancient Rome* (Princeton: Princeton University Press, 2004), 41–66.

23   "I have a friend": Roger Ebert, review of *Top Secret!*, in *Roger Ebert's Movie Home Companion 1980–85* (Kansas City: Andrews, McMeel & Parker, 1985), 346.

"Mrs. Seward, the draconian rhetoric teacher": Ibid., review of *Fame*, 117.

24   "would have cracked": Ebert, review of *The Opposite Sex*, in *I Hated, Hated, Hated This Movie* (Kansas City: Andrews McMeel Publishing, 2000), 269–70.

"Where's the quirkiness": Ebert, review of *The Chorus*, in *Roger Ebert's Movie Yearbook 2006* (Kansas City: Andrews McMeel Publishing, 2006), 114.

"gently suggested that the day": Ibid., 115.

"the schoolmarm's approach": Kael, "Trash, Art, and the Movies," *Going Steady* (Boston: Atlantic Monthly Press/Little, Brown, 1970), 92.

"Miss Fiske would have": Ebert, review of *84 Charing Cross Road*, in *Roger Ebert's Movie Home Companion: 1993 Edition* (Andrews and McMeel Publishing, 1993), 196.

"Sigh. Miss Fiske, who you may": Ibid.

25   "if maybe there were": Ebert, review of *Bad Dreams*, in *Roger Ebert's Movie Home Companion 1990 Edition* (Andrews and McMeel Publishing, 1989), 50.

"Just imagine if": Ebert, review of *Pennies from Heaven*, in *Roger Ebert's Movie Home Companion 1980–85*, 243.

"From the opening shot": Ebert, review of *8 Women*, in *Roger Ebert's Movie Yearbook 2004* (Kansas City: Andrews McMeel Publishing, 2004), 186.

"cheerful open-mindedness": Ebert, review of *Election*, in *Roger Ebert's Movie Yearbook 2001* (Kansas City: Andrews McMeel Publishing, 2000), 171.

"cheerfully acknowledges": Ebert, review of *Quest for Fire*, in *Roger Ebert's Movie Home Companion 1980–85*, 263.

"a director cheerfully willing": Ebert, review of *Mary Shelley's Frankenstein*, in *Roger Ebert's Video Companion 1996 Edition* (Kansas City: Andrews and McMeel Publishing, 1995), 453.

"bound together by their": Ebert, review of *Amarcord*, in *Roger Ebert's Movie Home Companion 1987 Edition* (Kansas City: Andrews, McMeel & Parker, 1986), 18.

"a pure and cheerful": Ibid., review of *10*, 525.

26   "seem to retain": Ebert, review of *Chloe in the Afternoon*, in *Roger Ebert's Four-Star Reviews 1967–2007* (Kansas City: Andrews McMeel Publishing, 2007), 146.

"There is a jolting surprise": Ebert, review of *Fat Girl*, in *Roger Ebert's Movie Yearbook 2003* (Kansas City: Andrews McMeel Publishing, 2002), 206.

"They were like": Ebert, review of *The Eyes of Tammy Faye*, in *Roger Ebert's Movie Yearbook 2002* (Kansas City: Andrews McMeel Publishing, 2001), 201.

27 "Can you, dear reader": Ebert, review of *Déjà Vu*, in *Roger Ebert's Movie Yearbook 2001* (Kansas City: Andrews McMeel Publishing, 2000), 136.

"Perfect love is almost always": Ibid.

"We know we want": Ebert, review of *Strange Days*, in *Roger Ebert's Video Companion 1997 Edition* (Kansas City: Andrews and McMeel Publishing, 1996), 735.

28 "human survival at a most": Ebert, review of *Man Push Cart*, in *Roger Ebert's Four-Star Reviews 1967–2007*, 464.

"How many times": Roger Ebert, at Ebertfest, following the screening of *Man Push Cart*, April 27, 2006.

"In almost every play": John Simon, "Artists as They Aren't" (review of *The Music Lovers*), in *Something to Declare: Twelve Years of Films from Abroad* (New York: Clarkson N. Potter, Inc., 1983), 33.

"competent by our": John Simon, "And Lo! The Twain Shall Meet" (review of *Prizzi's Honor*), in *John Simon on Film: Criticism, 1982–2001* (New York: Applause, 2005), 90.

29 "Last time I saw": Pauline Kael, "Round Up the Usual Suspects" (review of *The Getaway*), in *Reeling* (Boston: Atlantic Monthly Press/Little, Brown, 1976), 80.

"It's better to adopt": Ebert, review of *Two Much*, in *Roger Ebert's Movie Yearbook 1999* (Kansas City: Andrews McMeel Publishing, 1998), 602.

"asked to be loyal": Ebert, review of *Me, Myself & Irene*, in *Roger Ebert's Movie Yearbook 2002* (Kansas City: Andrews McMeel Publishing, 2001), 367.

"thankless": Ebert, review of *Father's Day*, in *Roger Ebert's Movie Yearbook 1999*, 184.

"Supporting roles are crucial": Ebert, review of *Working Girl*, in *Roger Ebert's Movie Home Companion 1990 Edition* (Kansas City: Andrews and McMeel Publishing, 1989), 846.

30 "thankless assignment: to show us": Ibid., review of *A Cry in the Dark*, 169.

"You know me": Ebert, review of *Exit to Eden*, in *Roger Ebert's Video Companion 1996 Edition* (Kansas City: Andrews and McMeel Publishing, 1995), 223.

"In a performance": Ebert, review of *Turbulence*, in *Roger Ebert's Movie Yearbook 1999*, 591.

31 "[Lauren] Holly's performance": Ibid.

"*Wildcats* is clearly": Ebert, review of *Wildcats*, in *Roger Ebert's Movie Home Companion 1988 Edition* (Kansas City: Andrews and McMeel Publishing, 1987), 648.

"Kate Hudson, who stars": Ebert, review of *Raising Helen*, in *Roger Ebert's Movie Yearbook 2006* (Kansas City: Andrews McMeel Publishing, 2006), 554.

32　"Reynolds is so popular": Ebert, review of *Cannonball Run*, in *Roger Ebert's Movie Home Companion 1980–85*, 55.

"As a director, Reynolds": Ibid., review of *Sharky's Machine*, 288.

"assembly-line product": Ibid., review of *Stroker Ace*, 317.

"Greater love hath": Ibid., review of *Cannonball Run II*, 56.

"This time, in the": Ebert, review of *Breaking In*, in *Roger Ebert's Movie Home Companion 1992 Edition* (Kansas City: Andrews and McMeel Publishing, 1991), 75.

33　"not in terms of physical details": Ebert, "20 Questions: Siskel & Ebert," interviewed by Bill Zehme, *Playboy*, June 1984, 176.

"Movies do not change": Ebert, review of *La Dolce Vita*, in *The Great Movies* (New York: Broadway Books, 2002), 243.

34　"Simon and Mason must not drink": Ebert, review of *Only When I Laugh*, in *Roger Ebert's Movie Home Companion 1980–85*, 237.

"Since surgery in July of 2006": Ebert, "My Name Is Roger, and I'm an Alcoholic," *Roger Ebert's Journal* (blog), *Chicago Sun-Times*, August 25, 2009. http://blogs.suntimes.com/ebert/2009/08/my_name_is_roger_and_im_an_alc.html

"There's a chance somebody" and "I began to realize": Ibid.

35　"is after all" and "His personal life": Ebert, review of *The Beaver*, *Chicago Sun-Times*, May 4, 2011. http://rogerebert.suntimes.com/apps/pbcs.dll/article?AID=/20110504/REVIEWS/110509994

"If you want AA": Ebert, "My Name Is Roger," *Roger Ebert's Journal* (blog), *Chicago Sun-Times*, August 25, 2009. http://blogs.suntimes.com/ebert/2009/08/my_name_is_roger_and_im_an_alc.html

Chapter 3: Close to Ebert

37　"Here's a basic rule": Ebert, review of *Lassiter*, in *Roger Ebert's Movie Home Companion 1980–85* (Kansas City: Andrews, McMeel & Parker, 1985), 184.

"The movie uses each half": Ebert, review of *Agnes of God*, in *Roger Ebert's Movie Home Companion 1987 Edition* (Kansas City: Andrews, McMeel & Parker, 1986), 6.

"It's a loosely structured film": Ebert, review of *Foxes*, in *Roger Ebert's Movie Home Companion 1980–85*, 139.

"*Foxes* is an ambitious movie": Ibid.

"It's a lot more serious": Ibid.

38   "*Flashdance* is like": Ibid., review of *Flashdance*, 130.

39   "I went expecting": Ebert, review of *9½ Weeks*, in *Roger Ebert's Movie Home Companion 1987 Edition*, 363.

"Their first meeting": Ibid.

"This everyday material": Ibid., 364.

40   "That's what makes": Ibid.

"owes more to improbable": Ibid.

"To buy a whip": Ibid.

"*The Hitcher* is": Ibid., 364–5.

41   "If she is not yet": Ebert, "Kim Basinger," in *Roger Ebert's Movie Home Companion 1989 Edition* (Kansas City: Andrews and McMeel Publishing, 1988), 781.

"a former director of fashion": Julie Salamon, "Where's the 'S' and Where's the 'M'?" (review of *9½ Weeks*), *Wall Street Journal*, February 20, 1986, 23.

"[H]is first feature film": Ibid.

"Mr. Lyne knows how": Ibid.

42   "*Fatal Attraction* is a spellbinding": Ebert, review of *Fatal Attraction*, in *Roger Ebert's Movie Home Companion 1989 Edition*, 216.

43   "whose ideas of love": Ibid.

"complete with the unforgivable": Ibid., 217.

"*Fatal Attraction* clearly had": Ibid.

"All sorts of endings": Ebert, "*Fatal Attraction*'s Fatal Flaw," in *Roger Ebert's Movie Home Companion 1989 Edition*, 753.

44   "[Lyne] prefers 'French films'": Ibid., 753–4.

45   "That movie was compromised": Ebert, "Glenn Close," in *Roger Ebert's Movie Home Companion 1990 Edition* (Kansas City: Andrews and McMeel Publishing, 1989), 868–9.

47   "You can talk about [Dan Gallagher's] weakness": David Thomson, "Michael Douglas: Business as Usual," *Film Comment*, January–February 1990, 19.

Chapter 4: The Total Effect

49　"In Herzog's *Nosferatu*": Ebert, review of *The Hunger*, in *Roger Ebert's Movie Home Companion 1980–85* (Kansas City: Andrews, McMeel & Parker, 1985), 170.

"There is more": Ibid., review of *Heaven's Gate*, 166.

"Even in the extremes": Ebert, review of *The Exorcist*, in *Roger Ebert's Movie Home Companion 1988 Edition* (Kansas City: Andrews and McMeel Publishing, 1987), 185.

"ennobles filmmaking": Ebert, review of *Dead Man Walking*, in *Roger Ebert's Video Companion 1997 Edition* (Kansas City: Andrews and McMeel Publishing, 1996), 191.

"This is the kind": Ibid.

50　"I can't imagine": Ebert, review of *Mommie Dearest*, in *Roger Ebert's Movie Home Companion 1980–85*, 212.

"the movie doesn't even": Ibid., 212–13.

51　"The sets look": Ibid., 213.

"Faye Dunaway gives": Pauline Kael, "Dunaway Assoluta" (review of *Mommie Dearest*), in *Taking It All In* (New York: Holt, Rinehart and Winston, 1984), 233.

52　"Does Faye Dunaway": Sidney Lumet, *Making Movies* (London: Bloomsbury, 1995), 94.

"She does": Ibid.

"frighteningly human": Kael, *Mommie Dearest*, 235.

53　"In the obit": Ibid., 237.

"when her falseness": Ibid.

"psychological intelligence": Richard Schickel, "Losing Face" (review of *Mommie Dearest*), *Time*, September 21, 1981, 73.

"an awareness of": Ibid.

"Confronted by": Ibid.

54　"taking, that is": Renata Adler, "The Perils of Pauline" (review of Kael's *When the Lights Go Down*), *New York Review of Books*, August 14, 1980, 34.

"amounts to a small": Janet Maslin, "Movie: Faye Dunaway Plays 'Mommie Dearest'" (review of *Mommie Dearest*), *New York Times*, September 18, 1981, C15.

"needn't have been": Ibid.

"After Michael Redgrave": Kael, *Mommie Dearest*, 237.

55   "Their roles reminded": Ebert, review of *Supergirl*, in *Roger Ebert's Movie Home Companion* (Kansas City: Andrews, McMeel & Parker, 1985), 319.

"The emotional violence": Kael, *Mommie Dearest*, 237.

"frozen": Faye Dunaway (with Betsy Sharkey), *Looking for Gatsby* (New York: Simon & Schuster, 1995), 340.

56   "The best that can": Kael, *Mommie Dearest*, 236.

"The scenes don't build": Ebert, *Mommie Dearest*, 213.

57   "There's a tiny detail": Ebert, review of *Silkwood*, in *Roger Ebert's Movie Home Companion* (Kansas City: Andrews, McMeel & Parker, 1985), 290.

"'goodies'": Patrick McGilligan, *Cagney: The Actor as Auteur* (San Diego: A. S. Barnes & Co., 1982), 23.

"another of": Ebert, *Silkwood*, 290.

"Meryl Streep imitates": Kael, "Busybody" (review of *Silkwood*), *State of the Art* (New York: E.P. Dutton, 1985), 107.

"If the young": Ibid.

58   "If Debra Winger": Ibid.

"the external details": Ibid.

"does a whole lot": Ibid.

"She has no natural": Ibid.

"Since [Streep] has reached": Ibid., 106.

"Meryl Streep has been quoted": Ibid., 110–11.

"first-ladyish": James Agee, review of *The Corn Is Green*, in *Agee on Film* (New York: Modern Library, 2000), 145.

60   "Part of being": Kael, ibid., 111.

"The movie isn't about": Ebert, *Silkwood*, 290.

61   "our own longings": Kael, "Quests for America" (review of *Peggy Sue Got Married*), in *Hooked* (New York: E.P. Dutton, 1989), 219.

"Certain times and places": Ebert, review of *Peggy Sue Got Married*, in *Roger Ebert's Movie Home Companion 1988 Edition* (Kansas City: Andrews and McMeel Publishing, 1987), 425.

"We walk like ghosts": Ibid.

"Imagine kissing someone": Ibid.

"How does she play": Ibid.

"Not by trying": Ibid.

63   "For most of the movie": Kael, *Peggy Sue*, 220.

"honorable but uneven": Ebert, review of *Peggy Sue Got Married*, 426.

"This was one of": Ibid.

"I came away with": Kael, *Peggy Sue*, 221.

"The tone at the end": Ibid.

64 "It is intended as a dramatic": Ebert, review of *Music Box*, in *Roger Ebert's Movie Home Companion 1992 Edition* (Kansas City: Andrews and McMeel Publishing, 1991), 400.

66 "with the pull": Kael, "Melodrama/Cartoon/Mess" (review of *Music Box*), *Movie Love* (New York: Plume, 1991), 240.

"has the knack of giving": Ibid.

"They have put her": Ebert, *Music Box*, 401.

"keeps the father from": Kael, *Music Box*, 241–2.

"I love the sound": Ibid., 240.

"That's her emotional sound": Ibid.

"What counts is": Ibid., 242.

Chapter 5: Lit Crit

69 "That night he told his son": Roger Ebert, at Ebertfest, April 30, 2006.

"I think it helps": Ebert, review of *Greystoke*, in *Roger Ebert's Movie Home Companion 1980–85* (Kansas City: Andrews, McMeel & Parker, 1985), 156.

70 "Reading Shakespeare, Milton and Chaucer": Vanessa Faurie, "Critical Concerns," *Illinois Quarterly*, January–February 1995, 34.

"The movie's very faithfulness": Ebert, review of *A Separate Peace*, *Chicago Sun-Times*, October 30, 1972, http://rogerebert.suntimes.com/apps/pbcs.dll/article?AID=/19721030/REVIEWS/210300301/1023.

"The movie's a challenge": Ebert, review of *The French Lieutenant's Woman*, in *Roger Ebert's Movie Home Companion 1980–85*, 142.

71 "for serious study": Ebert, review of *Dead Poets Society*, in *Roger Ebert's Movie Home Companion 1990 Edition* (Kansas City: Andrews and McMeel Publishing, 1989), 183.

"When the movie was over": Ebert, review of *La Lectrice*, in *Roger Ebert's Movie Home Companion 1992 Edition* (Kansas City: Andrews and McMeel Publishing, 1991), 328.

"*Charlotte Gray* is based on": Ebert, review of *Charlotte Gray*, in *Roger Ebert's Movie Yearbook 2004* (Kansas City: Andrews McMeel Publishing, 2004), 114.

72 "a cross between a parody": Ebert, review of *Love Story*, in *Roger Ebert's Movie Home Companion 1987 Edition* (Kansas City: Andrews, McMeel & Parker, 1986), 313.

"In the novel, Gatsby": Ebert, review of *The Great Gatsby*, ibid., 231.

"often looked at merely": Ebert, review of *The Scarlet Letter*, in *Roger Ebert's Video Companion 1997 Edition* (Kansas City: Andrews and McMeel Publishing, 1996), 676.

"Actually, it is more often": Ibid.

73 "a very dense": Ibid.

"Hollywood has taken": Ibid., 677.

74 "much more interesting": Ebert, review of *The Bonfire of the Vanities*, in *Roger Ebert's Movie Home Companion 1992 Edition*, 70.

"The beauty of the Wolfe book": Ibid., 70–1.

"The movie sees much": Ibid., 71.

"doesn't seem to despise": Ibid., 70.

"That means that the love affair": Ebert, review of *Endless Love*, in *Roger Ebert's Movie Home Companion 1980–85*, 106.

"is too handsome": Ibid.

75 "Apparently the filmmakers": Ibid.

"The result is to take": Ibid.

"excessively obvious cinema": David Bordwell, Janet Staiger and Kristin Thompson, *The Classical Hollywood Cinema: Film Style & Mode of Production to 1960* (New York: Columbia University Press, 1985), 3, 11.

"a great natural beauty": Ebert, *Endless Love*, 107.

"a strong, unaffected": Ibid.

76 "We all have a tendency": Ebert, review of *Big Bad Love*, in *Roger Ebert's Movie Yearbook 2004* (Kansas City: Andrews McMeel Publishing, 2004), 66.

"The movie is narrated": Ebert, review of *A Thousand Acres*, in *Roger Ebert's Movie Yearbook 1999* (Kansas City: Andrews McMeel Publishing, 1998), 576.

78 "... I was unable to say": Ibid., 575.

"Truly we were beyond": Jane Smiley, *A Thousand Acres* (New York: Alfred A. Knopf, 1997), 363.

"In the book, Theresa": Ebert, review of *Looking for Mr. Goodbar*, in *Roger Ebert's Movie Home Companion 1987 Edition* (Kansas City: Andrews, McMeel & Parker, 1986), 309.

"Keaton's Charlie is not": Ebert, review of *The Little Drummer Girl*, in *Roger Ebert's Movie Home Companion 1980–85*, 191.

79 "...we get so many smiles": Ebert, review of *The Good Mother*, in *Roger Ebert's Movie Home Companion 1990 Edition* (Kansas City: Andrews and McMeel Publishing, 1989), 301.

"One of the qualities": Ebert, review of *The Bostonians*, in *Roger Ebert's Movie Home Companion 1980–85*, 44.

80   "intelligent and subtle": Ibid., 45.

81   "The buried message": Ebert, review of *The Wings of the Dove*, in *Roger Ebert's Movie Yearbook 1999* (Kansas City: Andrews McMeel Publishing, 1998), 635.

82   "The value of Henry James": Ebert, review of *The Portrait of a Lady*, in *Roger Ebert's Video Companion 1998 Edition* (Kansas City: Andrews McMeel Publishing, 1997), 640.

"In *The Wings of the Dove*": Ebert, review of *The Wings of the Dove*, in *Roger Ebert's Movie Yearbook 1999*, 636.

Chapter 6: And I Still Can See *Blue Velvet*, Through My Tears

85   "It is not only bad": Ebert, review of *Last Rites*, in *I Hated, Hated, Hated This Movie* (Kansas City: Andrews McMeel Publishing, 2000), 210.

"*Very Bad Things* filled me": Ebert, review of *Very Bad Things*, in *Roger Ebert's Movie Yearbook 2000* (Kansas City: Andrews McMeel Publishing, 1999), 644.

86   "American movies have been": Ebert, review of *Blue Velvet*, in *Roger Ebert's Movie Home Companion 1988 Edition* (Kansas City: Andrews and McMeel Publishing, 1987), 65.

"Occasionally, perhaps": Ibid.

87   "In *Blue Velvet*, Rossellini": Ibid., 66.

88   "All right, and I have": Ebert, "Film Clip: David Lynch," in *Roger Ebert's Movie Home Companion 1988 Edition*, 68.

89   "people" and "bluenoses": Peter Ranier, "Psycho Dramas" (review of *Blue Velvet*), in *Love and Hisses: The National Society of Film Critics Sound Off on the Hottest Movie Controversies*, ed. Peter Rainer (San Francisco: Mercury House, 1992), 5–6. First published in *Los Angeles Herald Examiner*, September 19, 1986.

"précis": Ebert, "Film Clip: David Lynch," 68.

"She has a special physical quality": Pauline Kael, "Out There and In Here" (review of *Blue Velvet*), in *Hooked* (New York: E.P. Dutton, 1989), 205.

90   "You were concerned": Roger Ebert, *Two Weeks in the Midday Sun: A Cannes Notebook* (Kansas City: Andrews and McMeel Publishing, 1987), 31–2.

"I wish I'd found": Isabella Rossellini, *Some of Me* (New York: Random House, 1997), 67–8.

91   "Extraordinary. It is customary": Ebert, "A Memory of *Blue Velvet*," in *Roger Ebert's Movie Yearbook 1999* (Kansas City: Andrews McMeel Publishing, 1998), 681.

"movies do not change": Ebert, review of *La Dolce Vita*, in *The Great Movies* (New York: Broadway Books, 2002), 243.

"Where was Lynch?": Ebert, "A Memory of *Blue Velvet*," 681.

"Why does someone": Ebert, review of *Fast Times at Ridgemont High*, in *Roger Ebert's Movie Home Companion 1980–85* (Kansas City: Andrews, McMeel & Parker, 1985), 119.

92   "How would you feel": Ibid., review of *Fraternity Vacation*, 141.

"Let me make myself clear": Ebert, *Fast Times*, 119.

"have an absolute gift": Ibid.

"At times, hearing the things": Ebert, review of *The Good Son*, in *Roger Ebert's Video Companion 1995 Edition* (Kansas City: Andrews and McMeel Publishing, 1994), 280.

"This is not a suitable": Ibid., 281.

"are they envious?" and "Do they feel": Pauline Kael, "Back to the Ouija Board" (review of *The Exorcist*), in *Reeling* (Boston: Atlantic Monthly Press/Little, Brown, 1976), 251.

"in an amoral way" and "we were just": Richard Schickel, *For the Love of Movies: The Story of American Film Criticism*, directed by Gerald Peary (AG Films, 2009).

93   "'David is obsessed": Stephen Schiff, "The Weird Dreams of David Lynch," *Vanity Fair*, March, 1987, 155.

Chapter 7: Cross References

96   "I remember one discussion" and "What would happen": Scott Sawyer, "Roger Ebert: On Sin, Kim Novak and the Movies," *Inklings*, Summer 1994, 18.

97   "absolutely no curiosity": Roger Ebert, review of *King David*, in *Roger Ebert's Movie Home Companion 1987 Edition* (Kansas City: Andrews, McMeel & Parker, 1986), 285.

"They have paid Christ": Ebert, review of *The Last Temptation of Christ*, in *Roger Ebert's Movie Home Companion 1990 Edition* (Kansas City: Andrews and McMeel Publishing, 1989), 414.

98   "I see that this entire review": Ibid., 414–15.

99   "technically blasphemous" and "only to suggest that": Ebert, *Scorsese by Ebert* (Chicago: University of Chicago Press, 2008), 102.

"In the title role": Ibid.

"Scorsese makes no": Ibid., 103.

"is as much about": Ibid.

"What makes [it] one": 103–4.

"Christ is the film": Ibid., 104.

100   "Pay less attention to yourself": Flannery O'Connor, "A Symposium on the Short Story," in *Conversations with Flannery O'Connor*, ed. Rosemary M. Magee (Jackson: University Press of Mississippi, 1987), 17. First published in *Esprit* (Scranton: University of Scranton, Winter 1959), 8–13.

"This is the most violent": Ebert, review of *The Passion of the Christ*, in *Roger Ebert's Movie Yearbook 2006* (Kansas City: Andrews McMeel Publishing, 2006), 526.

"Anyone raised as a Catholic": Ibid., 527.

101   "each one representing": Ibid., 528.

"Is the film 'good'" and "I imagine each person's": Ibid.

103   "Movies are often" and "They try so little": Ebert, "The Rapture of *The Rapture*," in *Roger Ebert's Movie Home Companion 1993 Edition* (Kansas City: Andrews and McMeel Publishing, 1993), 807.

"The best work": Michael Tolkin, at Ebertfest, following the screening of *The New Age*, April 22, 2010.

104   "One of the very few": John Simon, "Pinpricks in the Panacea" (review of *Marjoe*), in *Reverse Angle: A Decade of American Films* (New York: Clarkson N. Potter, Inc., 1982), 90.

"the sin of pride": Ebert, review of *The Rapture*, in *Roger Ebert's Movie Home Companion 1993 Edition*, 537.

105   "The construction of the story": Ebert, review of *Frailty*, in *Roger Ebert's Movie Yearbook 2003* (Kansas City: Andrews McMeel Publishing, 2002), 221.

"Is Dad deluded" and "The movie offers": Ebert, "Questions for the Movie Answer Man: *Frailty*," in *Roger Ebert's Movie Yearbook 2003*, 775.

106   "the values of a more": Ebert, review of *Saved!*, in *Roger Ebert's Movie Yearbook 2005* (Kansas City: Andrews McMeel Publishing, 2004), 573.

"To obtain comedy": Ibid., review of *Raising Helen*, 537.

107   "smooth meticulousness" and "an aversion to": Kael, "Mirrors" (review of *Places in the Heart*), in *State of the Art* (New York: E.P. Dutton, 1985), 246.

"about America": Ibid.

"can't support such": Ebert, review of *Places in the Heart*, in *Roger Ebert's Movie Home Companion 1980–85* (Kansas City: Andrews, McMeel & Parker, 1985), 247–8.

"God knows it's got": Kael, *Places in the Heart*, 246.

108 "We have so many" and "What the movie leaves": Ebert, review of *The King*, in *Roger Ebert's Movie Yearbook 2007* (Kansas City: Andrews McMeel Publishing, 2007), 375.

Chapter 8: Turned On

112 "Pretty good in 1969": Roger Ebert, "Playboy Interview: Siskel & Ebert," interviewed by Lawrence Grobel, *Playboy*, February 1991, 58.

"best rock camp horror": Ebert, "Beyond the Valley of My Memories," in *Roger Ebert's Movie Yearbook 2004* (Kansas City: Andrews McMeel Publishing, 2004), 758.

113 "something for everyone": John Simon, review of *Beyond the Valley of the Dolls*, in *Movies Into Film: Film Criticism 1967–1970* (New York: The Dial Press, 1971), 160.

"plays like gangbusters": Ebert, *Playboy*, February 1991, 58.

"I feel vindicated today": Ebert, "Above, Beneath, and Beyond the Valley: The Making of a Musical-Horror-Sex-Comedy." Disc 2. *Beyond the Valley of the Dolls*, DVD. Directed by Russ Meyer. Beverly Hills, CA: Twentieth Century Fox Home Entertainment, 2006.

"I've never been that interested": Ebert, "Beyond the Valley of My Memories," in *Roger Ebert's Movie Yearbook 2004*, 758.

"Since women's breasts": Ebert, review of *Rapa Nui*, in *Roger Ebert's Video Companion 1996 Edition* (Kansas City: Andrews and McMeel Publishing, 1995), 601.

114 "in the pre-bunny period": Pauline Kael, "Bravo!" (review of *Funny Girl*), in *Going Steady* (Boston: Atlantic Monthly Press/Little, Brown, 1970), 134.

"Meyer reveled in revealing": Jimmy McDonough, *Big Bosoms and Square Jaws: The Biography of Russ Meyer, King of the Sex Film* (New York: Crown Publishers, 2005), 252–3.

115 "doesn't know how": Kael, "No Contest" (review of *Hardcore*), in *When the Lights Go Down* (New York: Holt, Rinehart and Winston, 1980), 546.

"*I Am Curious*": Ebert, review of *I Am Curious (Yellow)*, in *I Hated, Hated, Hated This Movie* (Kansas City: Andrews McMeel Publishing, 2000), 176.

"The one interesting aspect": Ibid., 177.

116 "What a letdown": Ebert, review of *Spring Break*, in *Roger Ebert's Movie Home Companion 1980–85* (Kansas City: Andrews, McMeel & Parker, 1985), 301.

"They say you never" and "I know something": Ebert, review of *Perfect*, in *Roger Ebert's Movie Home Companion 1987 Edition* (Kansas City: Andrews, McMeel & Parker, 1986), 395.

"Graphic detail" and "What's erotic is": Ebert, "20 Questions: Siskel & Ebert," interviewed by Bill Zehme, *Playboy*, June 1984, 176.

"There's romance in this": review of *An Officer and a Gentleman*, in *Roger Ebert's Movie Home Companion 1980–85*, 229.

"all the more erotic": Ebert, review of *The Big Easy*, in *Roger Ebert's Movie Home Companion 1989 Edition*, 58.

"a power that transcends": Ebert, review of *Body Heat*, in *The Great Movies* (New York: Broadway Books, 2002), 79.

117 "the movie stops" and "I think the moment occurs": Ibid., 79–80.

"This is not a movie": Ebert, review of *Basic Instinct*, in *Roger Ebert's Movie Home Companion: 1993 Edition* (Kansas City: Andrews and McMeel Publishing, 1993), 52.

"We engage in a conspiracy": Ebert, review of *Wild Orchid*, in *Roger Ebert's Movie Home Companion 1992 Edition* (Kansas City: Andrews and McMeel Publishing, 1991), 673.

"Critics are the worst": Ibid.

"Apparently the lesson": Ibid., 674.

"There are not two": Stephen M. Silverman, *Dancing on the Ceiling: Stanley Donen and His Movies* (New York: Alfred A. Knopf, 1996), 318.

118 "But in *10*": Ebert, review of *Blame It on Rio*, in *Roger Ebert's Movie Home Companion 1980–85*, 38.

"has the mind of a": Ibid.

"not a member of": Ebert, review of *The Devil in Miss Jones*, *Chicago Sun-Times*, June 13, 1973. http://rogerebert.suntimes.com/apps/pbcs.dll/article?AID=/19730613/REVIEWS/306130301/1023.

"Carefully deployed clothing": Ebert, review of *Emmanuelle*, in *Roger Ebert's Movie Home Companion 1987 Edition*, 167.

"the first movie": Ibid., 166.

"actually seems to be": Ebert, review of *The Devil in Miss Jones*.

"None of this will" and "But for those of us": Ibid.

"has really done it" and "He has stripped": Ebert, review of *The Devils*, in *I Hated, Hated, Hated This Movie* (Kansas City: Andrews McMeel Publishing, 2000), 98.

119   "Sex is an activity": Ebert, review of *Crimes of Passion*, in *Roger Ebert's Movie Home Companion 1980–85*, 83.

"because there is nothing": Ibid.

"*Whore* is not about": Ebert, review of *Whore*, in *Roger Ebert's Movie Home Companion: 1993 Edition*, 733.

"He may have a point": Ibid.

120   "[Jeanne] lends herself to": Pauline Kael, "Tango" (review of *Last Tango in Paris*), in *Reeling* (Boston: Atlantic Monthly Press/Little, Brown, 1976), 29.

"If Brando knows": Ibid., 32.

"For adults, it's like": Ibid., 34.

121   "the most powerfully erotic" and "the most liberating": Ibid., 28.

"Bertolucci has a remarkably": Ibid., 30.

"speeded-up history": Ibid., 29.

"The couple's Paris flat": John Simon, "In France We Do It Horizontally" (review of *Last Tango in Paris*), in *Something to Declare: Twelve Years of Films from Abroad* (New York: Clarkson N. Potter, Inc., 1983), 130.

"There are no real characters": Ibid., 131.

122   "as the revelation of ultimate": Ibid., 133.

"is still the supreme heartthrob": Ibid.

"one of the great emotional": Ebert, review of *Last Tango in Paris*, in *Roger Ebert's Movie Home Companion 1992 Edition*, 334.

"For the movie is": Ibid.

"tragic imbalance between": Ibid.

"tremendous dramatic tension": Ibid.

"just a physical function": Ibid., 335.

"has no difficulty": Ibid.

"the most powerfully": Kael, *Last Tango*, 28.

"the sex isn't the point": Ebert, *Last Tango*, 334.

"expresses the characters' drives": Kael, *Last Tango*, 28.

123   "the movie breakthrough": Ibid.

"movies are a past": Ibid., 33.

"Bertolucci wasn't surprised": Ibid., 31.

"If Brando knows": Ibid., 32.

"so they won't have to": Ibid., 31.

"We are watching *Brando*": Ibid., 32.

"is that there is" and "Faced with a passage": Ebert, *Last Tango*, 335.

"A lot has been said": Ibid., 334.

"It is said in some quarters": Ibid.

124 "Only an idiot": Ibid.

"seems to be muttering": Simon, *Last Tango*, 134.

"a bouquet of Renoir's": Kael, *Last Tango*, 33.

"buxom guttersnipe": Simon, *Last Tango*, 134.

"Schneider doesn't seem": Ebert, *Last Tango*, 335.

"On the basis of this": Ibid.

"just the sort of thing": Simon, *Last Tango*, 132.

125 "It was not the beginning": Ebert, review of *Last Tango*, in *Awake in the Dark: The Best of Roger Ebert* (Chicago: University of Chicago Press, 2006), 243.

"I once had a professor": Ibid., 244.

"her open-faced lack of experience": Ibid., 245.

"Both characters are enigmas": Ibid.

"the moment is wonderful": Ibid.

"is like revisiting the house": Ibid., 243.

"meets [Brando] in the middle": Ebert, review of *Last Tango*, in *The Great Movies III* (Chicago: University of Chicago Press, 2010), 219.

126 "is in scenes as an actor": Ebert, *Last Tango*, in *Awake in the Dark*, 245.

"Wrong again" and "They are both in scenes": Ebert, *Last Tango*, in *The Great Movies III*, 220.

"[I]sn't it remarkable": Ibid., 219.

"Her vision is clearly": Kathleen Murphy, "A Matter of Skin: Catherine Breillat's Metaphysics of Film and Flesh," *Film Comment*, September–October 1999, 16.

127 "The film avoids the temptation": Ebert, review of *Bliss*, in *Roger Ebert's Video Companion 1998 Edition*, 85.

"*Bliss* is a daring movie": Ibid.

128 "the key to the film's success": Ibid.

"not an 'adult film'": Ibid.

129 "That's *extremely* bad behavior" and "There was a time": Lawrence Grobel, "The Critic: Gene Siskel and Roger Ebert," in *Above the Line: Conversations About the Movies* (New York: Da Capo Press, 2000), 350.

"The movie gets four stars": Ibid., 353.

"If I were 13": Ebert, review of *Beowulf*, in *Roger Ebert's Movie Yearbook 2009* (Kansas City: Andrews McMeel Publishing, 2009), 56.

"to never wear any garment": Ebert, review of *Three to Tango*, in *Roger Ebert's Movie Yearbook 2001* (Kansas City: Andrews McMeel Publishing, 2000), 605.

130 "had forgotten about": Ebert, review of *Swordfish*, in *Roger Ebert's Movie Yearbook 2002* (Kansas City: Andrews McMeel Publishing, 2001), 561.

"is the way" and "This story is": Ebert, review of *Monster's Ball*, in *Roger Ebert's Movie Yearbook 2003* (Kansas City: Andrews McMeel Publishing, 2002), 410.

"what's erotic is": Ebert, "20 Questions," *Playboy*, June 1984, 176.

131 "Many of the crucial moments" and "At her great age": Ebert, review of *The Whales of August*, in *Roger Ebert's Movie Home Companion 1989 Edition*, 709.

"a brothelkeeper with delusions": John Simon, review of *Beyond the Valley of the Dolls*, in *Movies Into Film: Film Criticism 1967–1970* (New York: The Dial Press, 1971), 154.

Chapter 9: Misfires

133 "It's one of the central events": Ebert, review of *Apocalypse Now Redux*, in *Roger Ebert's Movie Yearbook 2003* (Kansas City: Andrews McMeel Publishing, 2002), 30.

134 "does as little with" and "(1) Jan becoming Maxie": Ebert, review of *Maxie*, in *Roger Ebert's Movie Home Companion 1987 Edition* (Kansas City: Andrews, McMeel & Parker, 1986), 328.

135 "*Extremities* is a film": Ebert, review of *Extremities*, in *Roger Ebert's Movie Home Companion 1988 Edition* (Kansas City: Andrews and McMeel Publishing, 1987), 191.

"the only scenes with any": Ibid.

"on the same shelf": Ibid.

136 "Fawcett is a woman" and "Those are the only": Ibid.

137 "Fawcett's performance" and "She doesn't seem": Ibid.

138 "any true electricity" and "seems more inspired": Ibid.

"By the film's last shot": Ibid.

139 "Fawcett is admirable" and "Her own beauty": Jack Kroll, "Beauty and the Beast" (review of *Extremities*), *Newsweek*, September 1, 1986, 86.

"anything but entertaining": John Walker, review of *Extremities*, in *Halliwell's: Film, DVD & Video Guide 2007* (London: HarperCollins, 2006), 375.

"With that much plot": Ebert, review of *In Dreams*, in *Roger Ebert's Movie Yearbook 2000* (Kansas City: Andrews McMeel Publishing, 1999), 286.

140 "cinematic hallucination": Kathleen Murphy, "A Study in Scarlet" (review of *In Dreams*), *Film Comment*, March–April 1990, 13.

"Jordan's flawed, gorgeous film" and "Imperfect as it is": Ibid., 12.

"One of the most": Ibid., 13.

141 "Scanning Jordan's slant-rhymes": Ibid., 13.

"Whole subplots," "Although the drowned village," and "And how many viewers": Ebert, *In Dreams*, 287.

142 "Over the top?" and "You betcha!": Murphy, *In Dreams*, 16.

"This is a wonderful film": Ebert, review of *Terms of Endearment*, in *Roger Ebert's Movie Home Companion 1980–85* (Kansas City: Andrews, McMeel & Parker, 1985), 331.

"You'll mention someone": Ibid., 330.

"This is a movie": Ibid., 331.

"It's exactly the kind" and "guides the actors": Pauline Kael, "Retro Retro" (review of *Terms of Endearment*), in *State of the Art* (New York: E.P. Dutton, 1985), 93.

143 "rattles on through farce" and "A more calculating": John Simon, "Little Big Screen" (review of *Terms of Endearment*), in *John Simon on Film: Criticism, 1982–2001* (New York: Applause, 2005), 63–4.

"life's like that": Ebert, *Terms of Endearment*, 330.

"She outdoes herself": Ibid., 331.

"All this retro-forties virtue": Kael, *Terms of Endearment*, 94.

"incredibly vivid" and "and she has fresh details": Ibid., 95.

"especially with actors": Simon, *Terms of Endearment*, 66.

144 "so firmly in control": Ebert, *Terms of Endearment*, 331.

"Aurora's surely not" and "She's a TV-museum piece": Kael, *Terms of Endearment*, 94.

"MacLaine plays": Simon, *Terms of Endearment*, 66.

"doesn't reach for effects": Ebert, *Terms of Endearment*, 331.

"There isn't a thing": Ibid.

"pious," "uses cancer," and "At the end": Kael, *Terms of Endearment*, 97.

145 "is bound to elicit": Simon, *Terms of Endearment*, 66.

146 "Don't trust any critic": Ebert, review of *My Dog Skip*, in *Roger Ebert's Movie Yearbook 2001* (Kansas City: Andrews McMeel Publishing, 2000), 398.

147 "Most American movies": Ebert, review of *The Contender*, in *Roger Ebert's Movie Yearbook 2002* (Kansas City: Andrews McMeel Publishing, 2001), 128.

"takes sides," "Its sentiments" and "frankly partisan": Ibid.

"There is a remarkable scene": Ibid.

"positive Republican portrayals": Ebert, "Questions for the Movie Answer Man: *The Contender*," in *Roger Ebert's Movie Yearbook 2002*, 753.

148 "When did liberals": Kael, "Mythologizing the Sixties" (review of *Coming Home*), in *When the Lights Go Down* (New York: Holt, Rinehart and Winston, 1980), 405.

"Can't educated liberals": Kael, "'I Still Love Going to the Movies': An Interview with Pauline Kael," interviewed by Leonard Quart, *Cineaste*, vol. XXV, no. 2, 9.

149 "unwholesome curiosity": Ebert, *Contender*, 128.

150 "'This isn't a film about Vietnam'": Ebert, review of *Apocalypse Now*, in *Roger Ebert's Movie Home Companion 1987 Edition*, 27.

"Such criticisms are made": Ibid., 28.

151 "war is hell" and "We do not go": Ibid.

"*Apocalypse Now* achieves greatness": Ibid.

"the narrative device" and "That's really why": Ibid.

"[W]e no longer think of" and "We don't think of being": Kael, "Pauline Kael on the New Hollywood," in *Conversations with Pauline Kael*, interviewed by Pat Aufderheide, ed. Will Brantley (Jackson: University Press of Mississippi, 1996), 48. First published in *In These Times*, May 7–13, 1980, 12, 23.

"in characters and images, something": Ebert, *Apocalypse Now*, 28.

152 "It doesn't look at the facts" and "Instead we are carriers": Kael, "Pauline Kael on the New Hollywood," 45.

"simultaneously numbing" and "As the rockets jar": Ebert, *Apocalypse Now*, 28.

"How can you go further": Kael, "Pauline Kael on the New Hollywood," 48.

153 "The movie's feeling for bombs" and "It sure doesn't make you": Ibid.

"with such sudden, fierce:" Ebert, *Apocalypse Now*, 28.

"[Y]ou want to say": Kael, "Pauline Kael on the New Hollywood," 48.

"The film has no structure" and "There's no possible confrontation": Ibid.

"Sheen is already": Ibid.

"in such a moral, physical": Richard T. Jameson, "Vietnam Hot Damn" (review of *Apocalypse Now*), in *Love and Hisses: The National Society of Film Critics Sound Off on the Hottest Movie Controversies*, ed. Peter Rainer (San Francisco: Mercury House, 1992), 474. First published in *The Weekly* (Seattle), October 17, 1979.

155 "war is hell": Ebert, *Apocalypse Now*, 28.

"White man—he-devil": Pauline Kael, "Why Are Movies So Bad? or, The Numbers" (review of *Apocalypse Now*), in *Taking It All In* (New York: Holt, Rinehart and Winston, 1984), 18.

"Battles may seduce the desperate": John Simon, "$30 Million in Search of an Author" (review of *Apocalypse Now*), in *Reverse Angle: A Decade of American Films* (New York: Clarkson N. Potter, Inc., 1982), 388.

"fence-sitting stance" and "A text without a context": Frank P. Tomasulo, "The Politics of Ambivalence: *Apocalypse Now* as Prowar and Antiwar Film," in *From Hanoi to Hollywood: The Vietnam War in American Film*, Linda Dittmar and Gene Michaud (eds) (New Brunswick: Rutgers University Press, 1990), 157.

"one hundred great moments": Ebert, "One Hundred Scenes in One Hundred Years," in *Roger Ebert's Video Companion 1996 Edition* (Kansas City: Andrews and McMeel Publishing, 1995), 913.

Chapter 10: I Ain't a Pretty Boy No More

157 "best single scene": Ebert, review of *Runaway Train*, in *Roger Ebert's Movie Home Companion 1988 Edition* (Kansas City: Andrews and McMeel Publishing, 1987), 495.

"Mickey Rourke's role": Ebert, review of *Once Upon a Time in Mexico*, in *Roger Ebert's Movie Yearbook 2005* (Kansas City: Andrews McMeel Publishing, 2004), 492.

"*Working Girl* is Mike Nichols": Ebert, review of *Working Girl*, in *Roger Ebert's Movie Home Companion 1990 Edition* (Kansas City: Andrews and McMeel Publishing, 1989), 847.

"This is Melanie Griffith's movie" and "She is not an obvious": Ibid., 846.

158 "A movie like this" and "We see them many times": Ebert, review of *Another Day in Paradise*, in *Roger Ebert's Movie Yearbook 2000* (Kansas City: Andrews McMeel Publishing, 1999), 22–23.

"Has anybody ever looked": Pauline Kael, "Doubling Up" (review of *Something Wild*), in *Hooked* (New York: E.P. Dutton, 1989), 229.

"the last rose of summer": Ebert, *Another Day*, 22.

159 "If I were going to compile": Ebert, *Two Weeks in the Midday Sun: A Cannes Notebook* (Kansas City: Andrews and McMeel Publishing, 1987), 21.

160 "those who persist": Ibid., 30.

"There seemed to be a family": Ibid., 32.

"'[The projectionist] was doing the best": Ibid., 89.

161 "It was in an obscure backwater": Ibid., 49.

"'Basically, I sell": Ibid.

"Nobody I knew dressed as cool": Ebert, review of *Hairspray*, in *Roger Ebert's Movie Home Companion 1990 Edition*, 314.

162 "God, 13 can be horrible" and "I remember": Ebert, review of *Cheaper by the Dozen 2*, in *Roger Ebert's Movie Yearbook 2007* (Kansas City: Andrews McMeel Publishing, 2007), 114.

"Then we'd be on the side" and "Plus, there's the sweet touch": Ebert, review of *Splash*, in *Roger Ebert's Movie Home Companion 1980–85* (Kansas City: Andrews, McMeel & Parker, 1985), 300.

"I was disappointed" and "Is it not possible": Ebert, review of *The Butcher's Wife*, in *Roger Ebert's Movie Home Companion: 1993 Edition* (Kansas City: Andrews and McMeel Publishing, 1993), 97.

"Do you think Roger": Carol Felsenthal, "A Life in Movies," *Chicago*, December 2005, 124.

"I'll never be lonely again": Ibid.

"I think that I am better": Hank Sartin, "Things to Do: Roger and Chaz," *Time Out Chicago*, September 22, 2008. http://timeoutchicago.com/things-to-do/59153/roger-chaz?package=96134.

163 "His wait for the perfect mate": Melissa Merli, "Perfect Mate," *The News-Gazette*, Tuesday, April 20, 2010, A-6.

164 "You *are* the Debbie Reynolds": Ebert, at Ebertfest, following the screening of *My Fair Lady*, April 26, 2006.

"I have had good times": Ebert, "Roger's Welcome," *Roger Ebert's Overlooked Film Festival Take 2*, April 26, 2000. http://www.ebertfest.com/two/2welcome.htm

166 "greatest thing that's ever happened" and "This *is* hard": Mark Zupan, at Ebertfest, following the screening of *Murderball*, April 21, 2005.

"It is routinely said" and "It is not only that": Ebert, "Elevating the Oscar Winners Part #2: Best Leading Actor" (blog), *Chicago Sun-Times*, January 26, 2009. http://rogerebert.suntimes.com/apps/pbcs.dll/article?AID=/20090126/OSCARS/901269995

167 "It was sheer good chance" and "The bleeding seemed impossible": Ebert, "'Death Panels.' A Most Excellent Term," *Roger Ebert's Journal* (blog), *Chicago Sun-Times*, August 17, 2009. http://blogs.suntimes.com/ebert/2009/08/death_panels_an_excellent_phra.html

168 "The original appeal": Ebert, "It Wouldn't Be Ebertfest Without Roger" (blog), *Chicago Sun-Times*, April 23, 2007. http://rogerebert.suntimes.com/apps/pbcs.dll/article?AID=/20070423/PEOPLE/70423001

Epilogue: Heroes

169 "lit by matches": Lee Server, *Robert Mitchum: Baby, I Don't Care* (New York: St. Martin's Press, 2001), 208.

170 "So, Mitchum or Stewart?" and "I cannot choose": Roger Ebert, "Mitch and Jimmy: Some Thoughts," in *Roger Ebert's Video Companion 1998 Edition* (Kansas City: Andrews McMeel Publishing, 1997), 927.

"if you prick him": Ebert, review of *Casino Royale*, in *Roger Ebert's Movie Yearbook 2009* (Kansas City: Andrews McMeel Publishing, 2009), 95.

"Early in the film" and "He thinks maybe he's": Ebert, review of *Defiance*, in *Roger Ebert's Movie Yearbook 2010* (Kansas City: Andrews McMeel Publishing, 2010), 102–3.

171 "later reviews are fully formed": Craig Seligman, *Sontag & Kael: Opposites Attract Me* (New York: Counterpoint, 2004), 191.

"crap, but crap on a motorcycle": Pauline Kael, "Neutered" (review of *An Officer and a Gentleman*), in *Taking It All In* (New York: Holt, Rinehart and Winston, 1984), 381.

"In truth, they drop" and "When I read Kael": Seligman, *Sontag & Kael*, 191.

"I have heard the mermaids": T. S. Eliot, "The Love Song of J. Alfred Prufrock," in *Selected Poems* (San Diego: Harcourt Brace, 1964), 16.

"Don't we all know that feeling?" and "That feeling that": Ebert, review of *I've Heard the Mermaids Singing*, in *Roger Ebert's Movie Home Companion 1989 Edition*, 323–4.

172 "This is the ultimate law" and "But the life": C. S. Lewis, *The Problem of Pain* (San Francisco: HarperSanFrancisco, 1996), 154.

"Geniuses, almost necessarily" and "There's something monstrous": Seligman, *Sontag & Kael*, 187.

173 "Forget it's a thriller" and "See it because": Ebert, review of *The Big Easy*, in *Roger Ebert's Movie Home Companion 1989 Edition*, 58.

"By the end": Ebert, review of *Everybody's All-American*, in *Roger Ebert's Movie Home Companion 1990 Edition* (Kansas City: Andrews and McMeel Publishing, 1989), 232.

"The typical newsroom": Ebert, review of *Shattered Glass*, in *Roger Ebert's Movie Yearbook 2005* (Kansas City: Andrews McMeel Publishing, 2004), 600.

"So, Mitchum or Stewart?" and "I cannot choose": Ebert, "Mitch and Jimmy: Some Thoughts," in *Roger Ebert's Movie Home Companion 1998 Edition*, 927.

Index